SEVEN FAMOUS GREEK PLAYS

MODERN LIBRARY COLLEGE EDITIONS

SEVEN FAMOUS GREEK PLAYS

EDITED, WITH INTRODUCTIONS, BY

Whitney J. Oates

AVALON PROFESSOR OF HUMANITIES,
PRINCETON UNIVERSITY, AND

Eugene O'Neill, Jr.

The Modern Library · New York

Reprinted by arrangement with George Allen & Unwin Ltd., for Gilbert Murray's translation of *The Frogs*; to Mrs. Harry Fine for Paul Elmer More's translation of *Prometheus Bound*; and to Mr. Richard Aldington for his own translation of *Alcestis*.

THE MODERN LIBRARY

is published by

RANDOM HOUSE, INC.

Manufactured in the United States of America

PREFACE

THE aim of this volume is to provide students and general readers with a representative selection of the extant Greek drama in the best available translations.

Every effort has been made to impress upon the reader the extreme importance of the musical element in the Greek plays. To accomplish this end, all choral or singing passages in the prose versions have been indented, and broken up into their various choric constituents. Likewise, speeches which are attributed to the Chorus in the manuscripts, if they are written in the regular meter of the dialogue passages, have been assigned to the Leader of the Chorus, who thus becomes almost another member of the cast. Furthermore, all passages which were sung or chanted, so far as can be determined by their meter in the original, have been so indicated in the present text.

The General Introduction attempts to present certain material, both historical and systematic, which is requisite to the understanding of the plays. It treats, for example, such subjects as the nature of the Greek theater, Greek Tragedy and Greek Comedy in general, and the lives and works of the individual dramatists. Accompanying each play is a short special introduction to that play, designed primarily to facilitate its understanding on the part of the reader. Each play also is accompanied by notes which endeavor to explain particular passages which otherwise might prove difficult to apprehend. A Glossary renders unnecessary a number of specific notes on the individual plays. It is hoped that the Glossary will prove a useful and valuable adjunct to the book.

The editors together assume the responsibility for the selection of translations. Mr. Oates edited the text and prepared the individual introductions for the plays of Aeschylus, Sophocles and Euripides. He also prepared that part of the General Introduction which deals with tragedy and the tragedians. Mr. O'Neill edited the text, revised the translation, and prepared the introduction for the play by Aristophanes, as well as that portion of the General Introduction which deals with comedy and the comic poets. He likewise compiled the Glossary.

The resources of the two-volume Random House edition of *The Complete Greek Drama*, which contains all of the surviving forty-seven plays written by Aeschylus, Sophocles, Euripides, Aristophanes and Menander, were drawn upon for this collection. The editors earnestly hope that this volume will further the understanding and appreciation of these masterpieces of Greek creative art.

WHITNEY J. OATES
EUGENE O'NEILL, JR.

CONTENTS

GENERAL INTRODUCTION

I. Tragedy

THE plays of Aeschylus, Sophocles and Euripides were written during the fifth century B.C. Behind them lies a rich literary and dramatic, or at least quasi-dramatic, tradition, which accounts in no small measure for the depth, scope and complexity of the art form which the plays embody. The problem of fully understanding the dramas is therefore not a simple one, since they cannot be divorced completely from the epic, lyric, and dramatic tradition which precedes them.

By far the most important factor in the tradition is the epic which we know chiefly through the *Iliad* and the *Odyssey*. In the interval between the epics of Homer, which scholars date variously from the tenth to the eighth century B.C., and the age of the three great tragic poets, thinkers began to explore the various phenomena of the external world and came to understand many aspects of nature which had hitherto been shrouded in complete mystery. The creative literary activity of this epoch likewise betokens on the part of the Greeks an increasingly higher level of self-understanding and self-consciousness, in the best sense of the word. At this time appeared a group of lyric poets, who had looked deeply within their own natures, and through the vehicle of their poetry made abundantly evident how thoroughly they understood the essential character of man's inner being. In Greek tragedy as we now have it we meet a fully developed dramatic form.

THE THEATER

It is absolutely necessary for anyone who desires to apprehend as completely as possible these Greek plays, to re-create them imaginatively as dramas, that is, as actual plays, produced dramatically before an audience. A spectator of a Greek dramatic performance in the latter half of the fifth century B.C. would find himself seated in the *theatron,* or *koilon,* a semicircular, curved bank of seats, resembling in some respects the closed end of a horseshoe stadium. He has climbed up the steps (*klimakes*) to reach his seat, which is in a section (*kerkis*). Probably he has in the process walked along the level aisle (*diazoma*) which divides the lower and the upper parts of the *theatron.* Below him, in the best location in the theater, is the throne of the priest of Dionysus, who presides in a sense over the whole performance, which is essentially religious in character. The *theatron* is large—in fact, the one in Athens, in the Theater of Dionysus, with its seats banked up on the south slope of the Acropolis, seated approximately 17,000 persons.

The spectator sees before him a level circular area called the *orchestra,* in the center of which stands an altar, which figures frequently as a stage-property in a number of the plays. A part of the dramatic action will take place in the *orchestra,* as well as the manoeuvres and dance figures performed by the Chorus as they present their odes. To the right and left of the *theatron* are the *parodoi,* which are used not only by the spectators for entering and leaving the theater, but also for the entrances and exits of actors and the Chorus.

Directly beyond the circular *orchestra* lies the *skene* or scene-building. In most plays the *skene* represents the façade of a house, a palace, or a temple, and normally had three doors which served as additional entrances and exits for the actors. Immediately in front of the scene-building was a level platform, called the *proskenion* or *logeion,* where much of the dramatic action of the plays takes place. Flanking the *proskenion* were two projecting wings, the so-called *paraskenia.*

Dramatic productions of the fifth century B.C. involved the use of two mechanical devices, with which the student of Greek drama should be familiar. One, the *eccyclema,* was developed in the fifth century. It was some kind of platform on wheels, which, so far as we can discover, was rolled out from the *skene,* and in this position was supposed to represent an interior scene. The other was the "machine." Frequently at the close of a play the dramatist introduced a god into the action, who would naturally be expected to appear from above. He apparently was brought in by some kind of crane or derrick, called the "machine." Inasmuch as the god who was thus introduced usually served to disentangle the complicated threads of the dramatic action, and on occasions seemed to be brought in quite gratuitously by a playwright unable to work out a dénouement from elements already in the situation, the term *deus ex machina,* "the god from the machine," has become standard in dramatic criticism.

THE PERFORMANCE

In Athens of the fifth century B.C. dramas were presented only on two occasions, both of which marked religious festivals. At other times plays were presented at rural festivals in various Greek communities, when the productions, so to speak, would "go on the road." In the city, the less important of the festivals, called the *Lenaea,* or Festival of the Wine-Press, was held in January/February of each year. The more important festival, however, was the so-called *Greater* or *City Dionysia,* which was celebrated annually in March/

April in honor of the god, Dionysus.[1] Large audiences attended the festival, and witnessed the various performances. Earlier in the century admission to the performances was free, but later the cost was two obols, which would be refunded by the State to anyone who could show legitimate need.

Three contests for poets were held in the *Greater Dionysia,* one in comedy, one in tragedy, and one in the dithyramb. Prior to the Peloponnesian War the festival apparently lasted six days. On the first took place the great ceremonial procession which was followed on the second by the competition for the dithyrambic choruses. The dithyramb was an elaborate choral ode sung and performed by a trained chorus of fifty, the song itself having a direct bearing upon the central religious orientation of the whole festival and its connection with the god, Dionysus. Ten dithyrambs were presented in the contest on this day. Five comic poets each submitted a play for the competition in comedy which occupied the third day. Three tragic poets each submitted a tetralogy for the contest in tragedy which filled the last three days of the festival. A tragic poet had to present a group of four plays, three of them tragedies, either on separate themes or all on the same subject, plus a somewhat lighter after-piece known as a satyr-play. During the days of the Peloponnesian War, 431-404 B.C., the festival was reduced from six to five days in length, and the number of

[1] Greek drama had a common close association with the spring festivals which were held to celebrate the worship of Dionysus. This god, as one of the Greek anthropomorphic divinities, symbolized the spirit of fertility, of generation and regeneration, which marks the season of spring, and he also came to be identified with the vine. Even in the fifth century the dramatic performances in the *Greater Dionysia* were still an integral part of a very elaborate religious service. The Theater of Dionysus in Athens lay within the sacred precinct of the god. The very altar in the center of the *orchestra* was not primarily a stage property, though the dramatists sometimes took advantage of its presence there, but it was a real religious altar. Behind the *skene* were temples dedicated to the god. Hence it is no wonder that the Greek drama tends to be more religious than secular.

comic competitors was diminished from five to three. During these years the program for the last three days contained a tragic tetralogy in the morning followed by a comedy in the afternoon.

Great care and expense went into the individual dramatic productions. The poet himself in many instances directed his own play, or even acted in it. In all probability he helped select his cast, all the parts of which were taken by male actors, coached them and supervised the training of the Chorus. Normally in the tragedies there were not more than three actors for each play, any one of whom might take more than one part if the exigencies of the piece demanded it. A wealthy citizen stood the cost of a play's production, a responsibility which was placed upon him by the State, and was regarded as a legitimate obligation of his position and citizenship.

The tragedies combined within them many variegated elements: rhythm in the poetry, vivid action, and brilliant color. There was also solo and choral singing, plus a strikingly posed and highly stylized dancing. A further effect was added by the fact that the actors all wore masks. This may have been partially because the audience was so far removed from the actors that it was impossible to achieve any effects through facial expressions.

THE STRUCTURE OF THE TRAGEDY

The typical Greek tragedy is divided into certain definite parts. The play opens with a *prologue,* a scene in which a single character may speak, or a dialogue may take place. In general in this short introductory scene, the poet acquaints the audience with the requisite information concerning the dramatic situation of the play.

After the *prologue* comes the *parodos,* the first appearance of the Chorus. The members of this group enter the *orches-*

tra, singing and dancing, clearly suiting the rhythm of their motion and their gesticulations to the gravity and import of the words they sing. As time passes in the fifth century the Chorus in tragedy steadily diminishes in importance. In Euripides, particularly in his later plays, the Chorus merely sings lyrical interludes which have little or no coherence with the play. Normally the members of the Chorus serve as interested commentators upon the action, sometimes functioning as a background of public opinion against which the situation of the particular play is projected, or again becoming the vehicle whereby the poet is able to make clearer the more universal significance of the action. At the conclusion of the *parodos,* the Chorus almost always remains "on stage" throughout the remainder of the play. In the tragedies there are usually fifteen members in the Chorus. One of this number normally acts as a leader who may do solo singing and dancing, or may become virtually another character in the *dramatis personae.* Sometimes the Chorus breaks into two groups which sing responsively.[2]

As soon as the opening choral song has been completed, there comes the first *episode.* This is the exact counterpart of the act or scene in a modern play. A *stasimon* or choral ode succeeds the *episode* and the remainder of the piece is made up of these two parts in alternation. A normal play contains four or five of each. On occasion a *commus* takes the place of a *stasimon.* The *commus* is a lyric passage, sung by an actor or actors together with the Chorus. Intricate meters distinguish the *stasimon* and *commus,* whereas the spoken passages of dialogue or monologue in the *episodes* are written in the iambic trimeter, a close equivalent to the

[2]It is possible in translation to give only an incomplete impression of the highly complicated rhythmic and metric structure of the choral passages. Suffice it to say that they had a carefully articulated and balanced symmetry of constituent parts, for which there were certain flexible conventions. The *strophe* is balanced by the *antistrophe;* the pair is sometimes followed by an *epode.* This basic pattern is varied on occasion by the use of repeated refrains and similar devices.

iambic pentameter or blank verse in English. After the series of *episodes* and *stasima,* there is the finale or *exodus,* the closing scene of the play at the end of which the Chorus leaves the view of the audience by way of the *parodoi.*

ARISTOTLE ON TRAGEDY

The most important document to come out of antiquity concerning Greek tragedy is of course the justly famous *Poetics* of Aristotle. In it, though it was written some fifty years after the heyday of Greek tragedy, Aristotle devotes himself almost exclusively to this form of art.

Upon analysis Aristotle concludes that there are in tragedy six basic elements which he calls Plot, Character, Diction, Thought, Spectacle, and Song. However, preliminary to his whole study in the *Poetics,* he introduces the conception of *mimesis,* or "imitation," which Plato had already used before him, as fundamental to the phenomena of art. In saying that the artist "imitates" his models, Aristotle does not use the word in its primary sense of "copying," but rather is seeking to give a secondary meaning to the term. By the word he seems to mean the process which takes place when an artist creates his work of art. It is through *mimesis* that form comes to be imposed upon the artist's material, broadly conceived. Aristotle insists that "poetry is something more philosophic and of graver import than history, since its statements are of the nature of universals, whereas those of history are singulars." Hence poetry "imitates" universals, and the process of *mimesis* produces a resultant work of art in which the "universal" aspect constitutes the very essence. Aristotle classifies the six basic elements according to the rôle each of them occupies in the process of artistic "imitation." He maintains that Diction and Song refer to the medium of "imitation," Spectacle to the manner of "imitation," while Plot, Character, and Thought refer to the objects of "imitation." Of the six elements Aristotle holds that Plot is the most important, with Character second.

An acquaintance with these six elements and with the Aristotelian conception of *mimesis* are necessary preliminaries to an understanding of his famous definition of tragedy: "Tragedy, then, is an imitation of an action that is serious, complete, and of a certain magnitude; in language embellished with each kind of artistic ornament, the several kinds being found in separate parts of the play; in the form of action, not of narrative; through pity and fear effecting the proper purgation of these and similar emotions." Aristotle's analysis and definition contain much that is valuable for one who is endeavoring to comprehend the inner nature of Greek tragedy. First, in his analysis of the elements he has shown that the dramatic synthesis is rich and complicated. He likewise properly emphasizes the elements of Plot and Character. Second, in the definition he insists upon its essential seriousness, its completeness, that is, its unity as an artistic whole, and its "magnitude," that is, its scale and elevation, which in some way raises it above the ordinary run of things human. Furthermore, he indicates what he believes the function of tragedy to be, the *catharsis*, or "proper purgation" of pity, fear, and similar emotions.

One more conception of Aristotle in the *Poetics*, his theory of the ideal tragic hero and the "tragic flaw," merits our attention. Aristotle says that tragedy must involve a change of fortune for a character, but this personage cannot be a completely virtuous man passing from fortune to misfortune, because this would be simply odious to the spectator. Nor can it involve a bad man passing from misery to happiness, because this would outrage our human feelings, our moral sense, and accordingly no appropriate tragic emotions would be aroused within us. Nor again can it involve a bad man passing from happiness to misery. Perhaps this would satisfy the moral sense, but it again would not arouse in us the appropriate tragic emotions. Hence Aristotle defines the ideal tragic hero in these words: "A man who is highly renowned and prosperous, but one who is not pre-eminently virtuous and just, whose misfortune, however, is brought upon him not by vice and depravity but by some error of judgment or frailty."

There are several points to be particularly noted concerning Aristotle's conception of tragedy. First of all, he emphasizes the human element and insists implicitly that tragedy involves human beings. Second, he emphasizes the single individual in his argument concerning the tragic hero. Furthermore, he recognizes in human life states of happiness and misery, fortune and misfortune, in and out of which men pass. Here also he both implicitly and explicitly rejects the mechanical conception of "poetic justice," that the good prosper and the evil suffer. Aristotle likewise assumes the existence of some kind of moral order in the universe, as well as, by implication, the element of chance or luck, which may be possibly extended to include fate or destiny. In summary, then, for Aristotle tragedy is serious and elevated. It involves emotions of a particular sort. It looks at man and his states, in a world in which there is an element of chance or fate, but in which, at least so far as man himself is concerned, there is a definite moral order in some sort, and not moral chaos.

AESCHYLUS

Of the many writers of Greek tragedy only Aeschylus, Sophocles, and Euripides are represented in the plays which have survived. Aeschylus, the earliest of the three, was born of a rather prominent family in Athens in 525 B.C., at a time long before the city had achieved much distinction among the peoples of the Greek area.

Aeschylus first competed in the dramatic contests in Athens in 499 B.C. He achieved his first victory in 484 B.C.

and continued from then on to be highly successful in the theater. Aside from his dramatic activity, he apparently gained distinction in military affairs, having fought both at Marathon and Salamis. In all, he wrote approximately ninety plays, of which only seven have survived. We are told that he won first prizes in competition on thirteen occasions, his last victory occurring in 458 B.C. with his great trilogy, the *Oresteia.* He died in 455 B.C. while in Sicily, where he had gone shortly after his final tragic competition.

The loftiness of Aeschylean language and imagery is most notable, even though on some occasions the poet comes dangerously near bombast, a fact on which Aristophanes capitalized with great comic effect in *The Frogs.* However, Aeschylus' images possess a poetic depth and intensity which could only come from a mind driving deeply into the essence of that which it was seeking to express. Aeschylus' primary interest is in religion and theology. To be sure, he considers human phenomena, but not on the human level, or as ends in themselves. Aeschylus rather studies human affairs as means of throwing light upon the problems of religion and theology, which he considered more universal and more significant.

EURIPIDES

For general purposes of exposition it seems best to pass by Sophocles for the moment and turn to Euripides, who in many ways lies at the opposite extreme from Aeschylus in his basic interests. Euripides was born between the years 485 and 480 B.C. During his lifetime Euripides presented approximately eighty-eight plays, though he wrote in all about ninety-two. In the contests he was successful only four times, probably because his somewhat new and unorthodox views did not find immediate favor with the public. Certainly there is a strong strain of scepticism in his writing, and one becomes aware of the increasing doubt and uncertainty which pervade the plays, particularly those written towards the close of the Peloponnesian War, when Athens, the great city of ante-bellum days, was tottering upon the brink of ruin. Though Euripides' plays were not well received during his life, it is evident that after his death, during the fourth century B.C. and later, he was by far the most popular of the three tragedians. Euripides left Athens for the court of King Archelaus of Macedonia in about 408 B.C. and died there in 406 B.C.

Euripides' greatest claims to fame rest on his superb studies of human problems considered on the human level, his penetrating psychological analyses of his characters, his capacity to create genuine pathos, his sense of the dramatic possibilities of an individual scene, and his ability by means of dramatic innovations to reinterpret the traditional legends upon which all the dramatists relied for their material.

Euripides had a profound influence upon the drama. He seems to have shaken the domination which the traditional sagas exerted upon the playwrights; he reduced the importance of the Chorus, until it only served to provide lyric interludes between actual dramatic scenes, but above all he raised to supreme importance the study of character. Unlike Aeschylus he is not predominantly interested in religion and theology, but rather in ethical problems, in human beings face to face with the pain and evil of human life, as they exhibit now strength and now pathetic weakness. Although he never consistently formulates his ideas concerning the gods or the superhuman elements in the universe, he nevertheless seems to believe that they exist and are relevant to human life in some way or other.

SOPHOCLES

There remains to consider Sophocles, the great mediating figure between Aeschylus and Euripides. He was born about

495 B.C., some ten years or so before the birth of Euripides, and lived to the great age of ninety, when he died about 405 B.C., surviving his younger contemporary by approximately a year. The poet's family was wealthy, and he himself served in public office on several occasions. In the main, however, he devoted himself completely to the theater and in all wrote about one hundred twenty-five plays of which now there are but seven extant, and unfortunately none of these derives from the first twenty-five years of his creative activity. His plays met with wide popular success, as is indicated by his twenty victories in tragic competition. Unlike Euripides, who, as we have already noted, became bitterly disillusioned towards the end of his life, and whose works show evidence of this change of temper, Sophocles in his plays seems to maintain a consistent and firm approach to the problems of tragedy.

Sophocles' mastery of dramatic technique is apparent in all his plays, most notably, of course, in *Oedipus the King*. Likewise in this tragedy, he demonstrated his ability to use with overwhelming effectiveness the device of dramatic irony. But his greatest excellence clearly lies in his general view of life, which can scarcely be communicated in the necessarily conceptual terms of criticism. It is, however, most clearly expressed in two great choral odes, one on the wonders of man in the *Antigone* and the other on the laws of Heaven in *Oedipus the King*. In the first of these Sophocles eloquently asserts the dignity, worth and value of man, even though there is death that he cannot conquer. In the second the poet proclaims his belief in a mysterious and powerful force behind the universe which sets and ordains the eternal laws of the world, which are holy, though ultimately incomprehensible to man. These seem to be the two fundamental aspects of Sophocles' view of life: man the marvel working out his own destiny, making his own choices, but under the guidance of Heaven and its everlasting laws. Sophocles concentrates on the continual interaction of these two aspects. So struggles Oedipus, who has transgressed unwittingly a law of Heaven, but who through iron and inflexible will endeavors to work out his destiny and to assume his responsibility in a world in which human and divine elements are wholly interfused.

We have maintained that Aeschylus' basic orientation was towards theology and religion. On the other hand, we have insisted that Euripides was predominantly interested in human beings, on the human level, in their psychological states as they face the complex problems of human life. In a curious way Sophocles lies in a mean between these two poets, and seems to combine in himself their outstanding powers. He has the scale of Aeschylus plus Euripides' power of psychological analysis. He studies his human characters psychologically in their human environment, and yet he manages to approach the elevation of Aeschylus. He remains on the human level, yet always directs his gaze towards that which is superhuman. It is the miracle of Sophocles' genius which has enabled him to express this interpretation of life, so deep and comprehensive that it has rarely if ever been equalled in the creative literature of Western Europe.

W. J. O.

II. Comedy

In a number of its broadest aspects the comedy of the fifth century resembles tragedy. It was performed at festivals of Dionysus under the aegis of the Athenian state. Its expenses were met in the same manner as those of tragedy and the rivalry of the poets competing for the prizes was just as keen. It was performed in the same theater before the same type of audience, by a chorus of about the same size and by an equally limited number of actors. Its structure shows many of the characteristic features of the mature tragic drama, such as *prologue*, *parodos*, and *exodus*, and the main body of both types of play consists of a series of relatively short scenes separated by choral interludes. The *prologues* of fifth-century comedy are not usually composed with much care or skill, and the situation is often explained to the spectators by one of the actors in a long and undramatic speech reminiscent of the Euripidean *prologue*, but we nowhere find a comic *prologue* consisting entirely of such a speech. The comic *parodos* is much more complicated and dramatic than the one usually found in the tragic play, and it contains peculiarities of form that are unknown in tragedy. The special interest of the comic *exodus* derives not from its form, which is quite free. but from its content. It is in the choral interludes between scenes that the unique features of the form and the structure of comedy are most evident. Whereas in tragedy these performances of the Chorus, for all their differences in content and in meter, almost invariably have the standardized form of the *stasimon*, in comedy they exhibit astonishing variety and frequent specialization.

The typical fifth-century comedy falls into two well-defined parts, usually of more or less equal length. The first of these we find devoted to the creation of some incongruous situation, the second to the results of this, presented in a series of short scenes that have little dramatic coherence and no development.

The influence of tragedy on classic comedy is evident in the increasing preoccupation with subjects that are utopian or timeless, and the traditional satire on contemporary events and personages recedes more and more into the background. In the early fourth century we observe what appears to be a sudden decline in the importance of the Chorus. In the New Comedy (after 340 B.C.) the Chorus is merely an adventitious band of revellers which entertains the audience between the acts into which the plays of this period are divided.

ARISTOPHANES

As is so often the case with ancient writers, we know next to nothing about the life of Aristophanes. Born about 445 B.C. in Attica, he began to write when he was very young, and his first play was produced when he was eighteen. He composed about forty comedies in all, but we do not know how often he was victorious. On several occasions he brought out his plays under other names, but we do not know why he did this. The date of his death is uncertain, but it must have been later than 387 B.C.

There has never been anything quite like the comic drama of Aristophanes, and regrettably there will never be anything quite like it again. The effect of the initial impact of these plays is one of bewilderment. One rubs one's eyes and wonders whether it really can have happened. A closer acquaintance and a bit of sober reflection disclose a number of distinct reasons for astonishment. The first of these is the absolute freedom of speech which the comic poet of the fifth century enjoyed. He might make fun, banteringly or bitterly, thoroughly and repeatedly, of anything; no person, no institution, no god, enjoyed the slightest vestige of immunity, and the Athenian populace seems to have enjoyed these libels and slanders so hugely that they did not even require that they be always amusing.

Equally astonishing is the pervading obscenity, so abundant and so varied that it cannot be ignored or excised. It is so closely interwoven into almost every part of these plays that to expurgate is to destroy. A bowdlerized Aristophanes may offer a selection of passages well adapted to teach Attic Greek to schoolboys, but it is not Aristophanes. There is no escaping the fact that Aristophanes wrote just as obscenely as he could on every possible occasion. If we would appreciate him properly we should bear this in mind and endeavor to cultivate the same attitude that he had; the most unhealthy approach is the denial of the obvious in the name of healthiness.

The distinguishing characteristic of Aristophanes is his brilliant insouciance. Endowed by nature with an intellect of an exceptionally high order and an imagination inexhaustibly fertile, he exercised his talents in a medium ideally suited to them. His best comedies are concatenations of splendid and dazzling conceits which follow one another in breathless abundance. He is never at a loss what to invent next; indeed, he hardly ever has time fully to exploit the humorous possibilities of one motif before he is occupied with another. A mind of this sort has no use for consistency, and that stodgy virtue may best be cultivated by the lesser talents, who need all the virtues they can get.

It is from this point of view that we must approach him if we would avoid misunderstanding him, and we must not forget that Plato adored him. He has naturally been misunderstood, grossly and variously. He has a lot to say about himself, but hardly a word of it can be taken seriously. This would be an easy deduction from the quality of his mind, but he repeatedly proves it by his actions, for he blandly denies doing what he plainly and frequently does. His views on political and social questions have been eagerly and ponderously analyzed, but this is mostly a waste of time and energy. It is safe to say that whenever his wit is functioning properly we have no hope of discovering what his real feelings were.

Brilliance, however, was not his only gift, and his heart was as sensitive as his mind was keen. The soft side of his personality expresses itself in his lyrics, and here he astounds and delights us, at one moment with idyllic songs of the countryside, at another with lines of infinite tenderness and sympathy, particularly towards old men. Often in the midst of a lyric passage of great warmth and beauty something will touch off his wit, and a sentence that has begun in a gentle and sympathetic spirit will end with a devastating personal gibe or an uproarious bit of obscenity. The two sides of the poet's nature are not really separable; he can be both witty and lyrical, almost at one and the same moment. This strange and perfect blend of characteristics apparently so incompatible makes Aristophanes a wonderful man to read, and we begin to understand why Plato loved the old rogue as he did.

E. O'N., Jr.

BIBLIOGRAPHY

M. Bieber, *The History of the Greek and Roman Theater* (Princeton, 1961)

C. M. Bowra, *Sophoclean Tragedy* (Oxford, Clarendon Press, 1945)

F. M. Cornford, *The Origin of Attic Comedy* (London, Arnold, 1914)

R. F. Goheen, *The Imagery of Sophocles' Antigone* (Princeton, 1951)

L. H. G. Greenwood, *Aspects of Euripidean Tragedy* (Cambridge, 1953)

G. M. A. Grube, *The Drama of Euripides* (London, Methuen, 1941)

A. E. Haigh, *The Tragic Drama of the Greeks* (Oxford, Clarendon Press, 1896)

J. Jones, *On Aristotle and Greek Tragedy* (London, Chatto & Windus, 1962)

G. M. Kirkwood, *A Study of Sophoclean Drama* (Ithaca, N.Y., Cornell University Press, 1958)

H. D. F. Kitto, *Greek Tragedy: A Literary Study* (London, Methuen, 1950; 3rd ed., New York, Barnes & Noble, 1961)

———, *Form and Meaning in Drama* (London, Methuen, 1956; 2nd ed., New York, Barnes & Noble, 1959)

B. Knox, *Oedipus at Thebes* (New Haven, 1957)

———, *The Heroic Temper* (Berkeley, 1964)

R. Lattimore, *Story Patterns in Greek Tragedy* (Ann Arbor, University of Michigan Press, 1964)

A. M. G. Little, *Myth and Society in Attic Drama* (New York, Columbia University Press, 1942)

F. L. Lucas, *Euripides and his Influences* (Boston, Marshall Jones, 1923)

G. Murray, *Euripides and his Age* (New York, Holt, 1913)

———, *Aristophanes: A Study* (Oxford, Clarendon Press, 1933)

———, *Aeschylus: The Creator of Tragedy* (Oxford, Clarendon Press, 1940)

G. Norwood, *Greek Tragedy* (Boston, Luce, 1920)

———, *Greek Comedy* (Boston, Luce, 1932)

———, *Essays on Euripidean Drama* (Berkeley, 1954)

E. T. Owen, *The Harmony of Aeschylus* (Toronto, 1952)

A. W. Pickard-Cambridge, *The Theater of Dionysus in Athens* (Oxford, 1946)

———, *The Dramatic Festivals of Athens* (Oxford, 1953)

———, *Dithyramb: Tragedy and Comedy* (Oxford, 1962)

H. W. Smyth, *Aeschylean Tragedy* (Berkeley, 1924)

G. Thomson, *Aeschylus and Athens* (New York, International Publishers, 1950)

A. J. A. Waldock, *Sophocles the Dramatist* (Cambridge, 1951)

T. B. L. Webster, *Introduction to Sophocles* (Oxford, Clarendon Press, 1936)

C. H. Whitman, *Sophocles* (Cambridge, 1951)

———, *Aristophanes and the Comic Hero* (Cambridge, Mass., Harvard University Press, 1964)

PROMETHEUS BOUND

by

AESCHYLUS

Characters in the Play

Power
Force
Hephaestus
Prometheus
Chorus of the Daughters of Oceanus
Oceanus
Io
Hermes

INTRODUCTION

FEW GREEK tragedies present as many critical difficulties as does the *Prometheus Bound*. In the first place even its authenticity has been doubted, although this view has not commanded any general acceptance. Its date is likewise uncertain. Further, although the play is presumably one part of a trilogy, critics have not been able to determine with exactness what place it occupied in the larger dramatic unit and what was the content of its companion plays. Lastly, the question of its larger significance has provided ample material for critical debate.

So far as our information goes, we may with fair assurance accept the theory, now generally held, that the *Prometheus Bound* was the first play of the trilogy, followed by *Prometheus Unbound* and *Prometheus the Fire-Bearer*. In the trilogy the poet has treated in detail the legend of the great Titan, who took pity on the helplessness of men, and gave them the precious gift of fire which he stole from Heaven, wherewith they were able to improve their state and to learn the arts of civilization. Prometheus' theft contravened an ordinance of Zeus, the newly established Lord of Heaven, who had determined to destroy the race of men. Our play deals with Zeus' punishment of his rebellious subject, while the second of the series told of Prometheus' release, and the third, about which we have scarcely any knowledge, may have connected the legend with the institution of some religious festival of the Athenians.

In the *Prometheus Bound* Aeschylus was faced with a difficult problem of dramaturgy since he had to build a play in which his central character could not move, in a very literal sense of the word. Consequently the poet found himself considerably limited in scope and was forced practically to eliminate from his play anything which we might call "action." Aeschylus solves the problem by introducing several characters who in one way or another set off the central figure. He contrasts Prometheus now with Oceanus, now with Io his fellow-sufferer at the hands of Zeus, and finally with Hermes, the "lackey of Zeus" as Prometheus bitterly calls him. In and through the dialogues between Prometheus and his various interlocutors gradually emerges the poet's analysis of the questions he is raising in the play.

Since we do not possess the rest of the trilogy, any attempt to give a general interpretation of the *Prometheus Bound* is hazardous. At least some points are certain. Here we have a play whose dramatic date lies almost at the beginning of mythological time. Furthermore, all the characters, save Io, are superhuman. Hence the poet has given the play a greater elevation than is to be found elsewhere in the extant Greek drama. Of course, he loses in "realism," but, to compensate this loss, he has put himself in a position whence he may appropriately attack the central problem which he has before him. This problem appears to be "What is the nature of the divine power which lies behind the universe? If that power is benevolent, beneficent or good, why is it that man suffers? Why is there evil in the world?" Our play seems to contain only the preliminaries to some kind of resolution of this most difficult of all philosophical and religious problems. Prometheus, the benignant, the "Suffering Servant," the benefactor of mankind, is posed against Zeus, the malignant tyrant, omnipotent, though not omniscient. A quasi-allegory or partial symbolism may be present here in this opposition between wisdom and brute force.

PROMETHEUS BOUND

(SCENE:—*A rocky gorge in Scythia.* POWER *and* FORCE *enter, carrying* PROMETHEUS *as a captive. They are accompanied by* HEPHAESTUS.)

POWER

TO THIS far region of the earth, this pathless wilderness of Scythia, at last we are come. O Hephaestus, thine is the charge, on thee are laid the Father's commands in never-yielding fetters linked of adamant to bind this miscreant to the high-ridged rocks. For this is he who stole the flame of all-working fire, thy own bright flower, and gave to mortal men. Now for the evil done he pays this forfeit to the gods; so haply he shall learn some patience with the reign of Zeus and put away his love for human kind.

HEPHAESTUS

O Power and Force, your share in the command of Zeus is done, and for you nothing remains; but I—some part of courage still is wanting to bind with force a kindred god to this winter-bitten gorge. Yet must I summon daring to my heart, such dread dwells in the Father's word.—(*to* PROMETHEUS) O high magnanimous son of prudent Themis, against thy will and mine with brazen bonds no hand can loose I bind thee to this unvisited lonely rock. No human voice will reach thee here, nor any form of man be seen. Parched by the blazing fires of the sun thy skin shall change its pleasant hue; grateful to thee the starry-kirtled night shall come veiling the day, and grateful again the sun dispelling the morn's white frost. Forever the weariness of unremitting pain shall waste thy strength, for he is not born who can deliver thee. See now the profit of thy human charity: thou, a god not fearing the wrath of the gods, hast given to mortal men honors beyond their due; and therefore on this joyless rock thou must keep vigil, sleepless and weary-clinging, with unbended knees, pouring out thy ceaseless lamentations and unheeded cries; for the mind of Zeus knows no turning, and ever harsh the hand that newly grasps the sway.

POWER

It may be so, yet why seek delay in vainly spent pity? Feel you no hatred for this enemy of the gods, who hath betrayed to mortals your own chief honor?

HEPHAESTUS

Kinship and old fellowship will have their due.

POWER

'Tis true; but where is strength to disobey the Father's words? Fearest thou not rather this?

HEPHAESTUS

Ever merciless thou art, and steeped in cruelty.

POWER

It healeth nothing to weep for him. Take not up an idle burden wherein there is no profit.

HEPHAESTUS

Alas, my cherished craft, thrice hateful now!

POWER

Why hateful? In simple sooth thy art hath no blame for these present ills.

HEPHAESTUS

Yet would it were another's, not mine!

POWER

All toil alike in sorrow, unless one were lord of heaven; none is truly free, save only Zeus.

HEPHAESTUS

This task confirms it; I can nothing deny.

POWER

Make haste then to bind him in fetters, lest the father detect thee loitering.

HEPHAESTUS

Behold the curb; it is ready to hand.

POWER

Strongly with thy hammer, strongly weld it about his hands; make him fast to the rock.

HEPHAESTUS

The work goes on, it is well done.

POWER

Harder strike them, tighter draw the links, leave nothing loose; strange skill he hath to find a way where none appeared.

HEPHAESTUS

One arm is fastened, and none may loose it.

POWER

Fetter the other, make it sure; he shall learn how all his cunning is folly before Zeus.

HEPHAESTUS

Save now my art hath never wrought harm to any.

POWER

Now strongly drive the biting tooth of the adamantine wedge straight through his breast.

HEPHAESTUS

Alas, Prometheus! I groan for thy pangs.

POWER

Dost thou shrink? Wilt thou groan for the foes of Zeus? Take heed, lest thou groan for thyself.

HEPHAESTUS

Thou lookest upon a spectacle grievous to the eye.

POWER

I look upon one suffering as he deserves.—Now about his sides strain tight the girth.

HEPHAESTUS

It must needs be done; yet urge me not overmuch.

POWER

Yet will I urge and harry thee on.—Now lower; with force constrain his legs.

HEPHAESTUS

'Tis even done; nor was the labor long.

POWER

Weld fast the galling fetters; remember that he who appraises is strict to exact.

HEPHAESTUS

Cruel thy tongue, and like thy cruel face.

POWER

Be thine the tender heart! Rebuke not my bolder mood, nor chide my austerity.

HEPHAESTUS

Let us go; now the clinging web binds all his limbs.

(HEPHAESTUS *departs.*)

POWER

There, wanton, in thy insolence! Now for thy creatures of a day filch divine honors. Tell me, will mortal men drain for thee these tortures? Falsely the gods call thee Prometheus, the Contriver, for no cunning contrivance shall help thee to slip from this bondage.

(Power *and* Force *depart.*)

Prometheus (*alone, chanting*)

O air divine, and O swift-wingèd winds!
Ye river fountains, and thou myriad-twinkling
Laughter of ocean waves! O mother earth!
And thou, O all-discerning orb o' the sun!—
To you, I cry to you; behold what I,
A god, endure of evil from the gods.

Behold, with what dread torments
I through the slow-revolving
Ages of time must wrestle;
Such hideous bonds the new lord
Of heaven hath found for my torture.
Woe! woe! for the present disasters
I groan, and for those that shall come;
Nor know I in what far sky
The dawn of deliverance shall rise.

Yet what is this I say? All future things
I see unerring, nor shall any chance
Of evil overtake me unaware.
The will of Destiny we should endure
Lightly as may be, knowing still how vain
To take up arms against Necessity.
Silent I cannot keep, I cannot tongue
These strange calamities. Lo, I am he
Who, darkly hiding in a fennel reed
Fountains of fire, so secretly purloined
And gave to be the teacher of all arts
And giver of all good to mortal men.
And now this forfeit for my sin I pay,
Thus lodged in fetters under the bare sky.

Woe's me!
What murmur hovereth near?
What odor, where visible shape
Is none? Some god, or a mortal,
Or one of the middle race?
Hath he come to this world's-end
Idly to gloat o'er my toils,
Or what would he have?—Behold me
Fettered, the god ill-fated,
The foeman of Zeus, the detested
Of all who enter his courts,
And only because of my love,
My too-great love for mankind.
Ah me! once more the murmur
I hear as of hovering birds;
And the air is whirring with quick
Beating of wings. For me
There is fear, whatever approaches.

(*The* CHORUS OF THE DAUGHTERS OF OCEANUS *enter, drawn in a winged car.*)

CHORUS (*singing*)

strophe 1

Fear nothing; in friendship and eager
With wingèd contention of speed
Together we draw near thy rock.
Scarce we persuaded our father,
But now at last the swift breezes
Have brought us. Down in the depth
Of our sea-cave came the loud noise
Of the welding of iron; and wonderment
Banished our maiden shame;
All in haste, unsandalled; hither
We flew in this wingèd car.

PROMETHEUS

Ah me! ah me!
O all ye children of Tethys,
Daughters of father Oceanus
Who ever with tide unwearied
Revolveth the whole world round,—
Behold now prisoned in chains
On the dizzy verge of this gorge
Forever I keep sad watch.

CHORUS

antistrophe 1

I see, O Prometheus, thy body
In the toils and torture of bondage
Withering here on this rock;
And a mist as of terror, a cloud
Of tears o'erveils my eyes:
New helmsmen guide in the heavens,
And Zeus unlawfully rules
With new laws, and the might of old
He hath banished to uttermost darkness.

PROMETHEUS

Would that me too he had hurled,
Bound in these cruel, unyielding
Bonds, down, down under earth,
Beneath wide Hades, where go
The tribe of innumerable dead,
Down to the infinite depths
Of Tartarus! There no god,
No mortal would gloat o'er my ruin.
Now like a toy of the winds
I hang, my anguish a joy
To my foes.

CHORUS

strophe 2

Who of the gods is so hardened?
To whom is thy sorrow a joy?
Who save only Zeus
But feels the pang of thy torments?
But he, ever savage of soul,
Swayeth the children of heaven;
Nor ever will cease till his heart
Is satiate grown, or another
Snatches the empire by guile.

PROMETHEUS

Ay, and this Lord of the blessed
Shall call in the fulness of time
Upon me whom he tortures in bondage,
Shall implore me to utter the plot
That will rob him of honor and throne.
No sweet-lipped charm of persuasion
Then shall allure me, and never
In cringing fear of his threats
The knowledge will I impart,
Till first he has loosened these bonds,
And for all my anguish he too
Hath humbled his neck unto judgment.

CHORUS

antistrophe 2

Bold art thou, and calamity
Softens thee not, but ever
Thy thought is quick on thy tongue.
Terror pierceth my heart,
And fearing I ask what shore,
O wanderer tempest-tost,
Far-off of peace shall receive thee!
Stern is the son of Cronos,
And deaf his heart to beseeching.

PROMETHEUS

I know of his hardness, I know
That justice he holds in his palm;
Yet his pride shall be humbled, I think;
His hardness made soft, and his wrath
Shall bow to the blows of adversity;
He, too, in milder mood
Shall come, imploring of me
The friendship I willingly grant.

LEADER OF THE CHORUS

Unfold to us the whole story. For what crime does Zeus so shamefully and bitterly torture you? Tell us, if there is no harm in telling.

PROMETHEUS

Painful are these things to relate, painful is silence, and all is wretchedness. When first the gods knew wrath, and faction raised its head amongst them, and some would tear old Cronos from his throne that Zeus might take his place, and others were determined that Zeus should never reign over the gods, then I with wise counsel sought to guide the Titans, children of Earth and Sky,—but all in vain. My crafty schemes they disdained, and in their pride of strength thought it were easy to make themselves lords by force. Often to me my mother Themis (or call her Earth, for many names she hath, being one) had foretold in oracles what was to be, with warning that not by might or brutal force should victory come, but by guile alone. So I counselled them, but they turned their eyes from me in impatience. Of the courses which then lay open, far the best, it seemed, was to take my mother as my helper and to join my will with the will of Zeus. By my advice the cavernous gloom of Tartarus now hides in night old Cronos and his peers. Thus the new tyrant of heaven took profit of me, and thus rewards me with these torments. 'Tis the disease of tyranny, no more, to take no heed of friendship. You ask why he tortures me; hear now the reason. No sooner was he established on his father's throne than he began to award various offices to the different gods, ordering his government throughout. Yet no care was in his heart for miserable men, and he was fain to blot out the whole race and in their stead create another. None save me opposed his purpose; I only dared; I rescued mankind from the heavy blow that was to cast them into Hades. Therefore I am bowed down by this anguish, painful to endure, pitiable to behold. Mercy I had for mortals, but found no mercy for myself: so piteously I am disciplined, an ignoble spectacle for Zeus.

LEADER

Fashioned of rock is he, and iron is his heart, O Prometheus, who feels not indignation at thy disasters. Rather would I not have seen them at all, and seeing them I am sore of heart.

PROMETHEUS

To my very friends I am a spectacle of pity.

LEADER

Yet it may be—did thy transgressions end there?

PROMETHEUS

Through me mankind ceased to foresee death.

LEADER

What remedy could heal that sad disease?

PROMETHEUS

Blind hopes I made to dwell in them.

LEADER

O merciful boon for mortals.

PROMETHEUS

And more than all I gave them fire.

LEADER

And so in their brief life they are lords of flaming fire?

PROMETHEUS

Through it they will learn many arts.

LEADER

And was it for crimes like this Zeus—

PROMETHEUS

Tortures me, and ceases not nor relents.

LEADER

And is there no goal to the struggle before thee?

PROMETHEUS

There is none, save when it seems to him good.

LEADER

When shall it so seem? What hope? Seest thou not thy error? That thou hast erred, I say in sorrow and with sorrow to thee. But enough of that; seek thou some release from the conflict.

PROMETHEUS

How easy for one who fares in pleasant ways to admonish those in adversity. But all this I knew; with open eyes, with willing mind, I erred; I do not deny it. Mankind I helped, but could not help myself. Yet I dreamed not that here in this savage solitary gorge, on this high rock, I should waste away beneath such torments. Yet care not to bewail these present disasters; but descend to the earth, and hear of the woes to come and all that is to be. I pray you heed my word; have compassion on one who is now caught in the toils; for sorrow flitteth now to one and now to another, and visiteth each in his turn.

CHORUS (*singing*)

We list to your words, O Prometheus.—
Lo, with light foot I step
From the swift-rushing car; the pure air.
The highway I leave of the birds;
And now to the rugged earth

I descend, I listen, I wait
For thy story of pain and disaster.
(OCEANUS *enters, borne on a winged horse.*)

OCEANUS

To thee I come, O Prometheus;
Borne on this swift-wingèd bird
That knoweth the will of his rider
And needeth no curb, from afar
I have flown a wearisome way,
Weary but ended at last.
I am grieved with thy grief; I am drawn
By our kinship, and even without it
Thee more than all others I honor.
I speak simple sooth, and my tongue
Knows not to flatter in idleness.
Nay, tell me what aid I may render;
For never thy lips shall avow
Oceanus failed thee in friendship.

PROMETHEUS

Ho! What is this I look upon? What then, art thou too come to stare upon my ruin? What new daring has brought thee from thy ocean stream and thy rock-roofed unbuilded caverns hither to our earth, the mother of iron? Art thou come to view my fate with indignation for my calamities? Behold the spectacle! behold me, the friend of Zeus, who helped him to a throne, now bowed down by his torments.

OCEANUS

I see, Prometheus; and, though thou art thyself cunning in device, I would admonish thee to prudence. Learn to know thyself, put on the habit of new ways, for there is a new tyrant among the gods. If still thou hurlest forth these harsh and biting words, perchance from afar off, Zeus, sitting above, may hear thee, and thy present burden of sorrows will seem as the sport of children. But, O wretched sufferer, put away thy moody wrath, and seek some respite from thy ills. My advice may sound as the trite sayings of old, yet thou thyself canst see what are the wages of too bold a tongue. Thou hast not learned humility, nor to yield to evils, but rather wouldst add others new to thy present store. Take me for thy teacher, and kick not against the pricks, for there rules in heaven an austere monarch who is responsible to none. Now I will go and make trial to win thy release from this grievous state. Do thou keep thy peace, and restrain thy blustering speech. Or knowest thou not in thy wisdom what penalties overtake an idle tongue?

PROMETHEUS

I give you joy that, having shared and dared with me, you have still kept yourself free of blame. I bid you trouble not your peace; his will is immutable and you cannot persuade him. Even beware, lest by your going you bring sorrow upon yourself.

OCEANUS

Thou art wiser to think for others than for thyself, and this I infer from the events. But deter me not from going, for I boast, yes, I may boast, that Zeus will grant me this boon and deliver thee from these toils.

PROMETHEUS

I thank you with gratitude that shall never fail, for you lack nothing in zeal. But trouble not yourself; it is idle, and your care will avail me nothing, despite your zeal. Hold your peace, and keep your foot well from these snares. If I suffer, let me suffer alone. Yet not alone, for I am burdened by the fate of Atlas, my brother. He in the far western ways stands bearing on his shoulders the mighty pillar of earth and sky, a weary burden to hold. And I have seen with pity the earth-born dweller of the Cilician caves, the impetuous, the hundred-headed Typho, when he was bent by force. For he withstood the host of the gods hissing forth terror from his horrid throats, whilst Gorgonian fires flamed from his eyes, as if to take by violence the very throne of Zeus; but the unsleeping weapon of Zeus fell upon him, the down-rushing thunderbolt with breath of flame, and smote him from his loud-vaunted boastings; and stricken to the heart he was scorched to embers, and thunder rent from him his strength. Now a helpless sprawling bulk he lies near the ocean strait, buried beneath the roots of Aetna; whilst above on the utmost summit Hephaestus welds the molten ore. Thence some day, I ween, shall burst forth rivers of fire to devour with savage maw the wide fields of fair-fruited Sicily,—such wrath shall Typho, scorched by the thunder of Zeus, send up, a tempest, terrible, seething, with breath of flame.—But thou art not untried, and needest not me for a teacher. Save thyself, as thou best knowest how; and leave me to drain this flood of calamity, till the mind of Zeus grows light of its anger.

OCEANUS

Knowest thou not, Prometheus, there are words of healing foı a mind distempered?

PROMETHEUS

Ay, if in good time we soothe the heart, nor violently repress its tumid rage.

OCEANUS

In prudent zeal and daring combined, tell me what peril hidden lies.

PROMETHEUS

Labor in vain and vain simplicity.

OCEANUS

Leave me, I prythee, to my mind's disease; for it is well having wisdom not to appear wise.

PROMETHEUS

The folly of thy mission will seem mine.

OCEANUS

It is clear your words dismiss me home.

PROMETHEUS

Your tears for me might win hatred for yourself.

OCEANUS

His hatred you mean, who newly wears the sovereignty?

PROMETHEUS

Ay, his; beware that you vex not his heart.

OCEANUS

Your calamity, Prometheus, is my teacher.

PROMETHEUS

Be gone, take yourself off, keep your present mind.

OCEANUS

I am gone even with your urgent words. See, the winged beast flutters the broad path of the air; gladly would he bend the weary knee in his stall at home.

(OCEANUS *departs as the* CHORUS *begins its song*)

CHORUS

strophe 1

I mourn, O Prometheus, for thee,
I wail for thy hapless fate;
And tears in a melting flood
Flow down from the fount of my eyes,
Drenching my cheeks. O insolent
Laws, O sceptre of Zeus,
How over the gods of old
Ye wield despotic might!

antistrophe 1

Lo, all the land groans aloud;
And the people that dwell in the West
Lament for thy time-honored reign
And the sway of thy kindred, Prometheus;
And they who have builded their homes
In holy Asia to the wail
Of thine anguish lament.

strophe 2

And they
Of the Colchian land, the virgins
Exulting in war; and the Scythians
By the far Maeotian Lake
In the uttermost regions of earth;

antistrophe 2

And the martial flower of Arabia,
Whose battle resounds with the crashing
Of brazen spears, they too
In their citadel reared aloft
Near Caucasus groan for thy fate.

epode

One other, a Titan god,
I have seen in his anguish,
Atlas, the mighty one, bound
In chains adamantine, who still
With groaning upholds on his back
The high-arched vault of the skies.

epode

While ever the surge of the sea
Moans to the sound of his cry,
And the depths of its waters lament;
The fountains of hallowed rivers
Sigh for his anguish in pity;
While from its dark abyss
The unseen world far below
Mutters and rumbles in concert.

PROMETHEUS

Think not I am silent through pride or insolence; dumb rage gnaws at my very heart for this outrage upon me. Yet who but I established these new gods in their honors? But I speak not of this, for already you are aware of the truth. Rather listen to the sad story of mankind, who like children lived until I gave them understanding and a portion of reason; yet not in disparagement of men I speak, but meaning to set forth the greatness of my charity. For seeing they saw not, and hearing they understood not, but like as shapes in a dream they wrought all the days of their life in confusion. No houses of brick raised in the warmth of the sun they had, nor fabrics of wood, but like the little ants they dwelt underground in the sunless depth of caverns. No certain sign of approaching winter they knew, no harbinger of flowering spring or fruitful summer; ever they labored at random, till I taught them to discern the seasons by the rising and the obscure setting of the stars. Numbers I invented for them, the chiefest of all discoveries; I taught them the grouping of letters, to be a memorial and record of the past, the mistress of the arts and mother of the Muses. I first brought under the yoke beasts of burden, who by draft and carrying relieved men of their hardest labors; I yoked the proud horse to the chariot, teaching him obedience to the reins, to be the adornment of wealth and luxury. I too contrived for sailors sea-faring vessels with their flaxen wings. Alas for me! such inventions I devised for mankind, but for myself I have no cunning to escape disaster.

LEADER OF THE CHORUS

Sorrow and humiliation are your portion: you have failed in understanding and gone astray; and like a poor physician falling into sickness you despond and know not the remedies for your own disease.

PROMETHEUS

Hear but the rest, and you will wonder more at my inventions and many arts. If sickness visited them, they had no healing drug, no salve or soothing potion, but wasted away for want of remedies, and this was my greatest boon; for I revealed to them the mingling of bland medicaments for the banishing of all diseases. And many modes of divination I appointed: from dreams I first taught them to judge what should befall in waking state; I found the subtle interpretation of words half heard or heard by chance, and of meetings by the way; and the flight of taloned birds with their promise of fortune or failure I clearly denoted, their various modes of life, their mutual feuds, their friendships and consortings; I taught men to observe the smooth plumpness of entrails, and the color of the gall pleasing to the gods, and the mottled symmetry of liver-lobe. Burning the thigh-bones wrapt in fat and the long chine, I guided mankind to a hidden art, and read to them the intimations of the altar-flames that before were meaningless. So much then for these inventions. And the secret treasures of the earth, all benefits to men, copper, iron, silver, gold,—who but I could boast their discovery? No one, I ween, unless in idle vaunting. Nay, hear the whole matter in a word,—all human arts are from Prometheus.

LEADER

Care not for mortals overmuch, whilst you neglect your own profit. Indeed, I am of good hope that yet some day, freed from bondage, you shall equal the might of Zeus.

PROMETHEUS

Not yet hath all-ordaining Destiny decreed my release; but after many years, broken by a world of disaster and woe, I shall be delivered. The craft of the forger is weaker far than Necessity.

LEADER

Who then holds the helm of Necessity?

PROMETHEUS

The Fates triform and the unforgetting Furies.

LEADER

And Zeus, is he less in power than these?

PROMETHEUS

He may not avoid what is destined.

LEADER

What is destined for Zeus but endless rule?

PROMETHEUS

Ask not, neither set thy heart on knowing.

LEADER

Some solemn secret thou wouldst clothe in mystery.

PROMETHEUS

Speak no more of it; the time is not yet to divulge it, and the secret must still be deeply shrouded. Harbouring this I shall one day escape from this outrage and ignominy of bondage.

CHORUS (*singing*)

strophe 1

May never Zeus, the all-wielder,
Against my feeble will
Set his strength; nor ever may I
By the stanchless flood of my father,
By the shores of Oceanus, cease
With hallowed offering of oxen
To worship the gods. May never
My tongue give offence, but always
This purpose abide in my soul.

antistrophe 1

Ah, sweet to prolong our days
In the courage of hope, and sweet
With ever dawning delights
To nourish the heart. I shudder,
Prometheus, for thee, for thy weight
Of myriad-pilèd woe;
Ay, fearing not Zeus, in self-will
Too much thou honourest mortals;

strophe 2

For thankless thy favor, O friend:
And where is the valour, what help
From men who appear and are gone?
Their weakness hast thou not discovered,
Their feeble blindness wherein
Like dreaming shadows they move?
Never their counsels shall break
Through the harmony ordered of Zeus.

antistrophe 2

I too have pondered this wisdom,
Beholding thy terrible ruin,
Prometheus. Ah me, for the change!
With what other notes I chanted
Thy bridal song, the shrill
Hymenean strains at the bath
And the couch, on the happy day
When our sister Hesione, won
By thy bounty, entered thy home!

(Io *enters, transformed in part to a heifer, followed by the Spectre of* ARGUS. *She is in a half-frenzied state.*)

Io (*chanting*)

What land have I reached? what people?
Who is this I behold in chains
On this storm-riven rock? What crime
Hath brought thee to perishing thus?
Ah whither, to what far regions
Hath misery borne me? Ah me!
Once more I am stung by the gadfly,
Pursued by the wraith of dead Argus.
Save me, O Earth! Once more
In my terror I see him, the watcher;
He is there, and his myriad eyes

Are upon me. Shall earth nevermore
Conceal her buried dead?
He hath come from the pit to pursue me,
He drives me weary and famished
Over the long sea sands;
And ever his shrill scrannel pipe,
Waxen-jointed, is droning forth
A slumberous strain.

Alas!

To what land far-off have I wandered?
What error, O Zeus, what crime
Is mine that thus I am yoked
Unto misery? Why am I stung
With frenzy that drives me unresting
Forever? Let fires consume me;
Let the deep earth yawning engulf me;
Or the monstrous brood of the sea
Devour; but O great King,
Hark to my pleading for respite!
I have wandered enough, I am weary,
And still I discern no repose.—

(*To* PROMETHEUS)

And thou, hast thou heard me, the virgin
Wearing these horns of a heifer?

PROMETHEUS

I hear the frenzied child of Inachus,
The maiden who with love could all inflame
Great Zeus's heart, and now by Hera's ha[illegible]
Forever flees before this stinging pest.

IO (*chanting*)

Thou knowest my father then?
And who, I prythee, art thou
That callest me thus by name,
Oh name most wretched! and tellest

The wasting plague heaven-sent
And the pest with its haunting sting?
Ah me! behold I am come
With leapings of madness, by hunger
And craving impelled, and subdued
By the crafty anger of Hera.
Who in this world of calamity,
Who suffers as I?—But thou,
If thou canst, declare what awaits me
Of sorrow; what healing balm
I may find. Speak thou, I implore thee,
I, the wandering virgin of sorrows.

PROMETHEUS

Clearly I will set forth all you would learn; speaking not in dark riddles, but in full simplicity, as speech is due between friends. Behold, I whom you see am Prometheus, the giver of fire to mankind.

IO

You who appeared to men with all-sufficient bounty,—tell my why are you, O enduring Prometheus, given over to chastisement?

PROMETHEUS

But now I have ceased bewailing these calamities.

IO

And will you deny me this simple boon?

PROMETHEUS

What do you ask? You may learn all from me.

IO

Declare who chained you to this rocky gorge.

PROMETHEUS

The will of Zeus, but Hephaestus' hand.

IO

For what crimes are you punished thus?

PROMETHEUS

I have told you enough; ask no more.

IO

One further boon: what term shall end my wanderings? what time is ordained for my peace?

PROMETHEUS

Better for you not to know than to know.

IO

Yet hide not what remains for me to endure.

PROMETHEUS

So much alone I am willing to grant.

IO

Why then do you delay? I would know all.

PROMETHEUS

It is not churlishness; I am loth to bruise your heart.

IO

Spare me not further than I myself desire.

PROMETHEUS

Since you so crave, it is well; hear me then.

LEADER OF THE CHORUS

Nay, not yet. Grant me also a share in your grace. Let us first hear from her the story of her sorrow and the disasters that prey on her life. Then do you declare to her what struggle still remains.

PROMETHEUS

'Tis for thee, Io, to bestow this favor; and fittingly, for these are thy father's sisters. Time is not lost, I deem, in bewailing and mourning our fate when answering tears stand ready in the listener's eye.

Io

Hard would it be to disregard your wish;
And if my words have credit in your ears
The tale is rendered. Yet as one who speaks
And still laments, my sorrows I recount,—
How wild, perturbing wonders in my soul
Wrought by the will of heaven, and how in shape
This bestial transformation I endured.
For always in the drowsy hours of night
I, sleeping in my virgin chambers, saw
Strange visitations pass, and as they passed
Each smiled and whispered: O sweet-favored girl,
Why cherish long thy maiden loneliness,
When love celestial calleth? Fair art thou,
And thronèd Zeus, heart-smitten with desire,
Yearns from his heaven to woo thee. Nay, sweet child,
Disdain him not. Now to the meadow land
Of Lerna, where thy father's pastures lie
And the sleek cattle browse, do thou steal forth
Alone, and haply there thy yielding grace
May soothe the passion in the Sovereign's eye.—
Such dreams, filling with fear the hours of sleep,
Drove me at last to tell my father all.
And he was troubled; many times in doubt
To Pythian Delphi and the speaking oaks
Of far Dodona messengers he sent,
Inquiring by what act or pleasing word
The grace of heaven to win. But ever these
With oracles of shifting speech returned,
Inexplicably dark. Yet in the end
Came one clear cruel utterance, oh, too clear!
That bade him drive me forth from home and land,
An exile doomed in solitary ways
To wander to the confines of the world.
With such commands came words of dreadful import,
And threats of flaming thunderbolts from Zeus
With burning wrath to desolate his race,

If he durst disobey. Much doubted he,
But at the last Apollo's warning voice
And Zeus' curb upon his soul prevailed:
He drave me forth, and all my life's young joy
Ended in bitter grief for him and me.
Straightway my form this strange distortion knew,
With horns here on my front; and madly stung
By this insatiate fly, with antic bounds
I sped away to the sweet-flowing fount
Of Cenchreae and the Lernéan well;
While close upon me Argus, born of earth,
Savage and sleepless trailed, his wakeful eyes
Fixed on my track. And though a sudden fate
Him overmastered, yet this stinging fly
Still with his lash pursues from land to land.—
Such is my tale; and now if in thy wit
It lies to prophesy what toils remain,
So say, nor by false pitying speech misguide;
For glozing words I deem the worst disease.

CHORUS (*singing*)

Oh strange! Oh, more than incredible!
Never I thought such words
Surpassing the wildest belief
Should enter my ears, such a tale
Of horror and woe and calamity.
I am stung to the soul, and compassion
Benumbs my heart. O Fate!
Alas, O Fate! I shudder
Beholding the lot of this maiden.

PROMETHEUS

You are quick to lament and very prone to fear. Yet wait a little till you have heard what remains.

LEADER OF THE CHORUS

Speak, tell us all; to the sick it is sweet to know betimes what awaits them of pain.

PROMETHEUS

Lightly I granted your former request, for you desired first to hear from her lips the story of her conflict; hear now the evils that Hera hath still in store for this maiden;—and do you, O daughter of Inachus, take my words to your heart that you may know the goal of your wanderings.—Turn first toward the rising sun, and thitherward proceeding over unploughed fields you will reach the nomad Scythians, a people of mighty archers, who in their wicker-woven houses dwell aloft on smooth-rolling wagons. Approach not these, but pass on through the land, keeping ever near to the surf-beaten shores of the Euxine. To the left dwell the Chalybes, famous workers of iron; and of them you must beware, for they are a savage race and regard not strangers. Then will you come to the River of Violence, fierce as its name and treacherous to ford; cross not over it until you have reached the Caucasus, highest of mountains, where the river pours out its fury over the brows of the cliffs. Here over the star-neighboring summits you must toil and turn to the southern path: so in time you will reach the host of the Amazons, ever hostile to men, who one day shall inhabit Themiscyra on the Thermodon, where Salmydessus opens upon the sea her ravenous jaws, a terror to strange sailors, a cruel step-dame to ships. Gladly the Amazons will guide thee on thy way. And thou wilt come to the Cimmerian isthmus by the narrow gateway of the lake; and leaving this with brave heart thou wilt cross over the Maeotic strait, which ever after in memorial of thy crossing men shall call the Bosporus, the fording of the heifer. Thus thou wilt abandon the plain of Europe and venture on the continent of Asia.—Now doth not the tyrant of the gods seem to you altogether violent? Behold how this god, desiring to mingle with a mortal woman, hath imposed on her these wanderings.—Thou hast met, O maiden, a bitter claimant for thy favor; and the words thou hast heard are not even the prelude to what must follow.

IO

Alas, for me!

PROMETHEUS

Once more you cry out and groan; what will you do when you have learned the troubles that remain?

LEADER

Nay, have you calamities still to recount?

PROMETHEUS

As it were a stormy sea of lamentable woe.

IO

What profit have I in life? Why do I not hurl myself out of hand from this rude precipice, that broken on the plain below I may have speedy respite from my troubles? It were better to die once for all than to drag out my lingering days in anguish.

PROMETHEUS

How hardly would you endure my struggles, for death that would release me from my woes is denied me by Destiny. Now there is no goal before me of my conflict until Zeus is thrown from his supremacy.

IO

And shall Zeus ever fall from power?

PROMETHEUS

You would rejoice, I think, to see his overthrow.

IO

Why should I not, who am abused by Zeus?

PROMETHEUS

You may learn from me that your wish is truth.

IO

Who shall despoil him of the tyrant's sceptre?

PROMETHEUS

He shall himself despoil by his own folly.

IO

How may it be? Speak, if there is no harm.

PROMETHEUS

An ill-fated espousal shall work him grief.

IO

A spouse divine or human? tell if thou mayst.

PROMETHEUS

What is it to thee? I may not speak her name.

IO

His bride shall drag him from the throne?

PROMETHEUS

A son she shall bear, mightier than his father.

IO

Hath he no refuge from this doom?

PROMETHEUS

There is none, except I be loosed from my bonds.

IO

Who is to loose thee against the will of Zeus?

PROMETHEUS

Thy own children's child must do the deed.

IO

What sayest thou? my son shall end thy evils?

PROMETHEUS

The third after the tenth generation.

IO

Thy oracle is dark to my understanding.

PROMETHEUS

Pass it by; thy own ill fate is involved therein.

IO

The boon is offered, and straightway thou withdrawest it.

PROMETHEUS

I grant thee the knowledge of either of two desires.

IO

Tell me the twain, and let me choose.

PROMETHEUS

'Tis done; choose whether I tell thee plainly of thy coming tribulations or of him who is to deliver me.

LEADER

Yet rather bestow the one favor on her and the other on me, and be not chary of your words. To her set forth her future wanderings, and to me your deliverer, as I long to hear.

PROMETHEUS

Your eagerness compels me, and I will relate all you ask. To you first, Io, I will proclaim trials of wandering, and do you record them on the tablets of your brain.—When you have crossed the tide that bounds two continents, then toward the flaming sun-trodden regions of the dawn pass on beyond the surge of the sea till you reach the Gorgonean plains of Cisthene, the home of the Graeae, the three daughters of Phorcys, ancient virgins, possessing among them but one eye and one tooth, upon whom neither the sun looks down with his beams, nor ever the moon by night. And near by are the three other sisters, the winged, snake-haired, man-hating Gorgons, upon whom no mortal may look and live. Such wardens guard that land. Yet hear another spectacle of dread: beware the sharp-beaked hounds of Zeus that never bark, the griffins, and beware the one-eyed Arimaspian host of riders who dwell by the gold-washing tide of Pluto's stream; approach them not. And you will come to a far-off land, a swarthy people, who live by the fountain of the sun and Aethiopia's river. Follow its banks until you arrive at the Cataract where from the Bybline hills the Nile pours out its waters sweet and worshipful. This stream will guide you to the great Nilotic delta, where at the last fate bids you and your children, Io, establish your far-off home. Now if my speech seems stammering and hard to understand, still question me and be advised; for there is more leisure to me than I could wish.

CHORUS

If anything remains untold of her life of weary wanderings, now recount it to her, but if all is said, then grant us the favor we beg. You have not forgotten it.

PROMETHEUS

She has heard her journeyings to the end; yet that she may know my words are not spoken in vain, I will relate her toils before coming hither, and this shall be a witness to the truth of my prophecy. I will pass over the greater part of the tale, and come to the end of your wanderings. For thus you came at last to the Molossian plains and Dodona with its lofty ridges, where is the oracle and home of Thesprotian Zeus and that strange portent of the talking oaks which in language clear and void of riddles addressed you as the renowned future spouse of Zeus, and the memory of this must still speak in your breast. From thence, urged on by frenzy, you rushed by the sea-shore path to the great gulf of Rhea, and back returned like a vessel tempest-tost from port. Now no longer the gulf shall be known by its old name, but shall be called the Ionian Sea, as a memorial to all men of your journeying. This knowledge is a sign to you of my understanding, that it discerns more than meets the eye.—The rest I tell to you, daughters of Oceanus, and to her together, returning again to the track of my former tale. There is a city, Canobus, standing on the verge of the land at the very mouth and silted bar of the Nile, where at the last Zeus shall restore you to your mind with but the stroke and gentle touching of his hand. There you shall bear a child to Zeus, the swarthy Epaphus, "Touch-born," who shall gather as lord the fruit of all the valley of the broad-flowing Nile. The fourth generation after him, a band of fifty sisters shall return perforce to Argos, to flee the courtship of their fifty cousins. And these, like hawks that follow hard upon a flock of doves, shall pursue the maidens, seeking marriage ill to seek, for God shall grudge them the sweet pleasure of that love. In the Pelasgian land the maidens shall find a home, when in the watches of the night with deed of murderous revenge they, women as they are, have slain their suitors, each plunging her deadly blade into her new lord's throat—so might the Queen of Love appear to my foes! Yet longing shall soothe one maiden's heart to spare her fellow, and blunt the edge of her resolve, for of the twain it will please her rather to be called timid than bloodthirsty. And from her a royal race shall spring in Argos—time fails to tell the whole—and a mighty man of valor, renowned with the bow, who shall deliver me from these toils. All this my ancient mother, the Titan Themis, foretold to me in an oracle; but how it shall come to pass needs yet many words to relate, and the hearing would profit you nothing.

Io (*chanting*)

Eleleu! eleleu!
Once more the spasm, the madness
Smiteth my brain as a fire.
I am stung by the pest, I am pierced
With a dart never forged in the fire;
My seated heart at my ribs
Doth knock, and my straining eyes
Revolve in their orbs; I am borne
As a vessel is lashed by the tempest;
My tongue hath broke its control,
And my turbid words beat madly
In billows of horror and woe.

(Io *departs, as the* Chorus *begins its song.*)

Chorus

strophe

Wise among mortals I count him
Who weighed this truth in his mind
And divulged it: better the union
Of equal with equal in wedlock.
How shall the toiler, the craftsman,

Be lifted in idle desire
To mate with the glory of wealth
Or the honor of noble descent?

antistrophe

Never, O kindly powers,
Behold me the partner of Zeus;
Never may one of the gods
Descend from the skies for my love.
Horror sufficient I feel
For Io, the virgin, the outcast,
Who hateth her lord and is driven
By Hera to wander forlorn.

epode

Wedlock if equal I fear not;
But oh! may never a god
With love's irresistible glance
Constrain me! Hard were the battle,
For who were I to resist him?
What way of escape would remain
From the counsel and purpose of Zeus?

PROMETHEUS

Yet shall Zeus himself, the stubborn of soul, be humbled, for the union he purposes in his heart shall hurl him to outer darkness from his throne of supremacy. Then at last the curse of his father Cronos shall be fulfilled to the uttermost, the curse that he swore when thrown from his ancient seat. All this I know and how the curse shall work, and I only of the gods may point out a refuge from these disasters. Therefore let him sit boldly now, trusting in his thunders that reverberate through the sky, and wielding fiery darts in his hands; they shall avail him naught nor save him from falling in ruin unendurable. A mighty wrestler he is preparing against himself, an irresistible champion, who shall search out a fire more terrible than his lightning and a roaring noise to drown his thunder, and who shall break in pieces that sea-scourge and shaker of the earth, the trident-spear of Poseidon. And Zeus, broken on this rock, shall learn how far apart it is to rule and be a slave.

LEADER OF THE CHORUS

Thy bodings against Zeus are but thy own desire.

PROMETHEUS

I speak what is to be, and that is my desire.

LEADER

Must we look for one to reign above Zeus?

PROMETHEUS

Troubles more grievous to bear shall bow his neck.

LEADER

Thou tremblest not to utter such words?

PROMETHEUS

Why should I tremble whose fate is not to die?

LEADER

Yet he might still harder torments inflict.

PROMETHEUS

So let him; I am prepared for all.

LEADER

Yet the wise bow down to Nemesis.

PROMETHEUS

So worship, flatter, adore the ruler of the day; but I have no thought in my heart for Zeus. Let him act, let him reign his little while as he will; for he shall not long rule over the gods.—(HERMES *enters*.) But I see here the lackey of Zeus, the servant of the new tyrant. No doubt he has come with tidings of some new device.

HERMES

Thee, the wise, the bitter beyond bitterness, the thief of fire, who hast revolted against the gods and betrayed their honors to thy creatures of a day,—to thee I speak. The father bids thee declare the chance of wedlock thou vauntest, that shall bereave him of his sceptre; and this thou art to state clearly and not involve thy speech in riddles. Put me out, O Prometheus, to double my journey; thou seest that Zeus is not appeased by dubious words.

PROMETHEUS

Haughty thy speech and swollen with pride, as becomes a servant of the gods. Ye are but young in tyranny, and think to inhabit a citadel unassaulted of grief; yet have I not seen two tryants fall therefrom? And third I shall behold this present lord cast down in utter ruin. Do I seem to cower and quail before these new gods? Hardly, I think; there is no fear in me. But do you trudge back the road you came; for all your pains of asking are in vain.

HERMES

Yet forget not such insolence has brought you to this pass of evil.

PROMETHEUS

Be assured I would not barter my hard lot for your menial service.

HERMES

It is better no doubt to serve this rock than to be the trusted herald of Zeus.

PROMETHEUS

I but answered insult with insult.

HERMES

You seem to glory in your present state.

PROMETHEUS

What, I? So might I see my enemies glory,—and you among them!

HERMES

You blame me too for your calamities?

PROMETHEUS

In simple sooth I count all the gods my foes, who requited my benefits with injuries.

HERMES

Your madness I see is a deep-rooted disease.

PROMETHEUS

If hatred of foes is madness, I am mad.

HERMES

Who could endure you in prosperity!

PROMETHEUS

Alas, prosperity!

HERMES

Zeus has not learned that cry, alas.

PROMETHEUS

Time, growing ever older, teaches all things.

HERMES

It has not taught you wisdom yet.

PROMETHEUS

Else I should hardly talk with you, a slave.

HERMES

It seems you will not answer the father's demands.

PROMETHEUS

My debt of gratitude I fain would pay.

HERMES

You have reviled and scorned me as a child.

PROMETHEUS (*in supreme anger*)

And are you not simpler than a child if you hope to learn aught from me? There is no torment or contrivance in the power of Zeus to wring this utterance from me, except these bonds are loosened. Therefore let him hurl upon me the red levin, let him confound the reeling world with tempest of white-feathered snow and subterranean thunders; none of these things shall extort from me the knowledge that may ward off his overthrow.

HERMES

Consider if you shall profit by this.

PROMETHEUS

I have considered long since and formed my plan.

HERMES

Yet subdue thyself in time, rash fool, to regard thy present ills in wisdom.

PROMETHEUS

You vex me to no purpose, as one might waste his words on a wave of the sea. Dream not that ever in fear of Zeus's will I shall grow woman-hearted, and raise my supine hands in supplication to my hated foe for deliverance from these bonds;—it is not in my nature.

HERMES

Though I speak much, my words will all be wasted; my appeals have no power to soften and appease your heart, but champing the bit like a new-yoked colt you are restive and struggle against the reins. There is no strength of wisdom in your savage mood, for mere self-will in a foolish man avails nothing. And consider, if thou disregard my words, what a tempest of evils, wave on wave inevitable, shall break upon thee; for first the father will smite this rugged cliff with rending of thunder and hurtling fires, and in its harsh and rock-ribbed embrace enfold thy hidden body. Then after a weary age of years once more thou shalt come forth to the light; and the winged hound of Zeus, the ravening eagle, with savage greed shall tear the mighty ruin of thy limbs, feasting all day an uninvited guest, and glutting his maw on thy black-gnawed liver. Neither look for any respite from this agony, unless some god shall appear as a voluntary successor to thy toils, and of his own free will goeth down to sunless Hades and the dark depths of Tartarus. Therefore take heed: for my words are not vain boasting, but all too truly spoken. The lips of Zeus know not to utter falsehood, but all that he saith he will accomplish. Do thou consider and reflect, and regard not vaunting pride as better than wise counsel.

LEADER

To us Hermes seems to utter words not untimely; for he admonishes you to abandon vaunting pride and seek for wise counsel. Obey him; it is shameful for a wise man to go astray.

PROMETHEUS (*chanting*)

All this ere he uttered his message
I knew; yet feel no dishonor
In suffering wrong from a foe.
Ay, let the lightning be launched
With curled and forkèd flame
On my head; let the air confounded
Shudder with thunderous peals
And convulsion of raging winds;
Let tempests beat on the earth
Till her rooted foundations tremble;
The boisterous surge of the sea
Leap up to mingle its crest
With the stars eclipsed in their orbs;
Let the whirling blasts of Necessity
Seize on my body and hurl it
Down to the darkness of Tartarus,—
Yet all he shall not destroy me!

HERMES

I hear the delirious cries
Of a mind unhinged; his prayer
Is frenzy, and all that he doth.—
But ye who condole with his anguish,
Be quick, I implore, and depart,
Ere the deafening roar of the thunder
Daze and bewilder your senses.

CHORUS

Waste not thy breath in vain warnings,
Nor utter a word unendurable;
For who art thou in the pathway
Of evil and falsehood to guide me?
Better I deem it to suffer
Whate'er he endures; for traitors
My soul abhorreth, their shame
I spew from my heart as a pest.

HERMES

Yet remember my counsel in season,
And blame not your fortune when caught
In the snare of Disaster, nor cry
Unto Zeus that he throws you unwarned
Into sorrow. Yourselves take the blame;
Foretaught and with eyes unveiled
You walk to be snared in the vast
And implicate net of Disaster.

(HERMES *goes out. A storm bursts, with thunder and lightning. The rocks are sundered;* PROMETHEUS *slowly sinks from sight, while the* CHORUS *scatters to right and left.*)

PROMETHEUS

Lo, in grim earnest the world
Is shaken, the roar of thunders
Reverberates, gleams the red levin,
And whirlwinds lick up the dust.
All the blasts of the winds leap out
And meet in tumultuous conflict,
Confounding the sea and the heavens.
'Tis Zeus who driveth his furies
To smite me with terror and madness.
O mother Earth all-honored,
O Air revolving thy light
A common boon unto all,
Behold what wrongs I endure.

AGAMEMNON

by

AESCHYLUS

Characters in the Play

A Watchman
Chorus of Argive Elders
Clytemnestra, *wife of* Agamemnon
A Herald
Agamemnon, *King of Argos*
Cassandra, *daughter of Priam, and slave of* Agamemnon
Aegisthus, *son of Thyestes, cousin of* Agamemnon
Servants, Attendants, Soldiers

INTRODUCTION

THE only trilogy in Greek tragedy which has come down to us complete is the so-called *Oresteia,* made up of the three plays, *Agamemnon, The Choephori,* and *The Eumenides.* Each individual play therefore must be regarded as a single large act of the whole tragedy. The trilogy is in all probability the last work which Aeschylus composed, and won the first prize in the tragic contest held in 458 B.C. There can be little question that it is Aeschylus' masterpiece and it deservedly holds its position at the forefront of Greek tragedy along with the great Oedipus plays of Sophocles.

In the *Oresteia* Aeschylus studies a curse upon a house. He turns to the legends of the House of Atreus which told how Atreus and Thyestes, sons of Pelops, became enemies, how Thyestes wronged Atreus's wife, how Atreus in revenge slew Thyestes' children, and served them to him in a ghastly banquet. The curse came into being as a result of these horrible crimes. Such was the inheritance of Agamemnon and Menelaus, the sons of Atreus. However, all went well with them until Helen, the wife of Menelaus, and reputedly the fairest of women in the world, deserted her husband to go with Paris to Troy. Then, at his brother's request, Agamemnon, the most powerful king in all Greece, marshalled a great Grecian host to invade the Troad and to regain Helen. The expedition assembled at Aulis, but the hostility of Artemis caused contrary winds to blow, and dissension and discontent arose among the Greeks, who were impatient to depart. Calchas, the seer to whom an appeal was made, announced that the expedition could sail only on condition that Agamemnon appease the wrath of Artemis by sacrificing his daughter, Iphigenia. Agamemnon, after a period of inner struggle, finally gave way, the maiden was sacrificed, and the host embarked. After ten years Troy fell, and the various Greek leaders began their journeys home.

The *Agamemnon* opens at this point. The scene is laid at Argos, where the queen, Clytemnestra, Agamemnon's wife, has not yet heard that the Greeks have captured Troy. Clytemnestra, in the king's absence and in anger at the loss of her daughter, Iphigenia, has taken as her lover, Aegisthus, Thyestes' sole surviving son, who is burning with a desire to revenge himself upon Agamemnon. The queen and her paramour have carefully laid a plot to murder the king upon his return. The events in the first play of the trilogy are the arrival of the news of Troy's capture, Agamemnon's homecoming and his subsequent murder. The second play, *The Choephori,* tells how Electra and Orestes, daughter and son of Agamemnon, slew their mother, Clytemnestra, and her lover, to avenge their father's death. The third play, *The Eumenides,* records how Orestes, driven by the Furies, who are quasi-symbols of conscience, ultimately was absolved of his guilt, and how the curse finally ceased to operate.

The *Agamemnon,* taken by itself, contains two aspects worthy of special consideration. The first is the masterly fashion in which Aeschylus has drawn the character of Clytemnestra. With sure hand, he reveals the tense psychological strain under which she is laboring, her adamantine calm as she first greets her husband, her wild triumph after the murder, when she glories in her deed, and her final exhausted reaction at the close of the play. Secondly, the so-called Cassandra scene is perhaps as intense dramatically as any in the literature of the theater. As Agamemnon's concubine and his chief spoil of the war, Cassandra follows him on the scene, remains motionless and silent until finally, after Agamemnon and Clytemnestra have entered the palace, she breaks into her half-crazed lament and prophecy, which none can believe. The variation in cadence and emotional tension of her lines in the scene account largely for its effectiveness.

It has already been stated that Aeschylus is studying the phenomenon of an ancestral curse. Here is the House of Atreus. Atreus and Thyestes sin. Agamemnon sins in his turn. He is murdered, and his murder begets another. When will the chain of crime cease? It seems undeniable that Aeschylus is focussing his attention upon this aspect of the problem of evil. Furthermore, Aeschylus attacks the question from the point of view of a monotheistic theology. God has ruled that man shall learn by suffering, such is the initial interpretation of the problem offered by Aeschylus at the outset of his drama. The tone continues in the other choral passages of the *Agamemnon,* though the interpretation tends to verge upon the theory that God's justice and his punishments are based upon the principle of "an eye for an eye." But in *The Eumenides* Orestes is acquitted and not for very logically convincing reasons, and with him justice seems to have been tempered with mercy. Orestes leaves the scene almost immediately, but the play continues, and it is in this closing passage that Aeschylus gives the final resolution to his problem. There are no human characters left, which suggests the idea that Aeschylus has used his human story merely to provide illustrative material for his analysis of the central issue. The Furies, who in their choral songs throughout the play have expressed themselves as uncompromising instruments of Fate and of divine vengeance — "an eye for an eye" — are won over by Athena, and mysteriously and mystically become Goddesses of Mercy. Aeschylus' resolution then is mystical and in a strange sense supra-rational. Its power is like in kind to and of the same order as that in the *Book of Job* when the Voice from the Whirlwind speaks. At the end of the *Oresteia* Aeschylus gives us a conception of a godhead which is at once merciful and just, in which both "Zeus" and "Fate" are fused, through whose wisdom man by suffering can achieve wisdom.

AGAMEMNON

(SCENE:—*Before the palace of* AGAMEMNON *in Argos. In front of the palace there are statues of the gods, and altars prepared for sacrifice. It is night. On the roof of the palace can be discerned a* WATCHMAN.)

WATCHMAN

I PRAY the gods to quit me of my toils,
To close the watch I keep, this livelong year;
For as a watch-dog lying, not at rest,
Propped on one arm, upon the palace-roof
Of Atreus' race, too long, too well I know
The starry conclave of the midnight sky,
Too well, the splendours of the firmament,
The lords of light, whose kingly aspect shows
What time they set or climb the sky in turn—
The year's divisions, bringing frost or fire.

And now, as ever, am I set to mark
When shall stream up the glow of signal-flame,
The bale-fire bright, and tell its Trojan tale—
Troy town is ta'en: such issue holds in hope
She in whose woman's breast beats heart of man.

Thus upon mine unrestful couch I lie,
Bathed with the dews of night, unvisited
By dreams—ah me!—for in the place of sleep
Stands Fear as my familiar, and repels
The soft repose that would mine eyelids seal.

And if at whiles, for the lost balm of sleep,
I medicine my soul with melody
Of trill or song—anon to tears I turn,
Wailing the woe that broods upon this home,
Not now by honour guided as of old.
But now at last fair fall the welcome hour
That sets me free, whene'er the thick night glow
With beacon-fire of hope deferred no more.
All hail!
(*A beacon-light is seen reddening the distant sky.*)
Fire of the night, that brings my spirit day,
Shedding on Argos light, and dance, and song,
Greetings to fortune, hail!

Let my loud summons ring within the ears
Of Agamemnon's queen, that she anon
Start from her couch and with a shrill voice cry
A joyous welcome to the beacon-blaze,
For Ilion's fall; such fiery message gleams
From yon high flame; and I, before the rest,
Will foot the lightsome measure of our joy;
For I can say, *My master's dice fell fair—*
Behold! the triple sice, the lucky flame!
Now be my lot to clasp, in loyal love,
The hand of him restored, who rules our home:
Home—but I say no more: upon my tongue
Treads hard the ox o' the adage.

Had it voice,
The home itself might soothliest tell its tale;
I, of set will, speak words the wise may learn,
To others, nought remember nor discern.

(*He withdraws. The* CHORUS OF ARGIVE ELDERS *enters, each leaning on a staff. During their song* CLYTEMNESTRA *appears in the background, kindling the altars.*)

CHORUS (*singing*)

Ten livelong years have rolled away,
Since the twin lords of sceptred sway,
By Zeus endowed with pride of place,
The doughty chiefs of Atreus' race,
  Went forth of yore,
To plead with Priam, face to face,
  Before the judgment-seat of War!

A thousand ships from Argive land
Put forth to bear the martial band,
That with a spirit stern and strong
Went out to right the kingdom's wrong—
Pealed, as they went, the battle-song,
  Wild as the vultures' cry;
When o'er the eyrie, soaring high,
In wild bereavèd agony,
Around, around, in airy rings,
They wheel with oarage of their wings,
But not the eyas-brood behold,
That called them to the nest of old;
But let Apollo from the sky,
Or Pan, or Zeus, but hear the cry,
The exile cry, the wail forlorn,
Of birds from whom their home is torn—
On those who wrought the rapine fell,
Heaven sends the vengeful fiends of hell.

Even so doth Zeus, the jealous lord
And guardian of the hearth and board,
Speed Atreus' sons, in vengeful ire,
'Gainst Paris—sends them forth on fire,
Her to buy back, in war and blood,
Whom one did wed but many woo'd!
And many, many, by his will,
The last embrace of foes shall feel,

And many a knee in dust he bowed,
And splintered spears on shields ring loud,
Of Trojan and of Greek, before
That iron bridal-feast be o'er!
But as he willed 'tis ordered all,
And woes, by heaven ordained, must fall—
Unsoothed by tears or spilth of wine
Poured forth too late, the wrath divine
Glares vengeance on the flameless shrine.

And we in grey dishonoured eld,
Feeble of frame, unfit were held
To join the warrior array
That then went forth unto the fray:
And here at home we tarry, fain
Our feeble footsteps to sustain,
Each on his staff—so strength doth wane,
And turns to childishness again.
For while the sap of youth is green,
And, yet unripened, leaps within,
The young are weakly as the old,
And each alike unmeet to hold
The vantage post of war!
And ah! when flower and fruit are o'er,
  And on life's tree the leaves are sere,
  Age wendeth propped its journey drear,
As forceless as a child, as light
And fleeting as a dream of night
Lost in the garish day!
But thou, O child of Tyndareus,
  Queen Clytemnestra, speak! and say
  What messenger of joy to-day
Hath won thine ear? what welcome news
That thus in sacrificial wise
E'en to the city's boundaries
Thou biddest altar-fires arise?

Each god who doth our city guard,
And keeps o'er Argos watch and ward
From heaven above, from earth below—
The mighty lords who rule the skies,
The market's lesser deities,
To each and all the altars glow,
Piled for the sacrifice!
And here and there, anear, afar,
Streams skyward many a beacon-star,
Conjur'd and charm'd and kindled well
By pure oil's soft and guileless spell,
Hid now no more
Within the palace' secret store.

O queen, we pray thee, whatsoe'er,
Known unto thee, were well revealed,
That thou wilt trust it to our ear,
And bid our anxious heart be healed!
That waneth now unto despair—
Now, waxing to a presage fair,
Dawns, from the altar, Hope—to scare
From our rent hearts the vulture Care.

strophe I

List! for the power is mine, to chant on high
The chiefs' emprise, the strength that omens gave!
List! on my soul breathes yet a harmony,
From realms of ageless powers, and strong to save!

How brother kings, twin lords of one command,
Led forth the youth of Hellas in their flower,
Urged on their way, with vengeful spear and brand,
By warrior-birds, that watched the parting hour.

Go forth to Troy, the eagles seemed to cry—
And the sea-kings obeyed the sky-kings' word,
When on the right they soared across the sky,
And one was black, one bore a white tail barre

High o'er the palace were they seen to soar,
  Then lit in sight of all, and rent and tare,
Far from the fields that she should range no more.
  Big with her unborn brood, a mother-hare.

(Ah woe and well-a-day! but be the issue fair!)

antistrophe I

And one beheld, the soldier-prophet true,
  And the two chiefs, unlike of soul and will,
In the twy-coloured eagles straight he knew,
  And spake the omen forth, for good and ill.

Go forth, he cried, *and Priam's town shall fall.*
  Yet long the time shall be; and flock and herd,
The people's wealth, that roam before the wall,
  Shall force hew down, when Fate shall give the word.

But O beware! lest wrath in Heaven abide,
  To dim the glowing battle-forge once more,
And mar the mighty curb of Trojan pride,
  The steel of vengeance, welded as for war!

For virgin Artemis bears jealous hate
  Against the royal house, the eagle-pair,
Who rend the unborn brood, insatiate—
  Yea, loathes their banquet on the quivering hare.

(Ah woe and well-a-day! but be the issue fair!)

epode

For well she loves—the goddess kind and mild—
  The tender new-born cubs of lions bold,
Too weak to range—and well the sucking child
  Of every beast that roams by wood and wold.

So to the Lord of Heaven she prayeth still,
  "Nay, if it must be, be the omen true!
Yet do the visioned eagles presage ill;
  The end be well, but crossed with evil too!"

Healer Apollo! be her wrath controll'd,
Nor weave the long delay of thwarting gales,
To war against the Danaans and withhold
From the free ocean-waves their eager sails!

She craves, alas! to see a second life
Shed forth a curst unhallowed sacrifice—
'Twixt wedded souls, artificer of strife,
And hate that knows not fear, and fell device.

At home there tarries like a lurking snake,
Biding its time, a wrath unreconciled,
A wily watcher, passionate to slake,
In blood, resentment for a murdered child.

Such was the mighty warning, pealed of yore—
Amid good tidings, such the word of fear,
What time the fateful eagles hovered o'er
The kings, and Calchas read the omen clear.

(In strains, like his, once more,
Sing woe and well-a-day! but be the issue fair!)

strophe [illegible]

Zeus—if to The Unknown
That name of many names seem good—
Zeus, upon Thee I call.
Thro' the mind's every road
I passed, but vain are all,
Save that which names thee Zeus, the Highest One,
Were it but mine to cast away the load,
The weary load, that weighs my spirit down.

antistrophe [illegible]

He that was Lord of old,
In full-blown pride of place and valour bold,
Hath fallen and is gone, even as an old tale told!

And he that next held sway,
By stronger grasp o'erthrown
Hath pass'd away!
And whoso now shall bid the triumph-chant arise
To Zeus, and Zeus alone,
He shall be found the truly wise.

strophe 3

'Tis Zeus alone who shows the perfect way
Of knowledge: He hath ruled,
Men shall learn wisdom, by affliction schooled.

In visions of the night, like dropping rain,
Descend the many memories of pain
Before the spirit's sight: through tears and dole
Comes wisdom o'er the unwilling soul—
A boon, I wot, of all Divinity,
That holds its sacred throne in strength, above the sky!

antistrophe 3

And then the elder chief, at whose command
The fleet of Greece was manned,
Cast on the seer no word of hate,
But veered before the sudden breath of Fate—

Ah, weary while! for, ere they put forth sail,
Did every store, each minish'd vessel, fail,
While all the Achaean host
At Aulis anchored lay,
Looking across to Chalcis and the coast
Where refluent waters welter, rock, and sway;

strophe 4

And rife with ill delay
From northern Strymon blew the thwarting blast—
Mother of famine fell,
That holds men wand'ring still

Far from the haven where they fain would be!—
And pitiless did waste
Each ship and cable, rotting on the sea,
And, doubling with delay each weary hour,
Withered with hope deferred th' Achaeans' warlike flower.

But when, for bitter storm, a deadlier relief,
And heavier with ill to either chief,
Pleading the ire of Artemis, the seer avowed,
The two Atreidae smote their sceptres on the plain,
And, striving hard, could not their tears restrain!

antistrophe 4

And then the elder monarch spake aloud—
Ill lot were mine, to disobey!
And ill, to smite my child, my household's love and pride!
To stain with virgin blood a father's hands, and slay
My daughter, by the altar's side!
'Twixt woe and woe I dwell—
I dare not like a recreant fly,
And leave the league of ships, and fail each true ally;
For rightfully they crave, with eager fiery mind,
The virgin's blood, shed forth to lull the adverse wind—
God send the deed be well!

strophe 5

Thus on his neck he took
Fate's hard compelling yoke;
Then, in the counter-gale of will abhorr'd, accursed,
To recklessness his shifting spirit veered—
Alas! that Frenzy, first of ills and worst,
With evil craft men's souls to sin hath ever stirred!

And so he steeled his heart—ah, well-a-day—
Aiding a war for one false woman's sake,
His child to slay,
And with her spilt blood make
An offering, to speed the ships upon their way!

antistrophe 5

Lusting for war, the bloody arbiters
Closed heart and ears, and would not hear nor heed
The girl-voice plead,
Pity me, Father! nor her prayers,
Nor tender, virgin years.
So, when the chant of sacrifice was done,
Her father bade the youthful priestly train
Raise her, like some poor kid, above the altar-stone,
From where amid her robes she lay
Sunk all in swoon away—
Bade them, as with the bit that mutely tames the steed,
Her fair lips' speech refrain,
Lest she should speak a curse on Atreus' home and seed,

strophe 6

So, trailing on the earth her robe of saffron dye,
With one last piteous dart from her beseeching eye
Those that should smite she smote—
Fair, silent, as a pictur'd form, but fain
To plead. *Is all forgot?*
How oft those halls of old,
Wherein my sire high feast did hold,
Rang to the virginal soft strain,
When I, a stainless child,
Sang from pure lips and undefiled,
Sang of my sire, and all
His honoured life, and how on him should fall
Heaven's highest gift and gain!

antistrophe 6

And then—but I beheld not, nor can tell,
What further fate befell:
But this is sure, that Calchas' boding strain
Can ne'er be void or vain.
This wage from Justice' hand do sufferers earn,
The future to discern:

And yet—farewell, O secret of To-morrow!
  Fore-knowledge is fore-sorrow.
Clear with the clear beams of the morrow's sun,
  The future presseth on.
Now, let the house's tale, how dark soe'er,
  Find yet an issue fair!—
So prays the loyal, solitary band
  That guards the Apian land.

(*They turn to* CLYTEMNESTRA, *who leaves the altars and comes forward.*)

LEADER OF THE CHORUS

O queen, I come in reverence of thy sway—
For, while the ruler's kingly seat is void,
The loyal heart before his consort bends.
Now—be it sure and certain news of good,
Or the fair tidings of a flatt'ring hope,
That bids thee spread the light from shrine to shrine,
I, fain to hear, yet grudge not if thou hide.

CLYTEMNESTRA

As saith the adage, *From the womb of Night*
Spring forth, with promise fair, the young child Light.
Ay—fairer even than all hope my news—
By Grecian hands is Priam's city ta'en!

LEADER

What say'st thou? doubtful heart makes treach'rous ear.

CLYTEMNESTRA

Hear then again, and plainly—Troy is ours!

LEADER

Thrills thro' my heart such joy as wakens tears.

CLYTEMNESTRA

Ay, thro' those tears thine eye looks loyalty.

LEADER

But hast thou proof, to make assurance sure?

CLYTEMNESTRA

Go to; I have—unless the god has lied.

LEADER

Hath some night-vision won thee to belief?

CLYTEMNESTRA

Out on all presage of a slumb'rous soul!

LEADER

But wert thou cheered by Rumour's wingless word?

CLYTEMNESTRA

Peace—thou dost chide me as a credulous girl.

LEADER

Say then, how long ago the city fell?

CLYTEMNESTRA

Even in this night that now brings forth the dawn.

LEADER

Yet who so swift could speed the message here?

CLYTEMNESTRA

From Ida's top Hephaestus, lord of fire,
Sent forth his sign; and on, and ever on,
Beacon to beacon sped the courier-flame.
From Ida to the crag, that Hermes loves,
Of Lemnos; thence unto the steep sublime
Of Athos, throne of Zeus, the broad blaze flared.
Thence, raised aloft to shoot across the sea,
The moving light, rejoicing in its strength,
Sped from the pyre of pine, and urged its way,
In golden glory, like some strange new sun,
Onward, and reached Macistus' watching heights.
There, with no dull delay nor heedless sleep,
The watcher sped the tidings on in turn,
Until the guard upon Messapius' peak

Saw the far flame gleam on Euripus' tide,
And from the high-piled heap of withered furze
Lit the new sign and bade the message on.
Then the strong light, far-flown and yet undimmed,
Shot thro' the sky above Asopus' plain,
Bright as the moon, and on Cithaeron's crag
Aroused another watch of flying fire.
And there the sentinels no whit disowned,
But sent redoubled on, the hest of flame—
Swift shot the light, above Gorgopis' bay,
To Aegiplanctus' mount, and bade the peak
Fail not the onward ordinance of fire.
And like a long beard streaming in the wind,
Full-fed with fuel, roared and rose the blaze,
And onward flaring, gleamed above the cape,
Beneath which shimmers the Saronic bay,
And thence leapt light unto Arachne's peak,
The mountain watch that looks upon our town.
Thence to th' Atreides' roof—in lineage fair,
A bright posterity of Ida's fire.
So sped from stage to stage, fulfilled in turn,
Flame after flame, along the course ordained,
And lo! the last to speed upon its way
Sights the end first, and glows unto the goal.
And Troy is ta'en, and by this sign my lord
Tells me the tale, and ye have learned my word.

LEADER

To heaven, O queen, will I upraise new song:
But, wouldst thou speak once more, I fain would hear
From first to last the marvel of the tale.

CLYTEMNESTRA

Think you—this very morn—the Greeks in Troy,
And loud therein the voice of utter wail!
Within one cup pour vinegar and oil,
And look! unblent, unreconciled, they war.

So in the twofold issue of the strife
Mingle the victor's shout, the captives' moan.
For all the conquered whom the sword has spared
Cling weeping—some unto a brother slain,
Some childlike to a nursing father's form,
And wail the loved and lost, the while their neck
Bows down already 'neath the captive's chain.
And lo! the victors, now the fight is done,
Goaded by restless hunger, far and wide
Range all disordered thro' the town, to snatch
Such victual and such rest as chance may give
Within the captive halls that once were Troy—
Joyful to rid them of the frost and dew,
Wherein they couched upon the plain of old—
Joyful to sleep the gracious night all through,
Unsummoned of the watching sentinel.
Yet let them reverence well the city's gods,
The lords of Troy, tho' fallen, and her shrines;
So shall the spoilers not in turn be spoiled.
Yea, let no craving for forbidden gain
Bid conquerors yield before the darts of greed.
For we need yet, before the race be won,
Homewards, unharmed, to round the course once more.
For should the host wax wanton ere it come,
Then, tho' the sudden blow of fate be spared,
Yet in the sight of gods shall rise once more
The great wrong of the slain, to claim revenge.
Now, hearing from this woman's mouth of mine,
The tale and eke its warning, pray with me,
Luck sway the scale, with no uncertain poise,
For my fair hopes are changed to fairer joys.

LEADER

A gracious word thy woman's lips have told,
Worthy a wise man's utterance, O my queen;
Now with clear trust in thy convincing tale

I set me to salute the gods with song,
Who bring us bliss to counterpoise our pain.

(CLYTEMNESTRA *goes into the palace.*)

CHORUS (*singing*)

Zeus, Lord of heaven! and welcome night
Of victory, that hast our might
With all the glories crowned!
On towers of Ilion, free no more,
Hast flung the mighty mesh of war,
And closely girt them round,
Till neither warrior may 'scape,
Nor stripling lightly overleap
The trammels as they close, and close,
Till with the grip of doom our foes
In slavery's coil are bound!

Zeus, Lord of hospitality,
In grateful awe I bend to thee—
'Tis thou hast struck the blow!
At Alexander, long ago,
We marked thee bend thy vengeful bow,
But long and warily withhold
The eager shaft, which, uncontrolled
And loosed too soon or launched too high,
Has wandered bloodless through the sky.

strophe 1

Zeus, the high God!—whate'er be dim in doubt,
This can our thought track out—
The blow that fells the sinner is of God,
And as he wills, the rod
Of vengeance smiteth sore. One said of old,
The gods list not to hold
A reckoning with him whose feet oppress
The grace of holiness—
An impious word! for whensoe'er the sire

Breathed forth rebellious fire—
What time his household overflowed the measure
Of bliss and health and treasure—
His children's children read the reckoning plain,
At last, in tears and pain.
On me let weal that brings no woe be sent,
And therewithal, content!
Who spurns the shrine of Right, nor wealth nor power
Shall be to him a tower,
To guard him from the gulf: there lies his lot,
Where all things are forgot.

antistrophe 1

Lust drives him on—lust, desperate and wild,
Fate's sin-contriving child—
And cure is none; beyond concealment clear,
Kindles sin's baleful glare.
As an ill coin beneath the wearing touch
Betrays by stain and smutch
Its metal false—such is the sinful wight.
Before, on pinions light,
Fair Pleasure flits, and lures him childlike on,
While home and kin make moan
Beneath the grinding burden of his crime;
Till, in the end of time,
Cast down of heaven, he pours forth fruitless prayer
To powers that will not hear.

And such did Paris come
Unto Atreides' home,
And thence, with sin and shame his welcome to repay,
Ravished the wife away—

strophe 2

And she, unto her country and her kin
Leaving the clash of shields and spears and arming ships,
And bearing unto Troy destruction for a dower

And overbold in sin,
Went fleetly thro' the gates, at midnight hour.
Oft from the prophets' lips
Moaned out the warning and the wail—Ah woe!
Woe for the home, the home! and for the chieftains, woe!
Woe for the bride-bed, warm
Yet from the lovely limbs, the impress of the form
Of her who loved her lord, awhile ago!
And woe! for him who stands
Shamed, silent, unreproachful, stretching hands
That find her not, and sees, yet will not see,
That she is far away!
And his sad fancy, yearning o'er the sea,
Shall summon and recall
Her wraith, once more to queen it in his hall.
And sad with many memories,
The fair cold beauty of each sculptured face—
And all to hatefulness is turned their grace,
Seen blankly by forlorn and hungering eyes!

antistrophe 2

And when the night is deep,
Come visions, sweet and sad, and bearing pain
Of hopings vain—
Void, void and vain, for scarce the sleeping sight
Has seen its old delight,
When thro' the grasps of love that bid it stay
It vanishes away
On silent wings that roam adown the ways of sleep.

Such are the sights, the sorrows fell,
About our hearth—and worse, whereof I may not tell.
But, all the wide town o'er,
Each home that sent its master far away
From Hellas' shore,
Feels the keen thrill of heart, the pang of loss, to-day.

For, truth to say,
The touch of bitter death is manifold!
Familiar was each face, and dear as life,
That went unto the war,
But thither, whence a warrior went of old,
Doth nought return—
Only a spear and sword, and ashes in an urn!

strophe 3

For Ares, lord of strife,
Who doth the swaying scales of battle hold,
War's money-changer, giving dust for gold,
Sends back, to hearts that held them dear,
Scant ash of warriors, wept with many a tear,
Light to the hand, but heavy to the soul;
Yea, fills the light urn full
With what survived the flame—
Death's dusty measure of a hero's frame!

Alas! one cries, *and yet alas again!*
Our chief is gone, the hero of the spear,
And hath not left his peer!
Ah woe! another moans—*my spouse is slain,*
The death of honour, rolled in dust and blood,
Slain for a woman's sin, a false wife's shame!
Such muttered words of bitter mood
Rise against those who went forth to reclaim;
Yea, jealous wrath creeps on against th' Atreides' name.

And others, far beneath the Ilian wall,
Sleep their last sleep—the goodly chiefs and tall,
Couched in the foeman's land, whereon they gave
Their breath, and lords of Troy, each in his Trojan grave.

antistrophe 3

Therefore for each and all the city's breast
Is heavy with a wrath supprest.

As deeply and deadly as a curse more loud
Flung by the common crowd:
And, brooding deeply, doth my soul await
Tidings of coming fate,
Buried as yet in darkness' womb.
For not forgetful is the high gods' doom
Against the sons of carnage: all too long
Seems the unjust to prosper and be strong,
Till the dark Furies come,
And smite with stern reversal all his home,
Down into dim obstruction—he is gone,
And help and hope, among the lost, is none!

O'er him who vaunteth an exceeding fame,
Impends a woe condign;
The vengeful bolt upon his eyes doth flame,
Sped from the hand divine.
This bliss be mine, ungrudged of God, to feel—
To tread no city to the dust,
Nor see my own life thrust
Down to a slave's estate beneath another's heel!

epode

Behold, throughout the city wide
Have the swift feet of Rumour hied,
Roused by the joyful flame:
But is the news they scatter, sooth?
Or haply do they give for truth
Some cheat which heaven doth frame?
A child were he and all unwise,
Who let his heart with joy be stirred.
To see the beacon-fires arise,
And then, beneath some thwarting word,
Sicken anon with hope deferred.
The edge of woman's insight still
Good news from true divideth ill:

Light rumours leap within the bound
Then fences female credence round,
But, lightly born, as lightly dies
The tale that springs of her surmise.

(Several days are assumed to have elapsed.)

LEADER OF THE CHORUS

Soon shall we know whereof the bale-fires tell,
The beacons, kindled with transmitted flame;
Whether, as well I deem, their tale is true,
Or whether like some dream delusive came
The welcome blaze but to befool our soul.
For lo! I see a herald from the shore
Draw hither, shadowed with the olive-wreath—
And thirsty dust, twin-brother of the clay,
Speaks plain of travel far and truthful news—
No dumb surmise, nor tongue of flame in smoke,
Fitfully kindled from the mountain pyre;
But plainlier shall his voice say, *All is well,*
Or—but away, forebodings adverse, now,
And on fair promise fair fulfilment come!
And whoso for the state prays otherwise,
Himself reap harvest of his ill desire!

(A HERALD *enters. He is an advance messenger from* AGAMEMNON'S *forces, which have just landed.)*

HERALD

O land of Argos, fatherland of mine!
To thee at last, beneath the tenth year's sun,
My feet return; the bark of my emprise,
Tho' one by one hope's anchors broke away,
Held by the last, and now rides safely here.
Long, long my soul despaired to win, in death,
Its longed-for rest within our Argive land:
And now all hail, O earth, and hail to thee,
New-risen sun! and hail our country's God,

High-ruling Zeus, and thou, the Pythian lord,
Whose arrows smote us once—smite thou no more!
Was not thy wrath wreaked full upon our heads,
O king Apollo, by Scamander's side?
Turn thou, be turned, be saviour, healer, now!
And hail, all gods who rule the street and mart
And Hermes hail! my patron and my pride,
Herald of heaven, and lord of heralds here!
And Heroes, ye who sped us on our way—
To one and all I cry, *Receive again*
With grace such Argives as the spear has spared.

Ah, home of royalty, belovèd halls,
And solemn shrines, and gods that front the morn!
Benign as erst, with sun-flushed aspect greet
The king returning after many days.
For as from night flash out the beams of day,
So out of darkness dawns a light, a king,
On you, on Argos—Agamemnon comes.
Then hail and greet him well! such meed befits
Him whose right hand hewed down the towers of Troy
With the great axe of Zeus who righteth wrong—
And smote the plain, smote down to nothingness
Each altar, every shrine; and far and wide
Dies from the whole land's face its offspring fair.
Such mighty yoke of fate he set on Troy—
Our lord and monarch, Atreus' elder son,
And comes at last with blissful honour home;
Highest of all who walk on earth to-day—
Not Paris nor the city's self that paid
Sin's price with him, can boast, *Whate'er befall,*
The guerdon we have won outweighs it all.
But at Fate's judgment-seat the robber stands
Condemned of rapine, and his prey is torn
Forth from his hands, and by his deed is reaped
A bloody harvest of his home and land

Gone down to death, and for his guilt and lust
His father's race pays double in the dust.

LEADER

Hail, herald of the Greeks, new-come from war.

HERALD

All hail! not death itself can fright me now.

LEADER

Was thine heart wrung with longing for thy land?

HERALD

So that this joy doth brim mine eyes with tears.

LEADER

On you too then this sweet distress did fall—

HERALD

How say'st thou? make me master of thy word.

LEADER

You longed for us who pined for you again.

HERALD

Craved the land us who craved it, love for love?

LEADER

Yea, till my brooding heart moaned out with pain.

HERALD

Whence thy despair, that mars the army's joy?

LEADER

Sole cure of wrong is silence, saith the saw.

HERALD

Thy kings afar, couldst thou fear other men?

LEADER

Death had been sweet, as thou didst say but now.

HERALD

'Tis true; Fate smiles at last. Throughout our toil,
These many years, some chances issued fair,
And some, I wot, were chequered with a curse.
But who, on earth, hath won the bliss of heaven,
Thro' time's whole tenor an unbroken weal?
I could a tale unfold of toiling oars,
Ill rest, scant landings on a shore rock-strewn,
All pains, all sorrows, for our daily doom.
And worse and hatefuller our woes on land;
For where we couched, close by the foeman's wall,
The river-plain was ever dank with dews,
Dropped from the sky, exuded from the earth,
A curse that clung unto our sodden garb,
And hair as horrent as a wild beast's fell.
Why tell the woes of winter, when the birds
Lay stark and stiff, so stern was Ida's snow?
Or summer's scorch, what time the stirless wave
Sank to its sleep beneath the noon-day sun?
Why mourn old woes? their pain has passed away;
And passed away, from those who fell, all care,
For evermore, to rise and live again.
Why sum the count of death, and render thanks
For life by moaning over fate malign?
Farewell, a long farewell to all our woes!
To us, the remnant of the host of Greece,
Comes weal beyond all counterpoise of woe;
Thus boast we rightfully to yonder sun,
Like him far-fleeted over sea and land.
The Argive host prevailed to conquer Troy,
And in the temples of the gods of Greece
Hung up these spoils, a shining sign to Time.
Let those who learn this legend bless aright
The city and its chieftains, and repay
The meed of gratitude to Zeus who willed
And wrought the deed. So stands the tale fulfilled.

LEADER

Thy words o'erbear my doubt: for news of good,
The ear of age hath ever youth enow:
But those within and Clytemnestra's self
Would fain hear all; glad thou their ears and mine.

(CLYTEMNESTRA *enters from the palace.*)

CLYTEMNESTRA

That night, when first the fiery courier came,
In sign that Troy is ta'en and razed to earth,
So wild a cry of joy my lips gave out,
That I was chidden—*Hath the beacon watch*
Made sure unto thy soul the sack of Troy?
A very woman thou, whose heart leaps light
At wandering rumours!—and with words like these
They showed me how I strayed, misled of hope.
Yet on each shrine I set the sacrifice,
And, in the strain they held for feminine,
Went heralds thro' the city, to and fro,
With voice of loud proclaim, announcing joy;
And in each fane they lit and quenched with wine
The spicy perfumes fading in the flame.
All is fulfilled: I spare your longer tale—
The king himself anon shall tell me all.

Remains to think what honour best may greet
My lord, the majesty of Argos, home.
What day beams fairer on a woman's eyes
Than this, whereon she flings the portal wide,
To hail her lord, heaven-shielded, home from war?
This to my husband, that he tarry not,
But turn the city's longing into joy!
Yea, let him come, and coming may he find
A wife no other than he left her, true
And faithful as a watch-dog to his home,
His foemen's foe, in all her duties leal,

Trusty to keep for ten long years unmarred
The store whereon he set his master-seal.
Be steel deep-dyed, before ye look to see
Ill joy, ill fame, from other wight, in me!

HERALD

'Tis fairly said: thus speaks a noble dame,
Nor speaks amiss, when truth informs the boast.
(CLYTEMNESTRA *withdraws again into the palace.*)

LEADER

So has she spoken—be it yours to learn
By clear interpreters her specious word.
Turn to me, herald—tell me if anon
The second well-loved lord of Argos comes?
Hath Menelaus safely sped with you?

HERALD

Alas—brief boon unto my friends it were,
To flatter them, for truth, with falsehoods fair!

LEADER

Speak joy, if truth be joy, but truth, at worst—
Too plainly, truth and joy are here divorced.

HERALD

The hero and his bark were rapt away
Far from the Grecian fleet; 'tis truth I say.

LEADER

Whether in all men's sight from Ilion borne,
Or from the fleet by stress of weather torn?

HERALD

Full on the mark thy shaft of speech doth light,
And one short word hath told long woes aright.

LEADER

But say, what now of him each comrade saith?
What their forebodings, of his life or death?

HERALD

Ask me no more: the truth is known to none,
Save the earth-fostering, all-surveying Sun.

LEADER

Say, by what doom the fleet of Greece was driven?
How rose, how sank the storm, the wrath of heaven?

HERALD

Nay, ill it were to mar with sorrow's tale
The day of blissful news. The gods demand
Thanksgiving sundered from solicitude.
If one as herald came with rueful face
To say, *The curse has fallen, and the host*
Gone down to death; and one wide wound has reached
The city's heart, and out of many homes
Many are cast and consecrate to death,
Beneath the double scourge, that Ares loves,
The bloody pair, the fire and sword of doom—
If such sore burden weighed upon my tongue,
'Twere fit to speak such words as gladden fiends.
But—coming as he comes who bringeth news
Of safe return from toil, and issues fair,
To men rejoicing in a weal restored—
Dare I to dash good words with ill, and say
How the gods' anger smote the Greeks in storm?
For fire and sea, that erst held bitter feud,
Now swore conspiracy and pledged their faith,
Wasting the Argives worn with toil and war.
Night and great horror of the rising wave
Came o'er us, and the blasts that blow from Thrace
Clashed ship with ship, and some with plunging prow
Thro' scudding drifts of spray and raving storm
Vanished, as strays by some ill shepherd driven.
And when at length the sun rose bright, we saw
Th' Aegaean sea-field flecked with flowers of death,
Corpses of Grecian men and shattered hulls.

For us indeed, some god, as well I deem,
No human power, laid hand upon our helm,
Snatched us or prayed us from the powers of air,
And brought our bark thro' all, unharmed in hull:
And saving Fortune sat and steered us fair,
So that no surge should gulf us deep in brine,
Nor grind our keel upon a rocky shore.

So 'scaped we death that lurks beneath the sea,
But, under day's white light, mistrustful all
Of fortune's smile, we sat and brooded deep,
Shepherds forlorn of thoughts that wandered wild
O'er this new woe; for smitten was our host,
And lost as ashes scattered from the pyre.
Of whom if any draw his life-breath yet,
Be well assured, he deems of us as dead,
As we of him no other fate forebode.
But heaven save all! If Menelaus live,
He will not tarry, but will surely come:
Therefore if anywhere the high sun's ray
Descries him upon earth, preserved by Zeus,
Who wills not yet to wipe his race away,
Hope still there is that homeward he may wend.
Enough—thou hast the truth unto the end.

(*The* HERALD *departs.*)

CHORUS (*singing*)

strophe I

Say, from whose lips the presage fell?
Who read the future all too well,
  And named her, in her natal hour,
  Helen, the bride with war for dower?
'Twas one of the Invisible,
  Guiding his tongue with prescient power.
On fleet, and host, and citadel,
  War, sprung from her, and death did lour.

When from the bride-bed's fine-spun veil
She to the Zephyr spread her sail.
Strong blew the breeze—the surge closed o'er
The cloven track of keel and oar,
  But while she fled, there drove along,
  Fast in her wake, a mighty throng—
Athirst for blood, athirst for war,
  Forward in fell pursuit they sprung,
Then leapt on Simois' bank ashore,
  The leafy coppices among—
No rangers, they, of wood and field,
But huntsmen of the sword and shield.

antistrophe I

Heaven's jealousy, that works its will,
Sped thus on Troy its destined ill,
  Well named, at once, the Bride and Bane;
  And loud rang out the bridal strain;
But they to whom that song befell
  Did turn anon to tears again;
Zeus tarries, but avenges still
  The husband's wrong, the household's stain!
He, the hearth's lord, brooks not to see
Its outraged hospitality.

Even now, and in far other tone,
Troy chants her dirge of mighty moan,
  Woe upon Paris, woe and hate!
  Who wooed his country's doom for mate—
This is the burthen of the groan,
  Wherewith she wails disconsolate
The blood, so many of her own
  Have poured in vain, to fend her fate;
Troy! thou hast fed and freed to roam
A lion-cub within thy home!

strophe 2

A suckling creature, newly ta'en
From mother's teat, still fully fain
  Of nursing care; and oft caressed,
  Within the arms, upon the breast,
Even as an infant, has it lain;
  Or fawns and licks, by hunger pressed,
The hand that will assuage its pain;
  In life's young dawn, a well-loved guest,
A fondling for the children's play,
A joy unto the old and grey.

antistrophe 2

But waxing time and growth betrays
The blood-thirst of the lion-race,
  And, for the house's fostering care,
  Unbidden all, it revels there,
And bloody recompense repays—
  Rent flesh of kine, its talons tare:
A mighty beast, that slays, and slays,
  And mars with blood the household fair,
A God-sent pest invincible,
A minister of fate and hell.

strophe 3

Even so to Ilion's city came by stealth
  A spirit as of windless seas and skies,
A gentle phantom-form of joy and wealth,
  With love's soft arrows speeding from its eyes—
Love's rose, whose thorn doth pierce the soul in subtle wise.

Ah, well-a-day! the bitter bridal-bed,
  When the fair mischief lay by Paris' side!
What curse on palace and on people sped
  With her, the Fury sent on Priam's pride,
By angered Zeus! what tears of many a widowed bride!

antistrophe 3

Long, long ago to mortals this was told,
How sweet security and blissful state
Have curses for their children—so men hold—
And for the man of all-too prosperous fate
Springs from a bitter seed some woe insatiate.

Alone, alone, I deem far otherwise;
Not bliss nor wealth it is, but impious deed,
From which that after-growth of ill doth rise!
Woe springs from wrong, the plant is like the seed—
While Right, in honour's house, doth its own likeness breed.

strophe 4

Some past impiety, some grey old crime,
Breeds the young curse, that wantons in our ill,
Early or late, when haps th' appointed time—
And out of light brings power of darkness still,
A master-fiend, a foe, unseen, invincible;

A pride accursed, that broods upon the race
And home in which dark Atè holds her sway—
Sin's child and Woe's, that wears its parents' face;

antistrophe 4

While Right in smoky cribs shines clear as day,
And decks with weal his life, who walks the righteous way.

From gilded halls, that hands polluted raise,
Right turns away with proud averted eyes,
And of the wealth, men stamp amiss with praise,
Heedless, to poorer, holier temples hies,
And to Fate's goal guides all, in its appointed wise.

(AGAMEMNON *enters, riding in a chariot and accompanied by a great procession.* CASSANDRA *follows in another chariot. The* CHORUS *sings its welcome.*)

Hail to thee, chief of Atreus' race,

Returning proud from Troy subdued!
How shall I greet thy conquering face?
How nor a fulsome praise obtrude,
Nor stint the meed of gratitude?
For mortal men who fall to ill
Take little heed of open truth,
But seek unto its semblance still:
The show of weeping and of ruth
To the forlorn will all men pay,
But, of the grief their eyes display,
Nought to the heart doth pierce its way.
And, with the joyous, they beguile
Their lips unto a feignèd smile,
And force a joy, unfelt the while;
But he who as a shepherd wise
  Doth know his flock, can ne'er misread
Truth in the falsehood of his eyes,
Who veils beneath a kindly guise
  A lukewarm love in deed.
And thou, our leader—when of yore
Thou badest Greece go forth to war
For Helen's sake—I dare avow
That then I held thee not as now;
That to my vision thou didst seem
Dyed in the hues of disesteem.
I held thee for a pilot ill,
And reckless, of thy proper will,
Endowing others doomed to die
With vain and forced audacity!
Now from my heart, ungrudgingly,
To those that wrought, this word be said—
Well fall the labour ye have sped—
Let time and search, O king, declare
What men within thy city's bound
Were loyal to the kingdom's care,
And who were faithless found.

AGAMEMNON (*still standing in the chariot*)

First, as is meet, a king's All-hail be said
To Argos, and the gods that guard the land—
Gods who with me availed to speed us home,
With me availed to wring from Priam's town
The due of justice. In the court of heaven
The gods in conclave sat and judged the cause,
Not from a pleader's tongue, and at the close,
Unanimous into the urn of doom
This sentence gave, *On Ilion and her men,*
Death: and where hope drew nigh to pardon's urn
No hand there was to cast a vote therein.
And still the smoke of fallen Ilion
Rises in sight of all men, and the flame
Of Atè's hecatomb is living yet,
And where the towers in dusty ashes sink,
Rise the rich fumes of pomp and wealth consumed
For this must all men pay unto the gods
The meed of mindful hearts and gratitude:
For by our hands the meshes of revenge
Closed on the prey, and for one woman's sake
Troy trodden by the Argive monster lies—
The foal, the shielded band that leapt the wall,
What time with autumn sank the Pleiades.
Yea, o'er the fencing wall a lion sprang
Ravening, and lapped his fill of blood of kings.

Such prelude spoken to the gods in full,
To you I turn, and to the hidden thing
Whereof ye spake but now: and in that thought
I am as you, and what ye say, say I.
For few are they who have such inborn grace,
As to look up with love, and envy not,
When stands another on the height of weal.
Deep in his heart, whom jealousy hath seized,
Her poison lurking doth enhance his load;

For now beneath his proper woes he chafes,
And sighs withal to see another's weal.

I speak not idly, but from knowledge sure—
There be who vaunt an utter loyalty,
That is but as the ghost of friendship dead,
A shadow in a glass, of faith gone by.
One only—he who went reluctant forth
Across the seas with me—Odysseus—he
Was loyal unto me with strength and will,
A trusty trace-horse bound unto my car.
Thus—be he yet beneath the light of day,
Or dead, as well I fear—I speak his praise.

Lastly, whate'er be due to men or gods,
With joint debate, in public council held,
We will decide, and warily contrive
That all which now is well may so abide:
For that which haply needs the healer's art,
That will we medicine, discerning well
If cautery or knife befit the time.

Now, to my palace and the shrines of home,
I will pass in, and greet you first and fair,
Ye gods, who bade me forth, and home again—
And long may Victory tarry in my train!

CLYTEMNESTRA *enters from the palace, followed by maidens bearing crimson robes.*)

CLYTEMNESTRA

Old men of Argos, lieges of our realm,
Shame shall not bid me shrink lest ye should see
The love I bear my lord. Such blushing fear
Dies at the last from hearts of human kind.
From mine own soul and from no alien lips.
I know and will reveal the life I bore,

Reluctant, through the lingering livelong years,
The while my lord beleaguered Ilion's wall.

First, that a wife sat sundered from her lord,
In widowed solitude, was utter woe—
And woe, to hear how rumour's many tongues
All boded evil—woe, when he who came
And he who followed spake of ill on ill,
Keening *Lost, lost, all lost!* thro' hall and bower.
Had this my husband met so many wounds,
As by a thousand channels rumour told,
No network e'er was full of holes as he.
Had he been slain, as oft as tidings came
That he was dead, he well might boast him now
A second Geryon of triple frame,
With triple robe of earth above him laid—
For that below, no matter—triply dead,
Dead by one death for every form he bore.
And thus distraught by news of wrath and woe,
Oft for self-slaughter had I slung the noose,
But others wrenched it from my neck away.
Hence haps it that Orestes, thine and mine,
The pledge and symbol of our wedded troth,
Stands not beside us now, as he should stand.
Nor marvel thou at this: he dwells with one
Who guards him loyally; 'tis Phocis' king,
Strophius, who warned me erst, *Bethink thee, queen,*
What woes of doubtful issue well may fall!
Thy lord in daily jeopardy at Troy,
While here a populace uncurbed may cry,
"Down with the council, down!" bethink thee too,
'Tis the world's way to set a harder heel
On fallen power.
For thy child's absence then
Such mine excuse, no wily afterthought.
For me, long since the gushing fount of tears

Is wept away; no drop is left to shed.
Dim are the eyes that ever watched till dawn,
Weeping, the bale-fires, piled for thy return,
Night after night unkindled. If I slept,
Each sound—the tiny humming of a gnat,
Roused me again, again, from fitful dreams
Wherein I felt thee smitten, saw thee slain,
Thrice for each moment of mine hour of sleep.

All this I bore, and now, released from woe,
I hail my lord as watch-dog of a fold,
As saving stay-rope of a storm-tossed ship,
As column stout that holds the roof aloft,
As only child unto a sire bereaved,
As land beheld, past hope, by crews forlorn,
As sunshine fair when tempest's wrath is past,
As gushing spring to thirsty wayfarer.
So sweet it is to 'scape the press of pain.
With such salute I bid my husband hail!
Nor heaven be wroth therewith! for long and hard
I bore that ire of old.
                    Sweet lord, step forth,
Step from thy car, I pray—nay, not on earth
Plant the proud foot, O king, that trod down Troy!
Women! why tarry ye, whose task it is
To spread your monarch's path with tapestry?
Swift, swift, with purple strew his passage fair,
That justice lead him to a home, at last,
He scarcely looked to see.
(*The attendant women spread the tapestry.*)
                         For what remains,
Zeal unsubdued by sleep shall nerve my hand
To work as right and as the gods command.

AGAMEMNON (*still in the chariot*)

Daughter of Leda, watcher o'er my home,
Thy greeting well befits mine absence long,

For late and hardly has it reached its end.
Know, that the praise which honour bids us crave,
Must come from others' lips, not from our own:
See too that not in fashion feminine
Thou make a warrior's pathway delicate;
Not unto me, as to some Eastern lord,
Bowing thyself to earth, make homage loud,
Strew not this purple that shall make each step
An arrogance; such pomp beseems the gods,
Not me. A mortal man to set his foot
On these rich dyes? I hold such pride in fear,
And bid thee honour me as man, not god.
Fear not—such footcloths and all gauds apart,
Loud from the trump of Fame my name is blown;
Best gift of heaven it is, in glory's hour,
To think thereon with soberness: and thou—
Bethink thee of the adage, *Call none blest*
Till peaceful death have crowned a life of weal.
'Tis said: I fain would fare unvexed by fear.

CLYTEMNESTRA

Nay, but unsay it—thwart not thou my will!

AGAMEMNON

Know, I have said, and will not mar my word.

CLYTEMNESTRA

Was it fear made this meekness to the gods?

AGAMEMNON

If cause be cause, 'tis mine for this resolve.

CLYTEMNESTRA

What, think'st thou, in thy place had Priam done?

AGAMEMNON

He surely would have walked on broidered robes.

CLYTEMNESTRA

Then fear not thou the voice of human blame.

AGAMEMNON

Yet mighty is the murmur of a crowd.

CLYTEMNESTRA

Shrink not from envy, appanage of bliss.

AGAMEMNON

War is not woman's part, nor war of words.

CLYTEMNESTRA

Yet happy victors well may yield therein.

AGAMEMNON

Dost crave for triumph in this petty strife?

CLYTEMNESTRA

Yield; of thy grace permit me to prevail!

AGAMEMNON

Then, if thou wilt, let some one stoop to loose
Swiftly these sandals, slaves beneath my foot;
And stepping thus upon the sea's rich dye,
I pray, *Let none among the gods look down*
With jealous eye on me—reluctant all,
To trample thus and mar a thing of price,
Wasting the wealth of garments silver-worth.
Enough hereof: and, for the stranger maid,
Lead her within, but gently: God on high
Looks graciously on him whom triumph's hour
Has made not pitiless. None willingly
Wear the slave's yoke—and she, the prize and flower
Of all we won, comes hither in my train,
Gift of the army to its chief and lord.
—Now, since in this my will bows down to thine,
I will pass in on purples to my home.

(*He descends from the chariot, and moves toward the palace.*)

CLYTEMNESTRA

A Sea there is—and who shall stay its springs?
And deep within its breast, a mighty store,
Precious as silver, of the purple dye,
Whereby the dipped robe doth its tint renew.
Enough of such, O king, within thy halls
There lies, a store that cannot fail; but I—
I would have gladly vowed unto the gods
Cost of a thousand garments trodden thus,
(Had once the oracle such gift required)
Contriving ransom for thy life preserved.
For while the stock is firm the foliage climbs,
Spreading a shade, what time the dog-star glows;
And thou, returning to thine hearth and home,
Art as a genial warmth in winter hours,
Or as a coolness, when the lord of heaven
Mellows the juice within the bitter grape.
Such boons and more doth bring into a home
The present footstep of its proper lord.
Zeus, Zeus, Fulfilment's lord! my vows fulfil,
And whatsoe'er it be, work forth thy will!

(*She follows* AGAMEMNON *into the palace.*)

CHORUS (*singing*)

strophe 1

Wherefore for ever on the wings of fear
Hovers a vision drear
Before my boding heart? a strain,
Unbidden and unwelcome, thrills mine ear,
Oracular of pain.
Not as of old upon my bosom's throne
Sits Confidence, to spurn
Such fears, like dreams we know not to discern.
Old, old and grey long since the time has grown,
Which saw the linkèd cables moor
The fleet, when erst it came to Ilion's sandy shore;

antistrophe 1

And now mine eyes and not another's see
Their safe return.

Yet none the less in me
The inner spirit sings a boding song,
Self-prompted, sings the Furies' strain—
And seeks, and seeks in vain,
To hope and to be strong!

Ah! to some end of Fate, unseen, unguessed,
Are these wild throbbings of my heart and breast—
Yea, of some doom they tell—
Each pulse, a knell.
Lief, lief I were, that all
To unfulfilment's hidden realm might fall.

strophe 2

Too far, too far our mortal spirits strive,
Grasping at utter weal, unsatisfied—
Till the fell curse, that dwelleth hard beside,
Thrust down the sundering wall. Too fair they blow
The gales that waft our bark on Fortune's tide!
Swiftly we sail, the sooner all to drive
Upon the hidden rock, the reef of woe.
Then if the hand of caution warily
Sling forth into the sea
Part of the freight, lest all should sink below,
From the deep death it saves the bark: even so,
Doom-laden though it be, once more may rise
His household, who is timely wise.

How oft the famine-stricken field
Is saved by God's large gift, the new year's yield!

antistrophe 2

But blood of man once spilled,
Once at his feet shed forth, and darkening the plain,—
Nor chant nor charm can call it back again.

So Zeus hath willed:
Else had he spared the leech Asclepius, skilled
To bring man from the dead: the hand divine
Did smite himself with death—a warning and a sign—

Ah me! if Fate, ordained of old,
Held not the will of gods constrained, controlled,
Helpless to us-ward, and apart—
Swifter than speech my heart
Had poured its presage out!
Now, fretting, chafing in the dark of doubt,
'Tis hopeless to unfold
Truth, from fear's tangled skein; and, yearning to proclaim
Its thought, my soul is prophecy and flame.

(CLYTEMNESTRA *comes out of the palace and addresses* CASSANDRA, *who has remained motionless in her chariot.*)

CLYTEMNESTRA

Get thee within thou too, Cassandra, go!
For Zeus to thee in gracious mercy grants
To share the sprinklings of the lustral bowl,
Beside the altar of his guardianship,
Slave among many slaves. What, haughty still?
Step from the car; Alcmena's son, 'tis said,
Was sold perforce and bore the yoke of old.
Ay, hard it is, but, if such fate befall,
'Tis a fair chance to serve within a home
Of ancient wealth and power. An upstart lord,
To whom wealth's harvest came beyond his hope,
Is as a lion to his slaves, in all
Exceeding fierce, immoderate in sway.
Pass in: thou hearest what our ways will be.

LEADER OF THE CHORUS

Clear unto thee, O maid, is her command,
But thou—within the toils of Fate thou art—
If such thy will, I urge thee to obey;
Yet I misdoubt thou dost nor hear nor heed.

CLYTEMNESTRA

I wot—unless like swallows she doth use
Some strange barbarian tongue from oversea—
My words must speak persuasion to her soul.

LEADER

Obey: there is no gentler way than this.
Step from the car's high seat and follow her.

CLYTEMNESTRA

Truce to this bootless waiting here without!
I will not stay: beside the central shrine
The victims stand, prepared for knife and fire—
Offerings from hearts beyond all hope made glad.
Thou—if thou reckest aught of my command,
'Twere well done soon; but if thy sense be shut
From these my words, let thy barbarian hand
Fulfil by gesture the default of speech.

LEADER

No native is she, thus to read thy words
Unaided: like some wild thing of the wood,
New-trapped, behold! she shrinks and glares on thee.

CLYTEMNESTRA

'Tis madness and the rule of mind distraught,
Since she beheld her city sink in fire,
And hither comes, nor brooks the bit, until
In foam and blood her wrath be champed away.
See ye to her; unqueenly 'tis for me,
Unheeded thus to cast away my words.

(CLYTEMNESTRA *enters the palace.*)

LEADER

But with me pity sits in anger's place.
Poor maiden, come thou from the car; no way
There is but this—take up thy servitude.

CASSANDRA (*chanting*)

Woe, woe, alas! Earth, Mother Earth! and thou
Apollo, Apollo!

LEADER

Peace! shriek not to the bright prophetic god,
Who will not brook the suppliance of woe.

CASSANDRA (*chanting*)

Woe, woe, alas! Earth, Mother Earth! and thou
Apollo, Apollo!

LEADER

Hark, with wild curse she calls anew on him,
Who stands far off and loathes the voice of wail.

CASSANDRA (*chanting*)

Apollo, Apollo!
God of all ways, but only Death's to me,
Once and again, O thou, Destroyer named,
Thou hast destroyed me, thou, my love of old!

LEADER

She grows presageful of her woes to come,
Slave tho' she be, instinct with prophecy.

CASSANDRA (*chanting*)

Apollo, Apollo!
God of all ways, but only Death's to me,
O thou Apollo, thou Destroyer named!
What way hast led me, to what evil home?

LEADER

Know'st thou it not? The home of Atreus' race:
Take these my words for sooth and ask no more.

CASSANDRA (*chanting*)

Home cursed of God! Bear witness unto me,
  Ye visioned woes within—
The blood-stained hands of them that smite their kin—
The strangling noose, and, spattered o'er
With human blood, the reeking floor!

LEADER

How like a sleuth-hound questing on the track,
Keen-scented unto blood and death she hies!

CASSANDRA (*chanting*)

Ah! can the ghostly guidance fail,
Whereby my prophet-soul is onwards led?
Look! for their flesh the spectre-children wail,
Their sodden limbs on which their father fed!

LEADER

Long since we knew of thy prophetic fame,—
But for those deeds we seek no prophet's tongue.

CASSANDRA (*chanting*)

God! 'tis another crime—
Worse than the storied woe of olden time,
Cureless, abhorred, that one is plotting here—
A shaming death, for those that should be dear!
  Alas! and far away, in foreign land,
  He that should help doth stand!

LEADER

  I knew th' old tales, the city rings withal—
  But now thy speech is dark, beyond my ken.

CASSANDRA (*chanting*)

  O wretch, O purpose fell!
  Thou for thy wedded lord
  The cleansing wave hast poured—

A treacherous welcome!
How the sequel tell?
Too soon 'twill come, too soon, for now, even now,
She smites him, blow on blow!

LEADER

Riddles beyond my rede—I peer in vain
Thro' the dim films that screen the prophecy.

CASSANDRA (*chanting*)

God! a new sight! a net, a snare of hell,
Set by her hand—herself a snare more fell!
A wedded wife, she slays her lord,
Helped by another hand!
Ye powers, whose hate
Of Atreus' home no blood can satiate,
Raise the wild cry above the sacrifice abhorred!

CHORUS (*chanting*)

Why biddest thou some fiend, I know not whom,
Shriek o'er the house? Thine is no cheering word.
Back to my heart in frozen fear I feel
My wanning life-blood run—
The blood that round the wounding steel
Ebbs slow, as sinks life's parting sun—
Swift, swift and sure, some woe comes pressing on!

CASSANDRA (*chanting*)

Away, away—keep him away—
The monarch of the herd, the pasture's pride,
Far from his mate! In treach'rous wrath,
Muffling his swarthy horns, with secret scathe,
She gores his fenceless side!
Hark! in the brimming bath,
The heavy plash—the dying cry—
Hark—in the laver—hark, he falls by treachery!

CHORUS (*chanting*)

I read amiss dark sayings such as thine,
Yet something warns me that they tell of ill.
O dark prophetic speech,
Ill tidings dost thou teach
Ever, to mortals here below!
Ever some tale of awe and woe
Thro' all thy windings manifold
Do we unriddle and unfold!

CASSANDRA (*chanting*)

Ah well-a-day! the cup of agony,
Whereof I chant, foams with a draught for me.
Ah lord, ah leader, thou hast led me here—
Was't but to die with thee whose doom is near?

CHORUS (*chanting*)

Distraught thou art, divinely stirred,
And wailest for thyself a tuneless lay,
As piteous as the ceaseless tale
Wherewith the brown melodious bird
Doth ever Itys! Itys! wail,
Deep-bowered in sorrow, all its little life-time's day!

CASSANDRA (*chanting*)

Ah for thy fate, O shrill-voiced nightingale!
Some solace for thy woes did Heaven afford,
Clothed thee with soft brown plumes, and life apart from
wail—
But for my death is edged the double-biting sword!

CHORUS (*chanting*)

What pangs are these, what fruitless pain,
Sent on thee from on high?
Thou chantest terror's frantic strain,
Yet in shrill measured melody.
How thus unerring canst thou sweep along
The prophet's path of boding song?

CASSANDRA (*chanting*)

Woe, Paris, woe on thee! thy bridal joy
Was death and fire upon thy race and Troy!
And woe for thee, Scamander's flood!
Beside thy banks, O river fair,
I grew in tender nursing care
From childhood unto maidenhood!
Now not by thine, but by Cocytus' stream
And Acheron's banks shall ring my boding scream.

CHORUS (*chanting*)

Too plain is all, too plain!
A child might read aright thy fateful strain.
Deep in my heart their piercing fang
Terror and sorrow set, the while I heard
That piteous, low, tender word,
Yet to mine ear and heart a crushing pang.

CASSANDRA (*chanting*)

Woe for my city, woe for Ilion's fall!
Father, how oft with sanguine stain
Streamed on thine altar-stone the blood of cattle, slain
That heaven might guard our wall!
But all was shed in vain.
Low lie the shattered towers whereas they fell,
And I—ah burning heart!—shall soon lie low as well.

CHORUS (*chanting*)

Of sorrow is thy song, of sorrow still!
Alas, what power of ill
Sits heavy on thy heart and bids thee tell
In tears of perfect moan thy deadly tale?
Some woe—I know not what—must close thy pious wail.

CASSANDRA (*more calmly*)

List! for no more the presage of my soul,
Bride-like, shall peer from its secluding veil;
But as the morning wind blows clear the east,

More bright shall blow the wind of prophecy,
And as against the low bright line of dawn
Heaves high and higher yet the rolling wave,
So in the clearing skies of prescience
Dawns on my soul a further, deadlier woe,
And I will speak, but in dark speech no more.
Bear witness, ye, and follow at my side—
I scent the trail of blood, shed long ago.
Within this house a choir abidingly
Chants in harsh unison the chant of ill;
Yea, and they drink, for more enhardened joy,
Man's blood for wine, and revel in the halls,
Departing never, Furies of the home.
They sit within, they chant the primal curse,
Each spitting hatred on that crime of old,
The brother's couch, the love incestuous
That brought forth hatred to the ravisher.
Say, is my speech or wild and erring now,
Or doth its arrow cleave the mark indeed?
They called me once, *The prophetess of lies,*
The wandering hag, the pest of every door—
Attest ye now, *She knows in very sooth*
The house's curse, the storied infamy.

LEADER OF THE CHORUS

Yet how should oath—how loyally soe'er
I swear it—aught avail thee! In good sooth,
My wonder meets thy claim: I stand amazed
That thou, a maiden born beyond the seas,
Dost as a native know and tell aright
Tales of a city of an alien tongue.

CASSANDRA

That is my power—a boon Apollo gave.

LEADER

God though he were, yearning for mortal maid?

CASSANDRA

Ay! what seemed shame of old is shame no more.

LEADER

Such finer sense suits not with slavery.

CASSANDRA

He strove to win me, panting for my love.

LEADER

Came ye by compact unto bridal joys?

CASSANDRA

Nay—for I plighted troth, then foiled the god.

LEADER

Wert thou already dowered with prescience?

CASSANDRA

Yea—prophetess to Troy of all her doom.

LEADER

How left thee then Apollo's wrath unscathed?

CASSANDRA

I, false to him, seemed prophet false to all.

LEADER

Not so—to us at least thy words seem sooth.

CASSANDRA

Woe for me, woe! Again the agony—
Dread pain that sees the future all too well
With ghastly preludes whirls and racks my soul.
Behold ye—yonder on the palace roof
The spectre-children sitting—look, such things
As dreams are made on, phantoms as of babes,
Horrible shadows, that a kinsman's hand
Hath marked with murder, and their arms are full—
A rueful burden—see, they hold them up,
The entrails upon which their father fed!

For this, for this, I say there plots revenge
A coward lion, couching in the lair—
Guarding the gate against my master's foot—
My master—mine—I bear the slave's yoke now,
And he, the lord of ships, who trod down Troy,
Knows not the fawning treachery of tongue
Of this thing false and dog-like—how her speech
Glozes and sleeks her purpose, till she win
By ill fate's favour the desirèd chance,
Moving like Atè to a secret end.
O aweless soul! the woman slays her lord—
Woman? what loathsome monster of the earth
Were fit comparison? The double snake—
Or Scylla, where she dwells, the seaman's bane,
Girt round about with rocks? some hag of hell,
Raving a truceless curse upon her kin?
Hark—even now she cries exultingly
The vengeful cry that tells of battle turned—
How fain, forsooth, to greet her chief restored!
Nay then, believe me not: what skills belief
Or disbelief? Fate works its will—and thou
Wilt see and say in ruth, *Her tale was true.*

LEADER

Ah—'tis Thyestes' feast on kindred flesh—
I guess her meaning and with horror thrill,
Hearing no shadow'd hint of th' o'er-true tale,
But its full hatefulness: yet, for the rest,
Far from the track I roam, and know no more.

CASSANDRA

'Tis Agamemnon's doom thou shalt behold.

LEADER

Peace, hapless woman, to thy boding words!

CASSANDRA

Far from my speech stands he who saïns and saves

LEADER

Ay—were such doom at hand—which God forbid!

CASSANDRA

Thou prayest idly—these move swift to slay.

LEADER

What man prepares a deed of such despite?

CASSANDRA

Fool! thus to read amiss mine oracles.

LEADER

Deviser and device are dark to me.

CASSANDRA

Dark! all too well I speak the Grecian tongue.

LEADER

Ay—but in thine, as in Apollo's strains,
Familiar is the tongue, but dark the thought.

CASSANDRA

Ah, ah, the fire! it waxes, nears me now—
Woe, woe for me, Apollo of the dawn!

Lo, how the woman-thing, the lioness
Couched with the wolf—her noble mate afar—
Will slay me, slave forlorn! Yea, like some witch,
She drugs the cup of wrath, that slays her lord,
With double death—his recompense for me!
Ay, 'tis for me, the prey he bore from Troy,
That she hath sworn his death, and edged the steel!
Ye wands, ye wreaths that cling around my neck,
Ye showed me prophetess yet scorned of all—
I stamp you into death, or e'er I die—
Down, to destruction!
Thus I stand revenged—
Go, crown some other with a prophet's woe.

Look! it is he, it is Apollo's self
Rending from me the prophet-robe he gave.
God! while I wore it yet, thou saw'st me mocked
There at my home by each malicious mouth—
To all and each, an undivided scorn.
The name alike and fate of witch and cheat—
Woe, poverty, and famine—all I bore;
And at this last the god hath brought me here
Into death's toils, and what his love had made,
His hate unmakes me now: and I shall stand
Not now before the altar of my home,
But me a slaughter-house and block of blood
Shall see hewn down, a reeking sacrifice.
Yet shall the gods have heed of me who die,
For by their will shall one requite my doom.
He, to avenge his father's blood outpoured,
Shall smite and slay with matricidal hand.
Ay, he shall come—tho' far away he roam,
A banished wanderer in a stranger's land—
To crown his kindred's edifice of ill,
Called home to vengeance by his father's fall:
Thus have the high gods sworn, and shall fulfil.
And now why mourn I, tarrying on earth,
Since first mine Ilion has found its fate
And I beheld, and those who won the wall
Pass to such issue as the gods ordain?
I too will pass and like them dare to die!

(*She turns and looks upon the palace door.*)

Portal of Hades, thus I bid thee hail!
Grant me one boon—a swift and mortal stroke,
That all unwrung by pain, with ebbing blood
Shed forth in quiet death, I close mine eyes.

LEADER

Maid of mysterious woes, mysterious lore,
Long was thy prophecy: but if aright

Thou readest all thy fate, how, thus unscared,
Dost thou approach the altar of thy doom,
As fronts the knife some victim, heaven-controlled?

CASSANDRA

Friends, there is no avoidance in delay.

LEADER

Yet who delays the longest, his the gain.

CASSANDRA

The day is come—flight were small gain to me!

LEADER

O brave endurance of a soul resolved!

CASSANDRA

That were ill praise, for those of happier doom.

LEADER

All fame is happy, even famous death.

CASSANDRA

Ah sire, ah brethren, famous once were ye!
(*She moves to enter the house, then starts back.*)

LEADER

What fear is this that scares thee from the house?

CASSANDRA

Pah!

LEADER

What is this cry? some dark despair of soul?

CASSANDRA

Pah! the house fumes with stench and spilth of blood

LEADER

How? 'tis the smell of household offerings.

CASSANDRA

'Tis rank as charnel-scent from open graves.

LEADER

Thou canst not mean this scented Syrian nard?

CASSANDRA

Nay, let me pass within to cry aloud
The monarch's fate and mine—enough of life.
Ah friends!
Bear to me witness, since I fall in death,
That not as birds that shun the bush and scream
I moan in idle terror. This attest
When for my death's revenge another dies,
A woman for a woman, and a man
Falls, for a man ill-wedded to his curse.
Grant me this boon—the last before I die.

LEADER

Brave to the last! I mourn thy doom foreseen.

CASSANDRA

Once more one utterance, but not of wail,
Though for my death—and then I speak no more.

Sun! thou whose beam I shall not see again,
To thee I cry, Let those whom vengeance calls
To slay their kindred's slayers, quit withal
The death of me, the slave, the fenceless prey.

Ah state of mortal man! in time of weal,
A line, a shadow! and if ill fate fall,
One wet sponge-sweep wipes all our trace away—
And this I deem less piteous, of the twain.

(*She enters the palace.*)

CHORUS (*singing*)

Too true it is! our mortal state
With bliss is never satiate,

And none, before the palace high
And stately of prosperity,
Cries to us with a voice of fear,
Away! 'tis ill to enter here!

Lo! this our lord hath trodden down,
By grace of heaven, old Priam's town,
And praised as god he stands once more
On Argos' shore!
Yet now—if blood shed long ago
Cries out that other blood shall flow—
His life-blood, his, to pay again
The stern requital of the slain—
Peace to that braggart's vaunting vain,
Who, having heard the chieftain's tale,
Yet boasts of bliss untouched by bale!

(*A loud cry is heard from within.*)

VOICE OF AGAMEMNON

O I am sped—a deep, a mortal blow.

LEADER OF THE CHORUS

Listen, listen! who is screaming as in mortal agony?

VOICE OF AGAMEMNON

O! O! again, another, another blow!

LEADER

The bloody act is over—I have heard the monarch's cry—
Let us swiftly take some counsel, lest we too be doomed to die.

ONE OF THE CHORUS

'Tis best, I judge, aloud for aid to call,
"Ho! loyal Argives! to the palace, all!"

ANOTHER

Better, I deem, ourselves to bear the aid,
And drag the deed to light, while drips the blade.

ANOTHER

Such will is mine, and what thou say'st I say:
Swiftly to act! the time brooks no delay.

ANOTHER

Ay, for 'tis plain, this prelude of their song
Foretells its close in tyranny and wrong.

ANOTHER

Behold, we tarry—but thy name, Delay,
They spurn, and press with sleepless hand to slay.

ANOTHER

I know not what 'twere well to counsel now—
Who wills to act, 'tis his to counsel how.

ANOTHER

Thy doubt is mine: for when a man is slain,
I have no words to bring his life again.

ANOTHER

What? e'en for life's sake, bow us to obey
These house-defilers and their tyrant sway?

ANOTHER

Unmanly doom! 'twere better far to die—
Death is a gentler lord than tyranny.

ANOTHER

Think well—must cry or sign of woe or pain
Fix our conclusion that the chief is slain?

ANOTHER

Such talk befits us when the deed we see—
Conjecture dwells afar from certainty.

LEADER OF THE CHORUS

I read one will from many a diverse word,
To know aright, how stands it with our lord!

(*The central doors of the palace open, disclosing* Clytemnestra, *who comes forward. She has blood smeared upon her forehead. The body of* Agamemnon *lies, muffled in a long robe, within a silver-sided laver; the corpse of* Cassandra *is laid beside him.*)

Clytemnestra

Ho, ye who heard me speak so long and oft
The glozing word that led me to my will—
Hear how I shrink not to unsay it all!
How else should one who willeth to requite
Evil for evil to an enemy
Disguised as friend, weave the mesh straitly round him,
Not to be overleaped, a net of doom?
This is the sum and issue of old strife,
Of me deep-pondered and at length fulfilled.
All is avowed, and as I smote I stand
With foot set firm upon a finished thing!
I turn not to denial: thus I wrought
So that he could nor flee nor ward his doom.
Even as the trammel hems the scaly shoal,
I trapped him with inextricable toils,
The ill abundance of a baffling robe;
Then smote him, once, again—and at each wound
He cried aloud, then as in death relaxed
Each limb and sang to earth; and as he lay,
Once more I smote him, with the last third blow,
Sacred to Hades, saviour of the dead.
And thus he fell, and as he passed away,
Spirit with body chafed; each dying breath
Flung from his breast swift bubbling jets of gore,
And the dark sprinklings of the rain of blood
Fell upon me; and I was fain to feel
That dew—not sweeter is the rain of heaven
To cornland, when the green sheath teems with grain
Elders of Argos—since the thing stands so,

I bid you to rejoice, if such your will:
Rejoice or not, I vaunt and praise the deed,
And well I ween, if seemly it could be,
'Twere not ill done to pour libations here,
Justly—ay, more than justly—on his corpse
Who filled his home with curses as with wine,
And thus returned to drain the cup he filled.

LEADER

I marvel at thy tongue's audacity,
To vaunt thus loudly o'er a husband slain.

CLYTEMNESTRA

Ye hold me as a woman, weak of will,
And strive to sway me: but my heart is stout,
Nor fears to speak its uttermost to you,
Albeit ye know its message. Praise or blame,
Even as ye list,—I reck not of your words.
Lo! at my feet lies Agamemnon slain,
My husband once—and him this hand of mine,
A right contriver, fashioned for his death.
Behold the deed!

CHORUS (*chanting*)

Woman, what deadly birth,
What venomed essence of the earth
Or dark distilment of the wave,
To thee such passion gave,
Nerving thine hand
To set upon thy brow this burning crown,
The curses of thy land?
Our king by thee cut off, hewn down!
Go forth—they cry— *accursed and forlorn,*
To hate and scorn!

CLYTEMNESTRA

O ye just men, who speak my sentence now,
The city's hate, the ban of all my realm!

Ye had no voice of old to launch such doom
On him, my husband, when he held as light
My daughter's life as that of sheep or goat,
One victim from the thronging fleecy fold!
Yea, slew in sacrifice his child and mine,
The well-loved issue of my travail-pangs,
To lull and lay the gales that blew from Thrace.
That deed of his, I say, that stain and shame,
Had rightly been atoned by banishment;
But ye, who then were dumb, are stern to judge
This deed of mine that doth affront your ears.
Storm out your threats, yet knowing this for sooth,
That I am ready, if your hand prevail
As mine now doth, to bow beneath your sway:
If God say nay, it shall be yours to learn
By chastisement a late humility.

CHORUS (*chanting*)

Bold is thy craft, and proud
Thy confidence, thy vaunting loud;
Thy soul, that chose a murd'ress' fate,
Is all with blood elate—
Maddened to know
The blood not yet avenged, the damnèd spot
Crimson upon thy brow.
But Fate prepares for thee thy lot—
Smitten as thou didst smite, without a friend,
To meet thine end!

CLYTEMNESTRA

Hear then the sanction of the oath I swear—
By the great vengeance for my murdered child,
By Atè, by the Fury unto whom
This man lies sacrificed by hand of mine,
I do not look to tread the hall of Fear,
While in this hearth and home of mine there burns
The light of love—Aegisthus—as of old

Loyal, a stalwart shield of confidence—
As true to me as this slain man was false,
Wronging his wife with paramours at Troy,
Fresh from the kiss of each Chryseis there!
Behold him dead—behold his captive prize,
Seeress and harlot—comfort of his bed,
True prophetess, true paramour—I wot
The sea-bench was not closer to the flesh,
Full oft, of every rower, than was she.
See, ill they did, and ill requites them now.
His death ye know: she as a dying swan
Sang her last dirge, and lies, as erst she lay,
Close to his side, and to my couch has left
A sweet new taste of joys that know no fear.

CHORUS (*singing*)

strophe 1

Ah woc and well-a-day! I would that Fate—
  Not bearing agony too great,
Nor stretching me too long on couch of pain—
  Would bid mine eyelids keep
The morningless and unawakening sleep!
      For life is weary, now my lord is slain,
        The gracious among kings!
Hard fate of old he bore and many grievous things,
    And for a woman's sake, on Ilian land—
Now is his life hewn down, and by a woman's hand.

refrain I

      O Helen, O infatuate soul,
      Who bad'st the tides of battle roll,
      O'erwhelming thousands, life on life,
      'Neath Ilion's wall!
    And now lies dead the lord of all.
      The blossom of thy storied sin
      Bears blood's inexpiable stain,

O thou that erst, these halls within,
Wert unto all a rock of strife,
A husband's bane!

CLYTEMNESTRA (*chanting*)

Peace! pray not thou for death as though
Thine heart was whelmed beneath this woe,
Nor turn thy wrath aside to ban
The name of Helen, nor recall
How she, one bane of many a man,
Sent down to death the Danaan lords,
To sleep at Troy the sleep of swords,
And wrought the woe that shattered all.

CHORUS

antistrophe 1

Fiend of the race! that swoopest fell
Upon the double stock of Tantalus,
Lording it o'er me by a woman's will,
Stern, manful, and imperious—
A bitter sway to me!
Thy very form I see,
Like some grim raven, perched upon the slain,
Exulting o'er the crime, aloud, in tuneless strain!

CLYTEMNESTRA (*chanting*)

Right was that word—thou namest well
The brooding race-fiend, triply fell!
From him it is that murder's thirst,
Blood-lapping, inwardly is nursed—
Ere time the ancient scar can sain,
New blood comes welling forth again.

CHORUS

strophe 2

Grim is his wrath and heavy on our home,
That fiend of whom thy voice has cried

Alas, an omened cry of woe unsatisfied,
An all-devouring doom!

Ah woe, ah Zeus! from Zeus all things befall—
Zeus the high cause and finisher of all!—
Lord of our mortal state, by him are willed
All things, by him fulfilled!

refrain 2

Yet ah my king, my king no more!
What words to say, what tears to pour
Can tell my love for thee?
The spider-web of treachery
She wove and wound, thy life around,
And lo! I see thee lie,
And thro' a coward, impious wound
Pant forth thy life and die!
A death of shame—ah woe on woe!
A treach'rous hand, a cleaving blow!

CLYTEMNESTRA (*chanting*)

My guilt thou harpest, o'er and o'er!
I bid thee reckon me no more
As Agamemnon's spouse.
The old Avenger, stern of mood
For Atreus and his feast of blood,
Hath struck the lord of Atreus' house,
And in the semblance of his wife
The king hath slain.[1]—
Yea, for the murdered children's life,
A chieftain's in requital ta'en.

CHORUS

antistrophe 2

Thou guiltless of this murder, thou!
Who dares such thought avow?
Yet it may be, wroth for the parent's deed.

The fiend hath holpen thee to slay the son.
Dark Ares, god of death, is pressing on
Thro' streams of blood by kindred shed,
Exacting the accompt for children dead,
For clotted blood, for flesh on which their sire did feed.

refrain 2

Yet ah my king, my king no more!
What words to say, what tears to pour
Can tell my love for thee?
The spider-web of treachery
She wove and wound, thy life around,
And lo! I see thee lie,
And thro' a coward, impious wound
Pant forth thy life and die!
A death of shame—ah woe on woe!
A treach'rous hand, a cleaving blow!

CLYTEMNESTRA (*chanting*)

I deem not that the death he died
Had overmuch of shame:
For this was he who did provide
Foul wrong unto his house and name:
His daughter, blossom of my womb,
He gave unto a deadly doom,
Iphigenia, child of tears!
And as he wrought, even so he fares.
Nor be his vaunt too loud in hell;
For by the sword his sin he wrought,
And by the sword himself is brought
Among the dead to dwell.

CHORUS

strophe 3

Ah whither shall I fly?
For all in ruin sinks the kingly hall;
Nor swift device nor shift of thought have I,

To 'scape its fall.
A little while the gentler rain-drops fail;
I stand distraught—a ghastly interval,
Till on the roof-tree rings the bursting hail
Of blood and doom. Even now fate whets the steel
On whetstones new and deadlier than of old,
The steel that smites, in Justice' hold,
Another death to deal.
O Earth! that I had lain at rest
And lapped for ever in thy breast,
Ere I had seen my chieftain fall
Within the laver's silver wall,
Low-lying on dishonoured bier!
And who shall give him sepulchre,
And who the wail of sorrow pour?
Woman, 'tis thine no more!
A graceless gift unto his shade
Such tribute, by his murd'ress paid!
Strive not thus wrongly to atone
The impious deed thy hand hath done.
Ah who above the god-like chief
Shall weep the tears of loyal grief?
Who speak above his lowly grave
The last sad praises of the brave?

CLYTEMNESTRA (*chanting*)

Peace! for such task is none of thine.
By me he fell, by me he died,
And now his burial rites be mine!
Yet from these halls no mourners' train
Shall celebrate his obsequies;
Only by Acheron's rolling tide
His child shall spring unto his side,
And in a daughter's loving wise
Shall clasp and kiss him once again!

CHORUS

antistrophe 3

Lo! sin by sin and sorrow dogg'd by sorrow—
And who the end can know?
The slayer of to-day shall die to-morrow—
The wage of wrong is woe.
While Time shall be, while Zeus in heaven is lord,
His law is fixed and stern;
On him that wrought shall vengeance be outpoured–
The tides of doom return.
The children of the curse abide within
These halls of high estate—
And none can wrench from off the home of sin
The clinging grasp of fate.

CLYTEMNESTRA (*chanting*)

Now walks thy word aright, to tell
This ancient truth of oracle;
But I with vows of sooth will pray
To him, the power that holdeth sway
O'er all the race of Pleisthenes—
Tho' dark the deed and deep the guilt,
With this last blood, my hands have spilt,
I pray thee let thine anger cease!
I pray thee pass from us away
To some new race in other lands,
There, if thou wilt, to wrong and slay
The lives of men by kindred hands.

For me 'tis all sufficient meed,
Tho' little wealth or power were won,
So I can say, *'Tis past and done.*
The bloody lust and murderous,
The inborn frenzy of our house
Is ended, by my deed!

(Aegisthus *and his armed attendants enter.*)

Aegisthus

Dawn of the day of rightful vengeance, hail!
I dare at length aver that gods above
Have care of men and heed of earthly wrongs.
I, I who stand and thus exult to see
This man lie wound in robes the Furies wove,
Slain in the requital of his father's craft.
Take ye the truth, that Atreus, this man's sire,
The lord and monarch of this land of old,
Held with my sire Thyestes deep dispute,
Brother with brother, for the prize of sway,
And drave him from his home to banishment.
Thereafter, the lorn exile homeward stole
And clung a suppliant to the hearth divine,
And for himself won this immunity—
Not with his own blood to defile the land
That gave him birth. But Atreus, godless sire
Of him who here lies dead, this welcome planned—
With zeal that was not love he feigned to hold
In loyal joy a day of festal cheer,
And bade my father to his board, and set
Before him flesh that was his children once.
First, sitting at the upper board alone,
He hid the fingers and the feet, but gave
The rest—and readily Thyestes took
What to his ignorance no semblance wore
Of human flesh, and ate: behold what curse
That eating brought upon our race and name!
For when he knew what all unhallowed thing
He thus had wrought, with horror's bitter cry
Back-starting, spewing forth the fragments foul,
On Pelops' house a deadly curse he spake—
As darkly as I spurn this damnèd food,
So perish all the race of Pleisthenes!

Thus by that curse fell he whom here ye see,
And I—who else?—this murder wove and planned;
For me, an infant yet in swaddling bands,
Of the three children youngest, Atreus sent
To banishment by my sad father's side:
But Justice brought me home once more, grown now
To manhood's years; and stranger tho' I was,
My right hand reached unto the chieftain's life,
Plotting and planning all that malice bade.
And death itself were honour now to me,
Beholding him in Justice' ambush ta'en.

LEADER OF THE CHORUS

Aegisthus, for this insolence of thine
That vaunts itself in evil, take my scorn.
Of thine own will, thou sayest, thou hast slain
The chieftain, by thine own unaided plot
Devised the piteous death: I rede thee well,
Think not thy head shall 'scape, when right prevails.
The people's ban, the stones of death and doom.

AEGISTHUS

This word from thee, this word from one who rows
Low at the oars beneath, what time we rule,
We of the upper tier? Thou'lt know anon,
'Tis bitter to be taught again in age,
By one so young, submission at the word.
But iron of the chain and hunger's throes
Can minister unto an o'erswoln pride
Marvellous well, ay, even in the old.
Hast eyes, and seest not this? Peace—kick not thus
Against the pricks, unto thy proper pain!

LEADER

Thou womanish man, waiting till war did cease,
Home-watcher and defiler of the couch,
And arch-deviser of the chieftain's doom!

AEGISTHUS

Bold words again! but they shall end in tears.
The very converse, thine, of Orpheus' tongue:
He roused and led in ecstasy of joy
All things that heard his voice melodious;
But thou as with the futile cry of curs
Wilt draw men wrathfully upon thee. Peace!
Or strong subjection soon shall tame thy tongue.

LEADER

Ay, thou art one to hold an Argive down—
Thou, skilled to plan the murder of the king,
But not with thine own hand to smite the blow!

AEGISTHUS

That fraudful force was woman's very part,
Not mine, whom deep suspicion from of old
Would have debarred. Now by his treasure's aid
My purpose holds to rule the citizens.
But whoso will not bear my guiding hand,
Him for his corn-fed mettle I will drive
Not as a trace-horse, light-caparisoned,
But to the shafts with heaviest harness bound.
Famine, the grim mate of the dungeon dark,
Shall look on him and shall behold him tame.

LEADER

Thou losel soul, was then thy strength too slight
To deal in murder, while a woman's hand,
Staining and shaming Argos and its gods,
Availed to slay him? Ho, if anywhere
The light of life smite on Orestes' eyes,
Let him, returning by some guardian fate,
Hew down with force her paramour and her!

AEGISTHUS

How thy word and act shall issue, thou shalt shortly understand.

LEADER

Up to action, O my comrades! for the fight is hard at hand.
Swift, your right hands to the sword hilt! bare the weapon as for strife—

AEGISTHUS

Lo! I too am standing ready, hand on hilt for death or life.

LEADER

'Twas thy word and we accept it: onward to the chance of war!

CLYTEMNESTRA

Nay, enough, enough, my champion! we will smite and slay no more.
Already have we reaped enough the harvest-field of guilt:
Enough of wrong and murder, let no other blood be spilt.
Peace, old men! and pass away unto the homes by Fate decreed,
Lest ill valour meet our vengeance—'twas a necessary deed.
But enough of toils and troubles—be the end, if ever, now,
Ere thy talon, O Avenger, deal another deadly blow.
'Tis a woman's word of warning, and let who will list thereto.

AEGISTHUS

But that these should loose and lavish reckless blossoms of the tongue,
And in hazard of their fortune cast upon me words of wrong,
And forget the law of subjects, and revile their ruler's word—

LEADER

Ruler? but 'tis not for Argives, thus to own a dastard lord!

AEGISTHUS

I will follow to chastise thee in my coming days of sway.

LEADER

Not if Fortune guide Orestes safely on his homeward way.

AEGISTHUS

Ah, well I know how exiles feed on hopes of their return.

LEADER

Fare and batten on pollution of the right, while 'tis thy turn.

AEGISTHUS

Thou shalt pay, be well assurèd, heavy quittance for thy pride.

LEADER

Crow and strut, with her to watch thee, like a cock, his mate beside!

CLYTEMNESTRA

Heed not thou too highly of them—let the cur-pack growl and yell:
I and thou will rule the palace and will order all things well.

(AEGISTHUS *and* CLYTEMNESTRA *move towards the palace, as the* CHORUS *sullenly withdraws.*)

OEDIPUS THE KING

by

SOPHOCLES

Characters in the Play

Oedipus, *King of Thebes*
Priest of Zeus
Creon, *brother of* Jocasta
Teiresias, *the blind prophet*
Jocasta
First Messenger, *a shepherd from Corinth*
A Shepherd, *formerly in the service of Laius*
Second Messenger, *from the house*
Chorus of Theban Elders

Mute Persons

A train of Suppliants (old men, youths, and children)
The children Antigone *and* Ismene, *daughters of* Oedipus *and* Jocasta

INTRODUCTION

THE date of *Oedipus the King*, Sophocles' masterpiece, is unknown, though in all probability it must have been written when the poet's powers were at their zenith. The events of the story antecedent to the opening of the play emerge as its action advances. We hear of the oracle which warned Laius, the father of Oedipus, that a son would be born to him who would slay him. We hear how the son was born, was exposed, but rescued and reared by Polybus and Merope, King and Queen of Corinth, whom the boy regarded as his parents. We learn that Oedipus, in ignorance, slew Laius, came to Thebes, solved the riddle of the Sphinx, was made king, and married the recently widowed queen, Jocasta, who actually was his own mother. Many years have passed since their marriage, and two sons and two daughters were born to them. But presently a great calamity fell upon Thebes, a plague which was virtually destroying the city. Sophocles begins his tragedy at this point in the story, as a group of subjects appeal to their great king, Oedipus, to help them in their desolation. The action of the play reveals how Oedipus gradually came to learn the horrible truth that he had actually killed his father and married his mother.

Purely from the technical point of view, Sophocles' play is practically unrivalled in dramatic literature. With remarkable skill he allows Oedipus step by step to become acquainted with the facts of his past, at the same time exploiting to the full the possibilities for dramatic irony, since the audience always knows more of the truth than Oedipus at any given moment in the play. Furthermore, rarely does one find such perfect motivation for individual actions within the drama. Each move by each character emerges convincingly from what has happened immediately before. Because *Oedipus the King* possessed so many formal and technical excellences, it is not strange that Aristotle used it more frequently than any other Greek tragedy to illustrate his various critical theories.

The character of Oedipus naturally dominates the whole play. From it primarily Aristotle has derived his famous definition of the tragic hero, "a man who is highly renowned and prosperous, but one who is not pre-eminently virtuous and just, whose misfortune, however, is brought upon him not by vice and depravity but by some error of judgment or frailty." Much has been written on Oedipus' rashness and his temper. Critics have pointed to his erratic perceptions which are now keen, and now amazingly faulty, and to his intense power of concentration which enables him to see only one thing at a time, very often to his terrible detriment.

Oedipus the King has sometimes been called a tragedy of Fate, in which the characters are caught in a web of circumstance, from which they feebly and vainly try to extricate themselves. This may be partially true, but certainly there is a greater significance to the play than this theory would lead us to suspect. Oedipus in some sense is presented as master of his own destiny, or else it is meaningless that at the end of the play he does not excuse himself by pleading that he did not know what he was doing, but rather accepts full responsibility as a moral agent for all his acts, whether done in ignorance or not. In this point seems to lie the high distinction of the play, and its universal appeal.

OEDIPUS THE KING

(SCENE:—*Before the royal palace of Oedipus at Thebes. In front of the large central doors there is an altar; a smaller altar stands also near each of the two side-doors. Suppliants—old men, youths, and young children—are seated on the steps of the altars. They are dressed in white tunics and cloaks,—their hair bound with white fillets. On the altars they have laid down olive-branches wreathed with fillets of wool. The* PRIEST OF ZEUS, *a venerable man, is alone standing, facing the central doors of the palace. These are now thrown open. Followed by two attendants, who place themselves on either side of the doors,* OEDIPUS *enters, in the robes of a king. For a moment he gazes silently on the groups at the altars, and then speaks.*)

OEDIPUS

MY CHILDREN, latest-born to Cadmus who was of old, why are ye set before me thus with wreathed branches of suppliants, while the city reeks with incense, rings with prayers for health and cries of woe? I deemed it unmeet, my children, to hear these things at the mouth of others, and have come hither myself, I, Oedipus renowned of all.

Tell me, then, thou venerable man—since it is thy natural part to speak for these—in what mood are ye placed here, with what dread or what desire? Be sure that I would gladly give all aid; hard of heart were I, did I not pity such suppliants as these.

PRIEST OF ZEUS

Nay, Oedipus, ruler of my land, thou seest of what years we are who beset thy altars,—some, nestlings still too tender for far flights,—some, bowed with age, priests, as I of Zeus, —and these, the chosen youth; while the rest of the folk sit with wreathed branches in the market-places, and before the two shrines of Pallas, and where Ismenus gives answer by fire.

For the city, as thou thyself seest, is now too sorely vexed, and can no more lift her head from beneath the angry waves of death; a blight is on her in the fruitful blossoms of the land, in the herds among the pastures, in the barren pangs of women; and withal the flaming god, the malign plague, hath swooped on us, and ravages the town; by whom the house of Cadmus is made waste, but dark Hades rich in groans and tears.

It is not as deeming thee ranked with gods that I and these children are suppliants at thy hearth, but as deeming thee first of men, both in life's common chances, and when mortals have to do with more than man: seeing that thou camest to the town of Cadmus, and didst quit us of the tax that we rendered to the hard songstress; and this, though thou knewest nothing from us that could avail thee, nor hadst been schooled; no, by a god's aid, 'tis said and believed, didst thou uplift our life.

And now, Oedipus, king glorious in all eyes, we beseech thee, all we suppliants, to find for us some succour, whether by the whisper of a god thou knowest it, or haply as in the power of man; for I see that, when men have been proved in deeds past, the issues of their counsels, too, most often have effect.

On, best of mortals, again uplift our State! On, guard thy fame,—since now this land calls thee saviour for thy former zeal; and never be it our memory of thy reign that we were first restored and afterward cast down: nay, lift up this State in such wise that it fall no more!

With good omen didst thou give us that past happiness; now also show thyself the same. For if thou art to rule this land, even as thou art now its lord, 'tis better to be lord of men than of a waste: since neither walled town nor ship is anything, if it is void and no men dwell with thee therein.

OEDIPUS

Oh my piteous children, known, well known to me are the desires wherewith ye have come: well wot I that ye suffer all; yet, sufferers as ye are, there is not one of you whose suffering is as mine. Your pain comes on each one of you for himself alone, and for no other; but my soul mourns at once for the city, and for myself, and for thee.

So that ye rouse me not, truly, as one sunk in sleep: no, be sure that I have wept full many tears, gone many ways in wanderings of thought. And the sole remedy which, well pondering, I could find, this I have put into act. I have sent the son of Menoeceus, Creon, mine own wife's brother, to the Pythian house of Phoebus, to learn by what deed or word I might deliver this town. And already, when the lapse of days is reckoned, it troubles me what he doth; for he tarries strangely, beyond the fitting space. But when he comes, then shall I be no true man if I do not all that the god shows.

PRIEST

Nay, in season hast thou spoken; at this moment these sign to me that Creon draws near.

OEDIPUS

O king Apollo, may he come to us in the brightness of saving fortune, even as his face is bright!

PRIEST

Nay, to all seeming, he brings comfort; else would he not be coming crowned thus thickly with berry-laden bay.

OEDIPUS

We shall know soon: he is at range to hear.—(*Enter* CREON) Prince, my kinsman, son of Menoeceus, what news hast thou brought us from the god?

CREON

Good news: I tell thee that even troubles hard to bear,—if haply they find the right issue,—will end in perfect peace.

OEDIPUS

But what is the oracle? So far, thy words make me neither bold nor yet afraid.

CREON

If thou wouldest hear while these are nigh, I am ready to speak; or else to go within.

OEDIPUS

Speak before all: the sorrow which I bear is for these more than for mine own life.

CREON

With thy leave, I will tell what I heard from the god. Phoebus our lord bids us plainly to drive out a defiling thing, which (he saith) hath been harboured in this land, and not to harbour it, so that it cannot be healed.

OEDIPUS

By what rite shall we cleanse us? What is the manner of the misfortune?

CREON

By banishing a man, or by bloodshed in quittance of bloodshed, since it is that blood which brings the tempest on our city.

OEDIPUS

And who is the man whose fate he thus reveals?

CREON

Laius, king, was lord of our land before thou wast pilot of this State.

OEDIPUS

I know it well—by hearsay, for I saw him never.

CREON

He was slain; and the god now bids us plainly to wreak vengeance on his murderers—whosoever they be.

OEDIPUS

And where are they upon the earth? Where shall the dim track of this old crime be found?

CREON

In this land,—said the god. What is sought for can be caught; only that which is not watched escapes.

OEDIPUS

And was it in the house, or in the field, or on strange soil that Laius met this bloody end?

CREON

'Twas on a visit to Delphi, as he said, that he had left our land; and he came home no more, after he had once set forth.

OEDIPUS

And was there none to tell? Was there no comrade of his journey who saw the deed, from whom tidings might have been gained, and used?

CREON

All perished, save one who fled in fear, and could tell for certain but one thing of all that he saw.

OEDIPUS

And what was that? One thing might show the clue to many, could we get but a small beginning for hope.

CREON

He said that robbers met and fell on them, not in one man's might, but with full many hands.

OEDIPUS

How, then, unless there was some trafficking in bribes from here, should the robber have dared thus far?

CREON

Such things were surmised; but, Laius once slain, amid our troubles no avenger arose.

OEDIPUS

But, when royalty had fallen thus, what trouble in your path can have hindered a full search?

CREON

The riddling Sphinx had made us let dark things go, and was inviting us to think of what lay at our doors.

OEDIPUS

Nay, I will start afresh, and once more make dark things plain. Right worthily hath Phoebus, and worthily hast thou, bestowed this care on the cause of the dead; and so, as is meet, ye shall find me too leagued with you in seeking vengeance for this land, and for the god besides. On behalf of no far-off friend, no, but in mine own cause, shall I dispel this taint. For whoever was the slayer of Laius might wish to take vengeance on me also with a hand as fierce. Therefore, in doing right to Laius, I serve myself.

Come, haste ye, my children, rise from the altar-steps, and lift these suppliant boughs; and let some other summon hither the folk of Cadmus, warned that I mean to leave nought untried; for our health (with the god's help) shall be made certain—or our ruin.

PRIEST

My children, let us rise; we came at first to seek what this man promises of himself. And may Phoebus, who sent these oracles, come to us therewith, our saviour and deliverer from the pest.

(*Exeunt* OEDIPUS *and* PRIEST. *Enter* CHORUS OF THEBAN ELDERS.)

CHORUS (*singing*)

strophe 1

O sweetly-speaking message of Zeus, in what spirit hast thou come from golden Pytho unto glorious Thebes? I am on the rack, terror shakes my soul, O thou Delian healer to whom wild cries rise, in holy fear of thee, what thing thou wilt work for me, perchance unknown before, perchance renewed with the revolving years: tell me, thou immortal Voice, born of Golden Hope!

antistrophe 1

First call I on thee, daughter of Zeus, divine Athena, and on thy sister, guardian of our land, Artemis, who sits on her throne of fame, above the circle of our Agora, and on Phoebus the far-darter: O shine forth on me, my three-fold help against death! If ever aforetime, in arrest of ruin hurrying on the city, ye drove a fiery pest beyond our borders, come now also!

strophe 2

Woe is me, countless are the sorrows that I bear; a plague is on all our host, and thought can find no weapon for defence. The fruits of the glorious earth grow not; by no birth of children do women surmount the pangs in which they shriek; and life on life mayest thou see sped like bird on nimble wing, aye, swifter than resistless fire, to the shore of the western god.

antistrophe 2

By such deaths, past numbering, the city perishes: unpitied, her children lie on the ground, spreading pestilence, with none to mourn: and meanwhile young wives, and grey-haired mothers with them, uplift a wail at the steps of the altars, some here, some there, entreating for their weary woes. The prayer to the Healer rings clear, and blent therewith, the voice of lamentation: for these things, golden daughter of Zeus, send us the bright face of comfort.

strophe 3

And grant that the fierce god of death, who now with no brazen shields, yet amid cries as of battle, wraps me in the flame of his onset, may turn his back in speedy flight from our land, borne by a fair wind to the great deep of Amphitrite, or to those waters in which none find haven, even to the Thracian wave; for if night leave aught undone, day follows to accomplish this. O thou who wieldest the powers of the fire-fraught lightning, O Zeus our father, slay him beneath thy thunderbolt!

antistrophe 3

Lycean King, fain were I that thy shafts also, from thy bent bow's string of woven gold, should go abroad in their might, our champions in the face of the foe; yea, and the flashing fires of Artemis wherewith she glances through the Lycian hills. And I call him whose locks are bound with gold, who is named with the name of this land, ruddy Bacchus to whom Bacchants cry, the comrade of the Maenads, to draw near with the blaze of his blithe torch, our ally against the god unhonoured among gods.

(OEDIPUS *enters during the closing strains of the choral song.*)

OEDIPUS

Thou prayest: and in answer to thy prayer,—if thou wilt give a loyal welcome to my words and minister to thine own disease,—thou mayest hope to find succour and relief from woes. These words will I speak publicly, as one who has been a stranger to this report, a stranger to the deed; for I should not be far on the track, if I were tracing it alone, without a clue. But as it is,—since it was only after the time of the deed that I was numbered a Theban among Thebans,—to you, the Cadmeans all, I do thus proclaim.

Whosoever of you knows by whom Laius son of Labdacus was slain, I bid him to declare all to me. And if he is afraid, I tell him to remove the danger of the charge from his path by denouncing himself; for he shall suffer nothing else unlovely, but only leave the land, unhurt. Or if any one knows an alien, from another land, as the assassin, let him not keep silence; for I will pay his guerdon, and my thanks shall rest with him besides.

But if ye keep silence—if any one, through fear, shall seek to screen friend or self from my behest—hear ye what I then shall do. I charge you that no one of this land, whereof I hold the empire and the throne, give shelter or speak word unto that murderer, whosoever he be,—make him partner of his prayer or sacrifice, or serve him with the lustral rite; but that all ban him their homes, knowing that *this* is our defiling thing, as the oracle of the Pythian god hath newly shown me. I then am on this wise the ally of the god and of the slain. And I pray solemnly that the slayer, whoso he be, whether his hidden guilt is lonely or hath partners, evilly, as he is evil, may wear out his unblest life. And for myself I pray that if, with my privity, he should become an inmate of my house, I may suffer the same things which even now I called down upon others. And on you I lay it to make all these words good, for my sake, and for the sake of the god, and for our land's, thus blasted with barrenness by angry heaven.

For even if the matter had not been urged on us by a god, it was not meet that ye should leave the guilt thus unpurged, when one so noble, and he your king, had perished; rather were ye bound to search it out. And now, since 'tis I who hold the powers which once he held, who possess his bed and the wife who bare seed to him; and since, had his hope of issue not been frustrate, children born of one mother would have made ties betwixt him and me—but, as it was, fate swooped upon his head; by reason of these things will I uphold this cause, even as the cause of mine own sire, and will leave nought untried in seeking to find him whose hand shed that blood, for the honour of the son of Labdacus and of Polydorus and elder Cadmus and Agenor who was of old.

And for those who obey me not, I pray that the gods send them neither harvest of the earth nor fruit of the womb, but that they be wasted by their lot that now is, or by one yet more dire. But for all you, the loyal folk of Cadmus to whom these things seem good, may Justice, our ally, and all the gods be with you graciously for ever.

LEADER OF THE CHORUS

As thou hast put me on my oath, on my oath, O king, I will speak. I am not the slayer, nor can I point to him who slew. As for the question, it was for Phoebus, who sent it, to tell us this thing—who can have wrought the deed.

OEDIPUS

Justly said; but no man on the earth can force the gods to what they will not.

LEADER

I would fain say what seems to me next best after this.

OEDIPUS

If there is yet a third course, spare not to show it.

LEADER

I know that our lord Teiresias is the seer most like to our lord Phoebus; from whom, O king, a searcher of these things might learn them most clearly.

OEDIPUS

Not even this have I left out of my cares. On the hint of Creon, I have twice sent a man to bring him; and this long while I marvel why he is not here.

LEADER

Indeed (his skill apart) the rumours are but faint and old.

OEDIPUS

What rumours are they? I look to every story.

LEADER

Certain wayfarers were said to have killed him.

OEDIPUS

I, too, have heard it, but none sees him who saw it.

LEADER

Nay, if he knows what fear is, he will not stay when he hears thy curses, so dire as they are.

OEDIPUS

When a man shrinks not from a deed, neither is he scared by a word.

LEADER

But there is one to convict him. For here they bring at last the godlike prophet, in whom alone of men doth live the truth.

(*Enter* TEIRESIAS, *led by a boy.*)

OEDIPUS

Teiresias, whose soul grasps all things, the lore that may be told and the unspeakable, the secrets of heaven and the low things of earth,—thou feelest, though thou canst not see, what a plague doth haunt our State,—from which, great prophet, we find in thee our protector and only saviour. Now, Phoebus—if indeed thou knowest it not from the messengers—sent answer to our question that the only riddance from this pest which could come was if we should learn aright the slayers of Laius, and slay them, or send them into exile from our land. Do thou, then, grudge neither voice of birds nor any other way of seer-lore that thou hast, but rescue thyself and the State, rescue me, rescue all that is defiled by the dead. For we are in thy hand; and man's noblest task is to help others by his best means and powers.

TEIRESIAS

Alas, how dreadful to have wisdom where it profits not the wise! Aye, I knew this well, but let it slip out of mind; else would I never have come here.

OEDIPUS

What now? How sad thou hast come in!

TEIRESIAS

Let me go home; most easily wilt thou bear thine own burden to the end, and I mine, if thou wilt consent.

OEDIPUS

Thy words are strange, nor kindly to this State which nurtured thee, when thou withholdest this response.

TEIRESIAS

Nay, I see that thou, on thy part, openest not thy lips in season: therefore I speak not, that neither may I have thy mishap.

OEDIPUS

For the love of the gods, turn not away, if thou hast knowledge: all we suppliants implore thee on our knees.

TEIRESIAS

Aye, for ye are all without knowledge; but never will I reveal my griefs—that I say not thine.

OEDIPUS

How sayest thou? Thou knowest the secret, and wilt not tell it, but art minded to betray us and to destroy the State?

TEIRESIAS

I will pain neither myself nor thee. Why vainly ask these things? Thou wilt not learn them from me.

OEDIPUS

What, basest of the base,—for thou wouldest anger a very stone,—wilt thou never speak out? Can nothing touch thee? Wilt thou never make an end?

TEIRESIAS

Thou blamest my temper, but seest not that to which thou thyself art wedded: no, thou findest fault with me.

OEDIPUS

And who would not be angry to hear the words with which thou now dost slight this city?

TEIRESIAS

The future will come of itself, though I shroud it in silence.

OEDIPUS

Then, seeing that it must come, thou on thy part shouldst tell me thereof.

TEIRESIAS

I will speak no further; rage, then, if thou wilt, with the fiercest wrath thy heart doth know.

OEDIPUS

Aye, verily, I will not spare—so wroth I am—to speak all my thought. Know that thou seemest to me e'en to have helped in plotting the deed, and to have done it, short of slaying with thy hands. Hadst thou eyesight, I would have said that the doing, also, of this thing was thine alone.

TEIRESIAS

In sooth?—I charge thee that thou abide by the decree of thine own mouth, and from this day speak neither to these nor to me: *thou* art the accursed defiler of this land.

OEDIPUS

So brazen with thy blustering taunt? And wherein dost thou trust to escape thy due?

TEIRESIAS

I have escaped: in my truth is my strength.

OEDIPUS

Who taught thee this? It was not, at least, thine art.

TEIRESIAS

Thou: for thou didst spur me into speech against my will.

OEDIPUS

What speech? Speak again that I may learn it better.

TEIRESIAS

Didst thou not take my sense before? Or art thou tempting me to talk?

OEDIPUS

No, I took it not so that I can call it known:—speak again.

TEIRESIAS

I say that thou art the slayer of the man whose slayer thou seekest.

OEDIPUS

Now thou shalt rue that thou hast twice said words so dire.

TEIRESIAS

Wouldst thou have me say more, that thou mayest be more wroth?

OEDIPUS

What thou wilt; it will be said in vain.

TEIRESIAS

I say that thou hast been living in unguessed shame with thy nearest kin, and seest not to what woe thou hast come.

OEDIPUS

Dost thou indeed think that thou shalt always speak thus without smarting?

TEIRESIAS

Yes, if there is any strength in truth.

OEDIPUS

Nay, there is,—for all save thee; for thee that strength is not, since thou art maimed in ear, and in wit, and in eye.

TEIRESIAS

Aye, and thou art a poor wretch to utter taunts which every man here will soon hurl at thee.

OEDIPUS

Night, endless night hath thee in her keeping, so that thou canst never hurt me, or any man who sees the sun.

TEIRESIAS

No, thy doom is not to fall by *me:* Apollo is enough, whose care it is to work that out.

OEDIPUS

Are these Creon's devices, or thine?

TEIRESIAS

Nay, Creon is no plague to thee; thou art thine own.

OEDIPUS

O wealth, and empire, and skill surpassing skill in life's keen rivalries, how great is the envy that cleaves to you, if for the sake, yea, of this power which the city hath put into my hands, a gift unsought, Creon the trusty, Creon mine old friend, hath crept on me by stealth, yearning to thrust me out of it, and hath suborned such a scheming juggler as this, a tricky quack, who hath eyes only for his gains, but in his art is blind!

Come, now, tell me, where hast thou proved thyself a seer? Why, when the Watcher was here who wove dark song, didst thou say nothing that could free this folk? Yet the riddle, at least, was not for the first comer to read; there was need of a seer's skill; and none such thou wast found to have either by help of birds, or as known from any god: no, I came, I, Oedipus, the ignorant, and made her mute, when I had seized the answer by my wit, untaught of birds. And it is I whom thou art trying to oust, thinking to stand close to Creon's throne. Methinks thou and the plotter of these things will rue your zeal to purge the land. Nay, didst thou not seem to be an old man, thou shouldst have learned to thy cost how bold thou art.

LEADER

To our thinking, both this man's words and thine, Oedipus, have been said in anger. Not for such words is our need, but to seek how we shall best discharge the mandates of the god.

TEIRESIAS

King though thou art, the right of reply, at least, must be deemed the same for both; of that I too am lord. Not to thee do I live servant, but to Loxias; and so I shall not stand enrolled under Creon for my patron. And I tell thee—since thou hast taunted me even with blindness—that thou hast sight, yet seest not in what misery thou art, nor where thou dwellest, nor with whom. Dost thou know of what stock thou art? And thou hast been an unwitting foe to thy own kin, in the shades, and on the earth above; and the double lash of thy mother's and thy father's curse shall one day drive thee from this land in dreadful haste, with darkness then on the eyes that now see true.

And what place shall not be harbour to thy shriek, what of all Cithaeron shall not ring with it soon, when thou hast learnt the meaning of the nuptials in which, within that house, thou didst find a fatal haven, after a voyage so fair? And a throng of other ills thou guessest not, which shall make thee level with thy true self and with thine own brood.

Therefore heap thy scorns on Creon and on my message: for no one among men shall ever be crushed more miserably than thou.

OEDIPUS

Are these taunts to be indeed borne from *him?*—Hence, ruin take thee! Hence, this instant! Back!—away!—avaunt thee from these doors!

TEIRESIAS

I had never come, not I, hadst thou not called me.

OEDIPUS

I knew not that thou wast about to speak folly, or it had been long ere I had sent for thee to my house.

TEIRESIAS

Such am I,—as thou thinkest, a fool; but for the parents who begat thee, sane.

OEDIPUS

What parents? Stay . . . and who of men is my sire?

TEIRESIAS

This day shall show thy birth and shall bring thy ruin.

OEDIPUS

What riddles, what dark words thou always speakest!

TEIRESIAS

Nay, art not thou most skilled to unravel dark speech?

OEDIPUS

Make that my reproach in which thou shalt find me great.

TEIRESIAS

Yet 'twas just that fortune that undid thee.

OEDIPUS

Nay, if I delivered this town, I care not.

TEIRESIAS

Then I will go: so do thou, boy, take me hence.

OEDIPUS

Aye, let him take thee: while here, thou art a hindrance, thou, a trouble: when thou hast vanished, thou wilt not vex me more.

TEIRESIAS

I will go when I have done mine errand, fearless of thy frown: for thou canst never destroy me. And I tell thee—the man of whom thou hast this long while been in quest, uttering threats, and proclaiming a search into the murder of Laius—that man is here,—in seeming, an alien sojourner, but anon he shall be found a native Theban, and shall not be glad of his fortune. A blind man, he who now hath sight, a beggar, who now is rich, he shall make his way to a strange land, feeling the ground before him with his staff. And he shall be found at once brother and father of the children with whom he consorts; son and husband of the woman who bore him; heir to his father's bed, shedder of his father's blood.

So go thou in and think on that; and if thou find that I have been at fault, say thenceforth that I have no wit in prophecy.

(TEIRESIAS *is led out by the boy.* OEDIPUS *enters the palace.*)

CHORUS (*singing*)

strophe I

Who is he of whom the divine voice from the Delphian rock hath spoken, as having wrought with red hands horrors that no tongue can tell?

It is time that he ply in flight a foot stronger than the feet of storm-swift steeds: for the son of Zeus is springing on him, all armed with fiery lightnings, and with him come the dread, unerring Fates.

antistrophe I

Yea, newly given from snowy Parnassus, the message hath flashed forth to make all search for the unknown man. Into the wild wood's covert, among caves and rocks he is roaming, fierce as a bull, wretched and forlorn on his joyless path, still seeking to put from him the doom spoken at Earth's central shrine: but that doom ever lives, ever flits around him.

strophe 2

Dreadly, in sooth, dreadly doth the wise augur move me, who approve not, nor am able to deny. How to speak, I know not; I am fluttered with forebodings;

neither in the present have I clear vision, nor of the future. Never in past days, nor in these, have I heard how the house of Labdacus or the son of Polybus had, either against other, any grief that I could bring as proof in assailing the public fame of Oedipus, and seeking to avenge the line of Labdacus for the undiscovered murder.

antistrophe 2

Nay, Zeus indeed and Apollo are keen of thought, and know the things of earth; but that mortal seer wins knowledge above mine, of this there can be no sure test; though man may surpass man in lore. Yet, until I see the word made good, never will I assent when men blame Oedipus. Before all eyes, the winged maiden came against him of old, and he was seen to be wise; he bore the test, in welcome service to our State; never, therefore, by the verdict of my heart shall he be adjudged guilty of crime.

(*Enter* CREON)

CREON

Fellow-citizens, having learned that Oedipus the king lays dire charges against me, I am here, indignant. If, in the present troubles, he thinks that he has suffered from *me*, by word or deed, aught that tends to harm, in truth I crave not my full term of years, when I must bear such blame as this. The wrong of this rumour touches me not in one point alone, but has the largest scope, if I am to be called a traitor in the city, a traitor too by thee and by my friends.

LEADER OF THE CHORUS

Nay, but this taunt came under stress, perchance, of anger, rather than from the purpose of the heart.

CREON

And the saying was uttered, that *my* counsels won the seer to utter his falsehoods?

LEADER

Such things were said—I know not with what meaning

CREON

And was this charge laid against me with steady eyes and steady mind?

LEADER

I know not; I see not what my masters do: but here comes our lord forth from the house.

(*Enter* OEDIPUS)

OEDIPUS

Sirrah, how camest thou here? Hast thou a front so bold that thou hast come to my house, who art the proved assassin of its master,—the palpable robber of my crown? Come, tell me, in the name of the gods, was it cowardice or folly that thou sawest in me, that thou didst plot to do this thing? Didst thou think that I would not note this deed of thine creeping on me by stealth, or, aware, would not ward it off? Now is not thine attempt foolish,—to seek, without followers or friends, a throne,—a prize which followers and wealth must win?

CREON

Mark me now,—in answer to thy words, hear a fair reply, and then judge for thyself on knowledge.

OEDIPUS

Thou art apt in speech, but I have a poor wit for thy lessons, since I have found thee my malignant foe.

CREON

Now first hear how I will explain this very thing—

OEDIPUS

Explain me not one thing—that thou art not false

CREON

If thou deemest that stubbornness without sense is a good gift, thou art not wise.

OEDIPUS

If thou deemest that thou canst wrong a kinsman and escape the penalty, thou art not sane.

CREON

Justly said, I grant thee: but tell me what is the wrong that thou sayest thou hast suffered from me.

OEDIPUS

Didst thou advise, or didst thou not, that I should send for that reverend seer?

CREON

And now I am still of the same mind.

OEDIPUS

How long is it, then, since Laius—

CREON

Since Laius . . . ? I take not thy drift . . .

OEDIPUS

—was swept from men's sight by a deadly violence?

CREON

The count of years would run far into the past.

OEDIPUS

Was this seer, then, of the craft in those days?

CREON

Yea, skilled as now, and in equal honour.

OEDIPUS

Made he, then, any mention of me at that time?

CREON

Never, certainly, when I was within hearing.

OEDIPUS

But held ye not a search touching the murder?

CREON

Due search we held, of course—and learned nothing.

OEDIPUS

And how was it that this sage did not tell his story *then?*

CREON

I know not; where I lack light, 'tis my wont to be silent.

OEDIPUS

Thus much, at least, thou knowest, and couldst declare with light enough.

CREON

What is that? If I know it, I will not deny.

OEDIPUS

That, if he had not conferred with thee, he would never have named *my* slaying of Laius.

CREON

If so he speaks, thou best knowest; but I claim to learn from thee as much as thou hast now from me.

OEDIPUS

Learn thy fill: I shall never be found guilty of the blood.

CREON

Say, then—thou hast married my sister?

OEDIPUS

The question allows not of denial.

CREON

And thou rulest the land as she doth, with like sway?

OEDIPUS

She obtains from me all her desire.

CREON

And rank not I as a third peer of you twain?

OEDIPUS

Aye, 'tis just therein that thou art seen a false friend.

CREON

Not so, if thou wouldst reason with thine own heart as I with mine. And first weigh this,—whether thou thinkest that any one would choose to rule amid terrors rather than in unruffled peace,—granting that he is to have the same powers. Now I, for one, have no yearning in my nature to be a king rather than to do kingly deeds, no, nor hath any man who knows how to keep a sober mind. For now I win all boons from thee without fear; but, were I ruler myself, I should be doing much e'en against mine own pleasure.

How, then, could royalty be sweeter for me to have than painless rule and influence? Not yet am I so misguided as to desire other honours than those which profit. Now, all wish me joy; now, every man has a greeting for me; now, those who have a suit to thee crave speech with me, since therein is all their hope of success. Then why should I resign these things, and take those? No mind will become false, while it is wise. Nay, I am no lover of such policy, and, if another put it into deed, never could I bear to act with him.

And, in proof of this, first, go to Pytho, and ask if I brought thee true word of the oracle; then next, if thou find that I have planned aught in concert with the soothsayer, take and slay me, by the sentence not of one mouth, but of twain—by mine own, no less than thine. But make me not guilty in a corner, on unproved surmise. It is not right to adjudge bad men good at random, or good men bad. I count it a like thing for a man to cast off a true friend as to cast away the life in his own bosom, which most he loves. Nay, thou wilt learn these things with sureness in time, for time alone shows a just man; but thou couldst discern a knave even in one day.

LEADER

Well hath he spoken, O king, for one who giveth heed not to fall: the quick in counsel are not sure.

OEDIPUS

When the stealthy plotter is moving on me in quick sort, I, too, must be quick with my counterplot. If I await him in repose, his ends will have been gained, and mine missed.

CREON

What wouldst thou, then? Cast me out of the land?

OEDIPUS

Not so: I desire thy death—not thy banishment—that thou mayest show forth what manner of thing is envy.

CREON

Thou speakest as resolved not to yield or to believe?

OEDIPUS

No; for thou persuadest me not that thou art worthy of belief.

CREON

No, for I find thee not sane.

OEDIPUS

Sane, at least, in mine own interest.

CREON

Nay, thou shouldst be so in mine also.

OEDIPUS

Nay, thou art false.

CREON

But if thou understandest nought?

OEDIPUS

Yet must I rule.

CREON

Not if thou rule ill.

OEDIPUS

Hear him, O Thebes!

CREON

Thebes is for me also—not for thee alone.

(JOCASTA *enters from the palace.*)

LEADER

Cease, princes; and in good time for you I see Jocasta coming yonder from the house, with whose help ye should compose your present feud.

JOCASTA

Misguided men, why have ye raised such foolish strife of tongues? Are ye not ashamed, while the land is thus sick, to stir up troubles of your own? Come, go thou into the house, —and thou, Creon, to thy home,—and forbear to make much of a petty grief.

CREON

Kinswoman, Oedipus thy lord claims to do dread things unto me, even one or other of two ills,—to thrust me from the land of my fathers, or to slay me amain.

OEDIPUS

Yea; for I have caught him, lady, working evil, by ill arts, against my person.

CREON

Now may I see no good, but perish accursed, if I have done aught to thee of that wherewith thou chargest me!

JOCASTA

O, for the gods' love, believe it, Oedipus—first, for the awful sake of this oath unto the gods,—then for my sake and for theirs who stand before thee!

(*The following lines between the* CHORUS *and* OEDIPUS *and between the* CHORUS, JOCASTA, *and* OEDIPUS *are chanted responsively.*)

CHORUS

strophe 1

Consent, reflect, hearken, O my king, I pray thee!

OEDIPUS

What grace, then, wouldest thou have me grant thee?

CHORUS

Respect him who aforetime was not foolish, and who now is strong in his oath.

OEDIPUS

Now dost thou know what thou cravest?

CHORUS

Yea.

OEDIPUS

Declare, then, what thou meanest.

CHORUS

That thou shouldest never use an unproved rumour to cast a dishonouring charge on the friend who has bound himself with a curse.

OEDIPUS

Then be very sure that, when thou seekest this, for me thou art seeking destruction, or exile from this land.

CHORUS

strophe 2

No, by him who stands in the front of all the heavenly host, no, by the Sun! Unblest, unfriended, may I die by the uttermost doom, if I have that thought! But my unhappy soul is worn by the withering of the land, and again by the thought that our old sorrows should be crowned by sorrows springing from you twain.

OEDIPUS

Then let him go, though I am surely doomed to death, or to be thrust dishonoured from the land. Thy lips, not his, move my compassion by their plaint; but he, where'er he be, shall be hated.

CREON

Sullen in yielding art thou seen, even as vehement in the excesses of thy wrath; but such natures are justly sorest for themselves to bear.

OEDIPUS

Then wilt thou not leave me in peace, and get thee gone?

CREON

I will go my way; I have found thee undiscerning, but in the sight of these I am just.

(*Exit* CREON)

CHORUS

antistrophe I

Lady, why dost thou delay to take yon man into the house?

JOCASTA

I will do so, when I have learned what hath chanced.

CHORUS

Blind suspicion, bred of talk, arose; and, on the other part, injustice wounds.

JOCASTA

It was on both sides?

CHORUS

Aye.

JOCASTA

And what was the story?

CHORUS

Enough, methinks, enough—when our land is already vexed—that the matter should rest where it ceased.

OEDIPUS

Seest thou to what thou hast come, for all thy honest purpose, in seeking to slack and blunt my zeal?

CHORUS

antistrophe 2

King, I have said it not once alone—be sure that I should have been shown a madman, bankrupt in sane counsel, if I put thee away—thee, who gavest a true course to my beloved country when distraught by troubles—thee, who now also art like to prove our prospering guide.

JOCASTA

In the name of the gods, tell me also, O king, on what account thou hast conceived this steadfast wrath.

OEDIPUS

That will I; for I honour thee, lady, above yonder men:—the cause is Creon, and the plots that he hath laid against me.

JOCASTA

Speak on—if thou canst tell clearly how the feud began.

OEDIPUS

He says that I stand guilty of the blood of Laius.

JOCASTA

As on his own knowledge? Or on hearsay from another?

OEDIPUS

Nay, he hath made a rascal seer his mouthpiece; as for himself, he keeps his lips wholly pure.

JOCASTA

Then absolve thyself of the things whereof thou speakest; hearken to me, and learn for thy comfort that nought of mortal birth is a sharer in the science of the seer. I will give thee pithy proof of that.

An oracle came to Laius once—I will not say from Phoebus himself, but from his ministers—that the doom should overtake him to die by the hand of his child, who should spring from him and me.

Now Laius,—as, at least, the rumour saith,—was murdered one day by foreign robbers at a place where three highways meet. And the child's birth was not three days past, when Laius pinned its ankles together, and had it thrown, by others' hands, on a trackless mountain.

So, in that case, Apollo brought it not to pass that the babe should become the slayer of his sire, or that Laius should die—the dread thing which he feared—by his child's hand. Thus did the messages of seer-craft map out the future. Regard them, thou, not at all. Whatsoever needful things the god seeks, he himself will easily bring to light.

OEDIPUS

What restlessness of soul, lady, what tumult of the mind hath just come upon me since I heard thee speak!

JOCASTA

What anxiety hath startled thee, that thou sayest this?

OEDIPUS

Methought I heard this from thee,—that Laius was slain where three highways meet.

JOCASTA

Yea, that was the story; nor hath it ceased yet.

OEDIPUS

And where is the place where this befell?

JOCASTA

The land is called Phocis; and branching roads lead to the same spot from Delphi and from Daulia.

OEDIPUS

And what is the time that hath passed since these things were?

JOCASTA

The news was published to the town shortly before thou wast first seen in power over this land.

OEDIPUS

O Zeus, what hast thou decreed to do unto me?

JOCASTA

And wherefore, Oedipus, doth this thing weigh upon thy soul?

OEDIPUS

Ask me not yet; but say what was the stature of Laius, and how ripe his manhood.

JOCASTA

He was tall,—the silver just lightly strewn among his hair; and his form was not greatly unlike to thine.

OEDIPUS

Unhappy that I am! Methinks I have been laying myself even now under a dread curse, and knew it not.

JOCASTA

How sayest thou? I tremble when I look on thee, my king.

OEDIPUS

Dread misgivings have I that the seer can see. But thou wilt show better if thou wilt tell me one thing more.

JOCASTA

Indeed—though I tremble—I will answer all thou askest, when I hear it.

OEDIPUS

Went he in small force, or with many armed followers, like a chieftain?

JOCASTA

Five they were in all,—a herald one of them; and there was one carriage, which bore Laius.

OEDIPUS

Alas! 'Tis now clear indeed.—Who was he who gave you these tidings lady?

JOCASTA

A servant—the sole survivor who came home.

OEDIPUS

Is he haply at hand in the house now?

JOCASTA

No, truly; so soon as he came thence, and found thee reigning in the stead of Laius, he supplicated me, with hand laid on mine, that I would send him to the fields, to the pastures of the flocks, that he might be far from the sight of this town. And I sent him; he was worthy, for a slave, to win e'en a larger boon than that.

OEDIPUS

Would, then, that he could return to us without delay!

JOCASTA

It is easy: but wherefore dost thou enjoin this?

OEDIPUS

I fear, lady, that mine own lips have been unguarded; and therefore am I fain to behold him.

JOCASTA

Nay, he shall come. But I too, methinks, have a claim to learn what lies heavy on thy heart, my king.

OEDIPUS

Yea, and it shall not be kept from thee, now that my forebodings have advanced so far. Who, indeed, is more to me than thou, to whom I should speak in passing through such a fortune as this?

My father was Polybus of Corinth,—my mother, the Dorian Merope; and I was held the first of all the folk in that town, until a chance befell me, worthy, indeed, of wonder, though not worthy of mine own heat concerning it. At a banquet, a man full of wine cast it at me in his cups that I was not the true son of my sire. And I, vexed, restrained myself for that day as best I might; but on the next I went to my mother and father, and questioned them; and they were wroth for the taunt with him who had let that word fly. So on their part I had comfort; yet was this thing ever rankling in my heart; for it still crept abroad with strong rumour. And, unknown to mother or father, I went to Delphi; and Phoebus sent me forth disappointed of that knowledge for which I came, but in his response set forth other things, full of sorrow and terror and woe; even that I was fated to defile my mother's bed; and that I should show unto men a brood which they could not endure to behold; and that I should be the slayer of the sire who begat me.

And I, when I had listened to this, turned to flight from the land of Corinth, thenceforth wotting of its region by the stars alone, to some spot where I should never see fulfilment of the infamies foretold in mine evil doom. And on my way I came to the regions in which thou sayest that this prince perished. Now, lady, I will tell thee the truth. When in my journey I was near to those three roads, there met me a herald, and a man seated in a carriage drawn by colts, as thou hast described; and he who was in front. and the old man himself, were for thrusting me rudely from the path. Then, in anger, I struck him who pushed me aside—the driver; and the old man, seeing it, watched the moment when I was passing, and, from the carriage, brought his goad with two teeth down full upon my head. Yet was he paid with interest; by one swift blow from the staff in this hand he was rolled right out of the carriage, on his back; and I slew every man of them.

But if this stranger had any tie of kinship with Laius, who is now more wretched than the man before thee? What mortal could prove more hated of heaven? Whom no stranger, no citizen, is allowed to receive in his house; whom it is unlawful that any one accost; whom all must repel from their homes! And this—this curse—was laid on me by no mouth but mine own! And I pollute the bed of the slain man with the hands by which he perished. Say, am I vile? Oh, am I not utterly unclean?—seeing that I must be banished, and in banishment see not mine own people, nor set foot in mine own land, or else be joined in wedlock to my mother, and slay my sire, even Polybus, who begat and reared me.

Then would not he speak aright of Oedipus, who judged these things sent by some cruel power above man? Forbid, forbid, ye pure and awful gods, that I should see that day! No, may I be swept from among men, ere I behold myself visited with the brand of such a doom!

LEADER OF THE CHORUS

To us, indeed, these things, O king, are fraught with fear; yet have hope, until at last thou hast gained full knowledge from him who saw the deed.

OEDIPUS

Hope, in truth, rests with me thus far alone; I can await the man summoned from the pastures.

JOCASTA

And when he has appeared—what wouldst thou have of him?

OEDIPUS

I will tell thee. If his story be found to tally with thine, I, at least, shall stand clear of disaster.

JOCASTA

And what of special note didst thou hear from me?

OEDIPUS

Thou wast saying that he spoke of Laius as slain by robbers. If, then, he still speaks, as before, of several, I was not the slayer: a solitary man could not be held the same with that band. But if he names one lonely wayfarer, then beyond doubt this guilt leans to me.

JOCASTA

Nay, be assured that thus, at least, the tale was first told; he cannot revoke that, for the city heard it, not I alone. But even if he should diverge somewhat from his former story, never, king, can he show that the murder of Laius, at least, is truly square to prophecy; of whom Loxias plainly said that he must die by the hand of my child. Howbeit that poor innocent never slew him, but perished first itself. So henceforth, for what touches divination, I would not look to my right hand or my left.

OEDIPUS

Thou judgest well. But nevertheless send some one to fetch the peasant, and neglect not this matter.

JOCASTA

I will send without delay. But let us come into the house: nothing will I do save at thy good pleasure.

(OEDIPUS *and* JOCASTA *go into the palace.*)

CHORUS (*singing*)

strophe I

May destiny still find me winning the praise of reverent purity in all words and deeds sanctioned by those laws of range sublime, called into life throughout the high clear heaven, whose father is Olympus alone; their parent was no race of mortal men, no, nor shall oblivion ever lay them to sleep; the god is mighty in them, and he grows not old.

antistrophe 1

Insolence breeds the tyrant; Insolence, once vainly surfeited on wealth that is not meet nor good for it, when it hath scaled the top-most ramparts, is hurled to a dire doom, wherein no service of the feet can serve. But I pray that the god never quell such rivalry as benefits the State; the god will I ever hold for our protector.

strophe 2

But if any man walks haughtily in deed or word, with no fear of Justice, no reverence for the images of gods, may an evil doom seize him for his ill-starred pride, if he will not win his vantage fairly, nor keep him from unholy deeds, but must lay profaning hands on sanctities.

Where such things are, what mortal shall boast any more that he can ward the arrows of the gods from his life? Nay, if such deeds are in honour, wherefore should we join in the sacred dance?

antistrophe 2

No more will I go reverently to earth's central and inviolate shrine, no more to Abae's temple or Olympia, if these oracles fit not the issue, so that all men shall point at them with the finger. Nay, king,—if thou art rightly called,—Zeus all-ruling, may it not escape thee and thine ever-deathless power!

The old prophecies concerning Laius are fading; already men are setting them at nought, and nowhere is Apollo glorified with honours; the worship of the gods is perishing.

(JOCASTA *comes forth, bearing a branch, wreatned with festoons of wool, which, as a suppliant, she is about to lay on the altar of the household god, Lycean Apollo, in front of the palace.*)

JOCASTA

Princes of the land, the thought has come to me to visit the shrines of the gods, with this wreathed branch in my hands, and these gifts of incense. For Oedipus excites his soul overmuch with all manner of alarms, nor, like a man of sense, judges the new things by the old, but is at the will of the speaker, if he speak terrors.

Since, then, by counsel I can do no good, to thee, Lycean Apollo, for thou art nearest, I have come, a suppliant with these symbols of prayer, that thou mayest find us some riddance from uncleanness. For now we are all afraid, seeing *him* affrighted, even as they who see fear in the helmsman of their ship.

(*While* JOCASTA *is offering her prayers to the god, a* MESSENGER, *evidently a stranger, enters and addresses the Elders of the* CHORUS.)

MESSENGER

Might I learn from you, strangers, where is the house of the king Oedipus? Or, better still, tell me where he himself is—if ye know.

LEADER OF THE CHORUS

This is his dwelling, and he himself, stranger, is within; and this lady is the mother of his children.

MESSENGER

Then may she be ever happy in a happy home, since she is his heaven-blest queen.

JOCASTA

Happiness to thee also, stranger! 'tis the due of thy fair greeting.—But say what thou hast come to seek or to tell.

MESSENGER

Good tidings, lady, for thy house and for thy husband.

JOCASTA

What are they? And from whom hast thou come?

MESSENGER

From Corinth: and at the message which I will speak anon thou wilt rejoice—doubtless; yet haply grieve.

JOCASTA

And what is it? How hath it thus a double potency?

MESSENGER

The people will make him king of the Isthmian land, as 'twas said there.

JOCASTA

How then? Is the aged Polybus no more in power?

MESSENGER

No, verily: for death holds him in the tomb.

JOCASTA

How sayest thou? Is Polybus dead, old man?

MESSENGER

If I speak not the truth, I am content to die.

JOCASTA

O handmaid, away with all speed, and tell this to thy master! O ye oracles of the gods, where stand ye now! This is the man whom Oedipus long feared and shunned, lest he should slay him; and now this man hath died in the course of destiny, not by his hand.

(OEDIPUS *enters from the palace.*)

OEDIPUS

Jocasta, dearest wife, why hast thou summoned me forth from these doors?

JOCASTA

Hear this man, and judge, as thou listenest, to what the awful oracles of the gods have come.

OEDIPUS

And he—who may he be, and what news hath he for me?

JOCASTA

He is from Corinth, to tell that thy father Polybus lives no longer, but hath perished.

OEDIPUS

How, stranger? Let me have it from thine own mouth.

MESSENGER

If I must first make these tidings plain, know indeed that he is dead and gone.

OEDIPUS

By treachery, or by visit of disease?

MESSENGER

A light thing in the scale brings the aged to their rest.

OEDIPUS

Ah, he died, it seems, of sickness?

MESSENGER

Yea, and of the long years that he had told.

OEDIPUS

Alas, alas! Why, indeed, my wife, should one look to the hearth of the Pythian seer, or to the birds that scream above our heads, on whose showing I was doomed to slay my sire? But he is dead, and hid already beneath the earth; and here am I, who have not put hand to spear.—Unless, perchance, he was killed by longing for me: thus, indeed, I should be the cause of his death. But the oracles as they stand, at least, Polybus hath swept with him to his rest in Hades: they are worth nought.

JOCASTA

Nay, did I not so foretell to thee long since?

OEDIPUS

Thou didst: but I was misled by my fear.

JOCASTA

Now no more lay aught of those things to heart.

OEDIPUS

But surely I must needs fear my mother's bed?

JOCASTA

Nay, what should mortal fear, for whom the decrees of Fortune are supreme, and who hath clear foresight of nothing? 'Tis best to live at random, as one may. But fear not thou touching wedlock with thy mother. Many men ere now have so fared in dreams also: but he to whom these things are as nought bears his life most easily.

OEDIPUS

All these bold words of thine would have been well, were not my mother living; but as it is, since she lives, I must needs fear—though thou sayest well.

JOCASTA

Howbeit thy father's death is a great sign to cheer us.

OEDIPUS

Great, I know; but my fear is of her who lives.

MESSENGER

And who is the woman about whom ye fear?

OEDIPUS

Merope, old man, the consort of Polybus.

MESSENGER

And what is it in her that moves your fear?

OEDIPUS

A heaven-sent oracle of dread import, stranger.

MESSENGER

Lawful, or unlawful, for another to know?

OEDIPUS

Lawful, surely. Loxias once said that I was doomed to espouse mine own mother, and to shed with mine own hands my father's blood. Wherefore my home in Corinth was long kept by me afar; with happy event, indeed,—yet still 'tis sweet to see the face of parents.

MESSENGER

Was it indeed for fear of this that thou wast an exile from that city?

OEDIPUS

And because I wished not, old man, to be the slayer of my sire.

MESSENGER

Then why have I not freed thee, king, from this fear, seeing that I came with friendly purpose?

OEDIPUS

Indeed thou shouldst have guerdon due from me.

MESSENGER

Indeed 'twas chiefly for this that I came—that, on thy return home, I might reap some good.

OEDIPUS

Nay, I will never go near my parents.

MESSENGER

Ah my son, 'tis plain enough that thou knowest not what thou doest.

OEDIPUS

How, old man? For the gods' love, tell me.

MESSENGER

If for these reasons thou shrinkest from going home.

OEDIPUS

Aye, I dread lest Phoebus prove himself true for me.

MESSENGER

Thou dreadest to be stained with guilt through thy parents?

OEDIPUS

Even so, old man—this it is that ever affrights me.

MESSENGER

Dost thou know, then, that thy fears are wholly vain?

OEDIPUS

How so, if I was born of those parents?

MESSENGER

Because Polybus was nothing to thee in blood.

OEDIPUS

What sayest thou? Was Polybus not my sire?

MESSENGER

No more than he who speaks to thee, but just so much.

OEDIPUS

And how can my sire be level with him who is as nought to me?

MESSENGER

Nay, he begat thee not, any more than I.

OEDIPUS

Nay, wherefore, then, called he me his son?

MESSENGER

Know that he had received thee as a gift from my hands of yore.

OEDIPUS

And yet he loved me so dearly, who came from another's hand?

MESSENGER

Yea, his former childlessness won him thereto.

OEDIPUS

And thou—hadst thou bought me or found me by chance, when thou gavest me to him?

MESSENGER

Found thee in Cithaeron's winding glens.

OEDIPUS

And wherefore wast thou roaming in those regions?

MESSENGER

I was there in charge of mountain flocks.

OEDIPUS

What, thou wast a shepherd—a vagrant hireling?

MESSENGER

But thy preserver, my son, in that hour.

OEDIPUS

And what pain was mine when thou didst take me in thine arms?

MESSENGER

The ankles of thy feet might witness.

OEDIPUS

Ah me, why dost thou speak of that old trouble?

MESSENGER

I freed thee when thou hadst thine ankles pinned together.

OEDIPUS

Aye, 'twas a dread brand of shame that I took from my cradle.

MESSENGER

Such, that from that fortune thou wast called by the name which still is thine.

OEDIPUS

Oh, for the gods' love—was the deed my mother's or father's? Speak!

MESSENGER

I know not; he who gave thee to me wots better of that than I.

OEDIPUS

What, thou hadst me from another? Thou didst not light on me thyself?

MESSENGER

No: another shepherd gave thee up to me.

OEDIPUS

Who was he? Art thou in case to tell clearly?

MESSENGER

I think he was called one of the household of Laius.

OEDIPUS

The king who ruled this country long ago?

MESSENGER

The same: 'twas in his service that the man was a herd.

OEDIPUS

Is he still alive, that I might see him?

MESSENGER

Nay, ye folk of the country should know best.

OEDIPUS

Is there any of you here present that knows the herd of whom he speaks—that hath seen him in the pastures or the town? Answer! The hour hath come that these things should be finally revealed.

LEADER OF THE CHORUS

Methinks he speaks of no other than the peasant whom thou wast already fain to see; but our lady Jocasta might best tell that.

OEDIPUS

Lady, wottest thou of him whom we lately summoned? Is it of him that this man speaks?

JOCASTA

Why ask of whom he spoke? Regard it not . . . waste not a thought on what he said . . . 'twere idle.

OEDIPUS

It must not be that, with such clues in my grasp, I should fail to bring my birth to light.

JOCASTA

For the gods' sake, if thou hast any care for thine own life, forbear this search! My anguish is enough.

OEDIPUS

Be of good courage; though I be found the son of servile mother,—aye, a slave by three descents,—*thou* wilt not be proved base-born.

JOCASTA

Yet hear me, I implore thee: do not thus.

OEDIPUS

I must not hear of not discovering the whole truth.

JOCASTA

Yet I wish thee well—I counsel thee for the best.

OEDIPUS

These best counsels, then, vex my patience.

JOCASTA

Ill-fated one! Mayst thou never come to know who thou art!

OEDIPUS

Go, some one, fetch me the herdsman hither,—and leave yon woman to glory in her princely stock.

JOCASTA

Alas, alas, miserable!—that word alone can I say unto thee, and no other word henceforth for ever.

(*She rushes into the palace.*)

LEADER

Why hath the lady gone, Oedipus, in a transport of wild grief? I misdoubt, a storm of sorrow will break forth from this silence.

OEDIPUS

Break forth what will! Be my race never so lowly, I must crave to learn it. Yon woman, perchance,—for she is proud with more than a woman's pride—thinks shame of my base source. But I, who hold myself son of Fortune that gives good, will not be dishonoured. She is the mother from whom I spring; and the months, my kinsmen, have marked me sometimes lowly, sometimes great. Such being my lineage, never more can I prove false to it, or spare to search out the secret of my birth.

CHORUS (*singing*)

strophe

If I am a seer or wise of heart, O Cithaeron, thou shalt not fail—by yon heaven, thou shalt not!—to know at tomorrow's full moon that Oedipus honours thee as native to him, as his nurse, and his mother, and that thou art celebrated in our dance and song, because thou art well-pleasing to our prince. O Phoebus to whom we cry, may these things find favour in thy sight!

antistrophe

Who was it, my son, who of the race whose years are many that bore thee in wedlock with Pan, the mountain-roaming father? Or was it a bride of Loxias that bore thee? For dear to him are all the upland pastures. Or perchance 'twas Cyllene's lord, or the Bacchants' god, dweller on the hill-tops, that received thee, a new-born joy, from one of the Nymphs of Helicon, with whom he most doth sport.

OEDIPUS

Elders, if 'tis for me to guess, who have never met with him, I think I see the herdsman of whom we have long been in quest; for in his venerable age he tallies with yon stranger's years, and withal I know those who bring him, methinks, as servants of mine own. But perchance thou mayest have the advantage of me in knowledge, if thou hast seen the herdsman before.

LEADER

Aye, I know him, be sure; he was in the service of Laius—trusty as any man, in his shepherd's place.

(*The* HERDSMAN *is brought in.*)

OEDIPUS

I ask thee first, Corinthian stranger, is this he whom thou meanest?

MESSENGER

This man whom thou beholdest.

OEDIPUS

Ho thou, old man—I would have thee look this way, and answer all that I ask thee. Thou wast once in the service of Laius?

HERDSMAN

I was—a slave not bought, but reared in his house.

OEDIPUS

Employed in what labour, or what way of life?

HERDSMAN

For the best part of my life I tended flocks.

OEDIPUS

And what the regions that thou didst chiefly haunt?

HERDSMAN

Sometimes it was Cithaeron, sometimes the neighbouring ground.

OEDIPUS

Then wottest thou of having noted yon man in these parts—

HERDSMAN

Doing what? . . . What man dost thou mean? . . .

OEDIPUS

This man here—or of having ever met him before?

HERDSMAN

Not so that I could speak at once from memory.

MESSENGER

And no wonder, master. But I will bring clear recollection to his ignorance. I am sure that he well wots of the time when we abode in the region of Cithaeron,—he with two flocks, I, his comrade, with one,—three full half-years, from spring to Arcturus; and then for the winter I used to drive my flock to mine own fold, and he took his to the fold of Laius. Did aught of this happen as I tell, or did it not?

HERDSMAN

Thou speakest the truth—though 'tis long ago.

MESSENGER

Come, tell me now—wottest thou of having given me a boy in those days, to be reared as mine own foster-son?

HERDSMAN

What now? Why dost thou ask the question?

MESSENGER

Yonder man, my friend, is he who then was young.

HERDSMAN

Plague seize thee—be silent once for all!

OEDIPUS

Ha! chide him not, old man—thy words need chiding more than his.

HERDSMAN

And wherein, most noble master, do I offend?

OEDIPUS

In not telling of the boy concerning whom he asks.

HERDSMAN

He speaks without knowledge—he is busy to no purpose.

OEDIPUS

Thou wilt not speak with a good grace, but thou shalt on pain.

HERDSMAN

Nay, for the gods' love, misuse not an old man!

OEDIPUS

Ho, some one—pinion him this instant!

HERDSMAN

Alas, wherefore? what more wouldst thou learn?

OEDIPUS

Didst thou give this man the child of whom he asks?

HERDSMAN

I did,—and would I had perished that day!

OEDIPUS

Well, thou wilt come to that, unless thou tell the honest truth.

HERDSMAN

Nay, much more am I lost, if I speak.

OEDIPUS

The fellow is bent, methinks, on more delays . . .

HERDSMAN

No, no!—I said before that I gave it to him.

OEDIPUS

Whence hadst thou got it? In thine own house, or from another?

HERDSMAN

Mine own it was not—I had received it from a man.

OEDIPUS

From whom of the citizens here? from what home?

HERDSMAN

Forbear, for the gods' love, master, forbear to ask more!

OEDIPUS

Thou art lost if I have to question thee again.

HERDSMAN

It was a child, then, of the house of Laius.

OEDIPUS

A slave? or one born of his own race?

HERDSMAN

Ah me—I am on the dreaded brink of speech.

OEDIPUS

And I of hearing; yet must I hear.

HERDSMAN

Thou must know, then, that 'twas said to be his own child —but thy lady within could best say how these things are.

OEDIPUS

How? She gave it to thee?

HERDSMAN

Yea, O king.

OEDIPUS

For what end?

HERDSMAN

That I should make away with it.

OEDIPUS

Her own child, the wretch?

HERDSMAN

Aye, from fear of evil prophecies.

OEDIPUS

What were they?

HERDSMAN

The tale ran that he must slay his sire.

OEDIPUS

Why, then, didst thou give him up to this old man?

HERDSMAN

Through pity, master, as deeming that he would bear him away to another land, whence he himself came; but he saved him for the direst woe. For if thou art what this man saith, know that thou wast born to misery.

OEDIPUS

Oh, oh! All brought to pass—all true! Thou light, may I now look my last on thee—I who have been found accursed in birth, accursed in wedlock, accursed in the shedding of blood!

(*He rushes into the palace.*)

CHORUS (*singing*)

strophe I

Alas, ye generations of men, how mere a shadow do I count your life! Where, where is the mortal who wins more of happiness than just the seeming, and, after the semblance, a falling away? Thine is a fate that warns me,—thine, thine, unhappy Oedipus—to call no earthly creature blest.

antistrophe I

For he, O Zeus, sped his shaft with peerless skill, and won the prize of an all-prosperous fortune; he slew the maiden with crooked talons who sang darkly; he arose for our land as a tower against death. And from that time, Oedipus, thou hast been called our king, and hast been honoured supremely, bearing sway in great Thebes.

strophe 2

But now whose story is more grievous in men's ears? Who is a more wretched captive to fierce plagues and troubles, with all his life reversed?

Alas, renowned Oedipus! The same bounteous place of rest sufficed thee, as child and as sire also, that thou shouldst make thereon thy nuptial couch. Oh, how can the soil wherein thy father sowed, unhappy one, have suffered thee in silence so long?

antistrophe 2

Time the all-seeing hath found thee out in thy despite: he judgeth the monstrous marriage wherein begetter and begotten have long been one.

Alas, thou child of Laius, would, would that I had never seen thee! I wail as one who pours a dirge from his lips; sooth to speak, 'twas thou that gavest me new life, and through thee darkness hath fallen upon mine eyes.

(*Enter* SECOND MESSENGER *from the palace.*)

SECOND MESSENGER

Ye who are ever most honoured in this land, what deeds shall ye hear, what deeds behold, what burden of sorrow shall be yours, if, true to your race, ye still care for the house of Labdacus! For I ween that not Ister nor Phasis could wash this house clean, so many are the ills that it shrouds, or will soon bring to light,—ills wrought not unwittingly, but of purpose. And those griefs smart most which are seen to be of our own choice.

LEADER

Indeed those which we knew before fall not short of claiming sore lamentation: besides them, what dost thou announce?

SECOND MESSENGER

This is the shortest tale to tell and to hear: our royal lady Jocasta is dead.

LEADER

Alas, hapless one! From what cause?

SECOND MESSENGER

By her own hand. The worst pain in what hath chanced is not for you, for yours it is not to behold. Nevertheless, so far as mine own memory serves, ye shall learn that unhappy woman's fate.

When, frantic, she had passed within the vestibule, she rushed straight towards her nuptial couch, clutching her hair with the fingers of both hands; once within the chamber, she dashed the doors together at her back; then called on the name of Laius, long since a corpse, mindful of that son, begotten long ago, by whom the sire was slain, leaving the mother to breed accursed offspring with his own.

And she bewailed the wedlock wherein, wretched, she had borne a two-fold brood, husband by husband, children by her child. And how thereafter she perished, is more than I know. For with a shriek Oedipus burst in, and suffered us not to watch her woe unto the end; on him, as he rushed around, our eyes were set. To and fro he went, asking us to give him a sword,—asking where he should find the wife who was no wife, but a mother whose womb had borne alike himself and his children. And, in his frenzy, a power above man was his guide; for 'twas none of us mortals who were nigh. And with a dread shriek, as though some one beckoned him on, he sprang at the double doors, and from their sockets forced the bending bolts, and rushed into the room.

There beheld we the woman hanging by the neck in a twisted noose of swinging cords. But he, when he saw her, with a dread, deep cry of misery, loosed the halter whereby she hung. And when the hapless woman was stretched upon the ground, then was the sequel dread to see. For he tore from her raiment the golden brooches wherewith she was decked, and lifted them, and smote full on his own eye-balls, uttering words like these: 'No more shall ye behold such horrors as I was suffering and working! long enough have ye looked on those whom ye ought never to have seen, failed in knowledge of those whom I yearned to know—henceforth ye shall be dark!'

To such dire refrain, not once alone but oft struck he his eyes with lifted hand; and at each blow the ensanguined eye-balls bedewed his beard, nor sent forth sluggish drops of gore, but all at once a dark shower of blood came down like hail.

From the deeds of twain such ills have broken forth, not on one alone, but with mingled woe for man and wife. The old happiness of their ancestral fortune was aforetime happiness indeed; but to-day—lamentation, ruin, death, shame, all earthly ills that can be named—all, all are theirs.

LEADER

And hath the sufferer now any respite from pain?

SECOND MESSENGER

He cries for some one to unbar the gates and show to all the Cadmeans his father's slayer, his mother's—the unholy word must not pass my lips,—as purposing to cast himself out of the land, and abide no more, to make the house accursed under his own curse. Howbeit he lacks strength, and one to guide his steps; for the anguish is more than man may bear. And he will show this to thee also; for lo, the bars of the gates are withdrawn, and soon thou shalt behold a sight which even he who abhors it must pity.

(*The central door of the palace is now opened.* OEDIPUS *comes forth, leaning on attendants; the bloody stains are still upon his face. The following lines between* OEDIPUS *and the* CHORUS *are chanted responsively.*)

CHORUS

O dread fate for men to see, O most dreadful of all that have met mine eyes! Unhappy one, what madness hath come on thee? Who is the unearthly foe that, with a bound of more than mortal range, hath made thine ill-starred life his prey?

Alas, alas, thou hapless one! Nay, I cannot e'en look on thee, though there is much that I would fain ask, fain learn, much that draws my wistful gaze,—with such a shuddering dost thou fill me!

OEDIPUS

Woe is me! Alas, alas, wretched that I am! Whither, whither am I borne in my misery? How is my voice swept abroad on the wings of the air? Oh my Fate, how far hast thou sprung!

CHORUS

To a dread place, dire in men's ears, dire in their sight.

OEDIPUS

strophe I

O thou horror of darkness that enfoldest me, visitant unspeakable, resistless, sped by a wind too fair!

Ay me! and once again, ay me!

How is my soul pierced by the stab of these goads, and withal by the memory of sorrows!

CHORUS

Yea, amid woes so many a twofold pain may well be thine to mourn and to bear.

OEDIPUS

antistrophe 1

Ah, friend, thou still art steadfast in thy tendance of me,—thou still hast patience to care for the blind man! Ah me! Thy presence is not hid from me—no, dark though I am, yet know I thy voice full well.

CHORUS

Man of dread deeds, how couldst thou in such wise quench thy vision? What more than human power urged thee?

OEDIPUS

strophe 2

Apollo, friends, Apollo was he that brought these my woes to pass, these my sore, sore woes: but the hand that struck the eyes was none save mine, wretched that I am! Why was I to see, when sight could show me nothing sweet?

CHORUS

These things were even as thou sayest.

OEDIPUS

Say, friends, what can I more behold, what can I love, what greeting can touch mine ear with joy? Haste, lead me from the land, friends, lead me hence, the utterly lost, the thrice accursed, yea, the mortal most abhorred of heaven!

CHORUS

Wretched alike for thy fortune and for thy sense thereof, would that I had never so much as known thee!

OEDIPUS

antistrophe 2

Perish the man, whoe'er he was, that freed me in the pastures from the cruel shackle on my feet, and saved me from death, and gave me back to life,—a thankless deed! Had I died then, to my friends and to thine own soul I had not been so sore a grief.

CHORUS

I also would have had it thus.

OEDIPUS

So had I not come to shed my father's blood, nor been called among men the spouse of her from whom I sprang: but now am I forsaken of the gods, son of a defiled mother, successor to his bed who gave me mine own wretched being: and if there be yet a woe surpassing woes, it hath become the portion of Oedipus.

CHORUS

I know not how I can say that thou hast counselled well: for thou wert better dead than living and blind.

OEDIPUS

Show me not at large that these things are not best done thus: give me counsel no more. For, had I sight, I know not with what eyes I could e'en have looked on my father, when I came to the place of the dead, aye, or on my miserable mother, since against both I have sinned such sins as strangling could not punish. But deem ye that the sight of children, born as mine were born, was lovely for me to look upon? No, no, not lovely to mine eyes for ever! No, nor was this town with its towered walls, nor the sacred statues of the gods, since I, thrice wretched that I am,—I, noblest of the sons of Thebes,—have doomed myself to know these no more, by mine own command that all should thrust away the impious one,—even him whom gods have shown to be unholy—and of the race of Laius!

After bearing such a stain upon me, was I to look with steady eyes on this folk? No, verily: no, were there yet a way to choke the fount of hearing, I had not spared to make a fast prison of this wretched frame, that so I should have known nor sight nor sound; for 'tis sweet that our thought should dwell beyond the sphere of griefs.

Alas, Cithaeron, why hadst thou a shelter for me? When I was given to thee, why didst thou not slay me straightway, that so I might never have revealed my source to men? Ah, Polybus,—ah, Corinth, and thou that wast called the ancient house of my fathers, how seeming-fair was I your nurseling, and what ills were festering beneath! For now I am found evil, and of evil birth. O ye three roads, and thou secret glen,—thou coppice, and narrow way where three paths met —ye who drank from my hands that father's blood which was mine own,—remember ye, perchance, what deeds I wrought for you to see,—and then, when I came hither, what fresh deeds I went on to do?

O marriage-rites, ye gave me birth, and when ye had brought me forth, again ye bore children to your child, ye created an incestuous kinship of fathers, brothers, sons,—brides, wives, mothers,—yea, all the foulest shame that is wrought among men! Nay, but 'tis unmeet to name what 'tis unmeet to do:—haste ye, for the gods' love, hide me somewhere beyond the land, or slay me, or cast me into the sea, where ye shall never behold me more! Approach,—deign to lay your hands on a wretched man;—hearken, fear not,—my plague can rest on no mortal beside.

(*Enter* CREON)

LEADER

Nay, here is Creon, in meet season for thy requests, crave they act or counsel; for he alone is left to guard the land in thy stead.

OEDIPUS

Ah me! how indeed shall I accost him? What claim to credence can be shown on my part? For in the past I have been found wholly false to him.

CREON

I have not come in mockery, Oedipus, nor to reproach thee with any bygone fault. (*To the attendants.*) But ye, if ye respect the children of men no more, revere at least the all-nurturing flame of our lord the Sun,—spare to show thus nakedly a pollution such as this,—one which neither earth can welcome, nor the holy rain, nor the light. Nay, take him into the house as quickly as ye may; for it best accords with piety that kinsfolk alone should see and hear a kinsman's woes.

OEDIPUS

For the gods' love—since thou hast done a gentle violence to my presage, who hast come in a spirit so noble to me, a man most vile—grant me a boon:—for thy good I will speak, not for mine own.

CREON

And what wish art thou so fain to have of me?

OEDIPUS

Cast me out of this land with all speed, to a place where no mortal shall be found to greet me more.

CREON

This would I have done, be thou sure, but that I craved first to learn all my duty from the god.

OEDIPUS

Nay, his behest hath been set forth in full,—to let me perish, the parricide, the unholy one, that I am.

CREON

Such was the purport; yet, seeing to what a pass we have come, 'tis better to learn clearly what should be done.

OEDIPUS

Will ye, then, seek a response on behalf of such a wretch as I am?

CREON

Aye, for thou thyself wilt now surely put faith in the god.

OEDIPUS

Yea; and on thee lay I this charge, to thee will I make this entreaty:—give to her who is within such burial as thou thyself wouldest; for thou wilt meetly render the last rites to thine own. But for me—never let this city of my sire be condemned to have me dwelling therein, while I live: no, suffer me to abide on the hills, where yonder is Cithaeron, famed as mine,—which my mother and sire, while they lived, set for my appointed tomb,—that so I may die by their decree who sought to slay me. Howbeit of thus much am I sure,—that neither sickness nor aught else can destroy me; for never had I been snatched from death, but in reserve for some strange doom.

Nay, let *my* fate go whither it will: but as touching my children,—I pray thee, Creon, take no care on thee for my sons; they are men, so that, be they where they may, they can never lack the means to live. But my two girls, poor hapless ones,—who never knew my table spread apart, or lacked their father's presence, but ever in all things shared my daily bread,—I pray thee, care for *them;* and—if thou canst—suffer me to touch them with my hands, and to indulge my grief. Grant it, prince, grant it, thou noble heart! Ah, could I but once touch them with my hands, I should think that they were with me, even as when I had sight. . .

(CREON'S *attendants lead in the children* ANTIGONE *and* ISMENE.)

Ha? O ye gods, can it be my loved ones that I hear sobbing,—can Creon have taken pity on me and sent me my children—my darlings? Am I right?

CREON

Yea: 'tis of my contriving, for I knew thy joy in them of old,—the joy that now is thine.

OEDIPUS

Then blessed be thou, and, for guerdon of this errand, may heaven prove to thee a kinder guardian than it hath to me! My children, where are ye? Come hither,—hither to the hands of him whose mother was your own, the hands whose offices have wrought that your sire's once bright eyes should be such orbs as these,—his, who seeing nought, knowing nought, became your father by her from whom he sprang! For you also do I weep—behold you I cannot—when I think of the bitter life in days to come which men will make you live. To what company of the citizens will ye go, to what festival, from which ye shall not return home in tears, instead of sharing in the holiday? But when ye are now come to years ripe for marriage, who shall he be, who shall be the man, my daughters, that will hazard taking unto him such reproaches as must be baneful alike to my offspring and to yours? For what misery is wanting? Your sire slew his sire, he had seed of her who bare him, and begat you at the sources of his own being! Such are the taunts that will be cast at you; and who then will wed? The man lives not, no, it cannot be, my children, but ye must wither in barren maidenhood.

Ah, son of Menoeceus, hear me—since thou art the only father left to them, for we, their parents, are lost, both of us,—allow them not to wander poor and unwed, who are thy kinswomen, nor abase them to the level of my woes. Nay, pity them, when thou seest them at this tender age so utterly forlorn, save for thee. Signify thy promise, generous man, by the touch of thy hand! To you, my children, I would have given much counsel, were your minds mature; but now I would have this to be your prayer—that ye live where occasion suffers, and that the life which is your portion may be happier than your sire's

CREON

Thy grief hath had large scope enough: nay, pass into the house.

OEDIPUS

I must obey, though 'tis in no wise sweet.

CREON

Yea: for it is in season that all things are good.

OEDIPUS

Knowest thou, then, on what conditions I will go?

CREON

Thou shalt name them; so shall I know them when I hear.

OEDIPUS

See that thou send me to dwell beyond this land.

CREON

Thou askest me for what the god must give.

OEDIPUS

Nay, to the gods I have become most hateful.

CREON

Then shalt thou have thy wish anon.

OEDIPUS

So thou consentest?

CREON

'Tis not my wont to speak idly what I do not mean.

OEDIPUS

Then 'tis time to lead me hence.

CREON

Come, then,—but let thy children go.

OEDIPUS

Nay, take not these from me!

CREON

Crave not to be master in all things: for the mastery which thou didst win hath not followed thee through life.

CHORUS (*singing*)

Dwellers in our native Thebes, behold, this is Oedipus, who knew the famed riddle, and was a man most mighty; on whose fortunes what citizen did not gaze with envy? Behold into what a stormy sea of dread trouble he hath come!

Therefore, while our eyes wait to see the destined final day, we must call no one happy who is of mortal race, until he hath crossed life's border, free from pain.

ANTIGONE

by

SOPHOCLES

Characters in the Play

ANTIGONE } *daughters of Oedipus*
ISMENE }
CREON, *King of Thebes*
EURYDICE, *his wife*
HAEMON, *his son*
TEIRESIAS, *the blind prophet*
GUARD, *set to watch the corpse of Polyneices*
FIRST MESSENGER
SECOND MESSENGER, *from the house*
CHORUS OF THEBAN ELDERS

INTRODUCTION

THREE of the extant plays of Sophocles interpret aspects of the familiar Theban saga. The *Antigone*, the earliest of the three, being written probably about 442 B.C., treats the latest events of the legend. The second, *Oedipus the King*, deals with the early part of the story, while the third, *Oedipus at Colonus*, the crowning achievement of Sophocles' old age, presents the last hours and death of Oedipus, which in the chronology of the legend fall between episodes of *Oedipus the King* and the *Antigone*. Although Sophocles follows in its general outlines the received version of the legend, he has not scrupled to alter it or change its emphases in order to serve his own particular dramatic purpose. For example, Creon is a very sympathetic character in *Oedipus the King*, whereas he is portrayed quite differently in the *Antigone.*

According to the legend, Eteocles, son of Oedipus and now king of Thebes, had exiled his brother, Polyneices, who also desired to hold the royal power. Polyneices had enlisted the support of Argos, and had led a tremendous host against Thebes in order to seize the throne. In the battle which then ensued, the brothers, who met in individual combat, fell each by the other's hand, and fulfilled thereby the curse which their father, Oedipus, had called down upon them just before his death. The Argive host has been repulsed, and Creon has assumed the vacant throne. The action of the *Antigone* takes place on the day after the battle. Creon has just issued a proclamation that the body of Eteocles shall be given the full funeral honors due a hero, while the corpse of Polyneices shall lie unburied. At this point the play opens.

The central conflict of the play between Antigone and

Creon is presented in simple terms, and derives, on the surface, from the conventional Greek attitude towards burial ritual. Creon has inflicted upon the dead Polyneices a punishment which the Greeks looked upon with peculiar terror, namely that his body should not receive the requisite funeral rites. The poet has universalized the conflict which arises from this particular situation, until it becomes basically a question whether man-made and tyrannically enforced law should take precedence over what any individual conceives in his heart to be divine law. Creon endeavors to impose his human law on Antigone, who disobeys out of respect for a higher law.

Creon is distinctly a tragic figure, who holds firmly to what he believes to be right and who has no doubts as to the absolute validity of his beliefs. Nothing shakes him, not even the criticism and open opposition of his son, Haemon, with whom Creon is sharply contrasted, until it is too late and the catastrophe has already occurred. Creon gains in stature at the conclusion because he realizes his guilt and assumes responsibility for it. As for Antigone, critics are divided in their interpretations. Some hold that she is guilty of pride, *hybris,* and that she is suffering from an absurd and stubborn desire to become a martyr. Others insist that she is unswervingly and magnificently devoted to her ideals for which she is willing to sacrifice her life, that she does not possess any "tragic flaw" in any sense of the word, and that her fate is completely undeserved. Whatever may be a satisfactory interpretation of her character, at least it is certain that Sophocles has created a living and vital figure in Antigone. Her devotion to her ideals may perhaps lead her to a somewhat uncompromising harshness towards her sister, but Sophocles makes it clear that she has within her a warmth and gentleness of spirit which she has suppressed but which are revealed, now in her love for Haemon, and now when she asks pathetically, as she is led away to death, why it is that she suffers.

ANTIGONE

(SCENE:—*The same as in the Oedipus the King, an open space before the royal palace, once that of Oedipus, at Thebes. The backscene represents the front of the palace, with three doors, of which the central and largest is the principal entrance into the house. The time is at daybreak on the morning after the fall of the two brothers, Eteocles and Polyneices, and the flight of the defeated Argives.* ANTIGONE *calls* ISMENE *forth from the palace, in order to speak to her alone.*)

ANTIGONE

ISMENE, sister, mine own dear sister, knowest thou what ill there is, of all bequeathed by Oedipus, that Zeus fulfils not for us twain while we live? Nothing painful is there, nothing fraught with ruin, no shame, no dishonour, that I have not seen in thy woes and mine.

And now what new edict is this of which they tell, that our Captain hath just published to all Thebes? Knowest thou aught? Hast thou heard? Or is it hidden from thee that our friends are threatened with the doom of our foes?

ISMENE

No word of friends, Antigone, gladsome or painful, hath come to me, since we two sisters were bereft of brothers twain, killed in one day by a twofold blow; and since in this last night the Argive host hath fled, I know no more, whether my fortune be brighter, or more grievous.

ANTIGONE

I knew it well, and therefore sought to bring thee beyond the gates of the court, that thou mightest hear alone.

ISMENE

What is it? 'Tis plain that thou art brooding on some dark tidings.

ANTIGONE

What, hath not Creon destined our brothers, the one to honoured burial, the other to unburied shame? Eteocles, they say, with due observance of right and custom, he hath laid in the earth, for his honour among the dead below. But the hapless corpse of Polyneices—as rumour saith, it hath been published to the town that none shall entomb him or mourn, but leave unwept, unsepulchred, a welcome store for the birds, as they espy him, to feast on at will.

Such, 'tis said, is the edict that the good Creon hath set forth for thee and for me,—yes, for *me,*—and is coming hither to proclaim it clearly to those who know it not; nor counts the matter light, but, whoso disobeys in aught, his doom is death by stoning before all the folk. Thou knowest it now; and thou wilt soon show whether thou art nobly bred, or the base daughter of a noble line.

ISMENE

Poor sister,—and if things stand thus, what could I help to do or undo?

ANTIGONE

Consider if thou wilt share the toil and the deed.

ISMENE

In what venture? What can be thy meaning?

ANTIGONE

Wilt thou aid this hand to lift the dead?

ISMENE

Thou wouldst bury him,—when 'tis forbidden to Thebes?

ANTIGONE

I will do my part,—and thine, if thou wilt not,—to a brother. False to him will I never be found.

ISMENE

Ah, over-bold! when Creon hath forbidden?

ANTIGONE

Nay, he hath no right to keep me from mine own.

ISMENE

Ah me! think, sister, how our father perished, amid hate and scorn, when sins bared by his own search had moved him to strike both eyes with self-blinding hand; then the mother wife, two names in one, with twisted noose did despite unto her life; and last, our two brothers in one day, —each shedding, hapless one, a kinsman's blood,—wrought out with mutual hands their common doom. And now *we* in turn—we two left all alone—think how we shall perish, more miserably than all the rest, if, in defiance of the law, we brave a king's decree or his powers. Nay, we must remember, first, that we were born women, as who should not strive with men; next, that we are ruled of the stronger, so that we must obey in these things, and in things yet sorer. I, therefore, asking the Spirits Infernal to pardon, seeing that force is put on me herein, will hearken to our rulers; for 'tis witless to be over busy.

ANTIGONE

I will not urge thee,—no, nor, if thou yet shouldst have the mind, wouldst thou be welcome as a worker with *me*. Nay, be what thou wilt; but I will bury him: well for me to die in doing that. I shall rest, a loved one with him whom I have loved, sinless in my crime; for I owe a longer allegiance to the dead than to the living: in that world I shall abide for ever. But if *thou* wilt, be guilty of dishonouring laws which the gods have stablished in honour

ISMENE

I do them no dishonour; but to defy the State,—I have no strength for that.

ANTIGONE

Such be thy plea:—I, then, will go to heap the earth above the brother whom I love.

ISMENE

Alas, unhappy one! How I fear for thee!

ANTIGONE

Fear not for me: guide thine own fate aright.

ISMENE

At least, then, disclose this plan to none, but hide it closely,—and so, too, will I.

ANTIGONE

Oh, denounce it! Thou wilt be far more hateful for thy silence, if thou proclaim not these things to all.

ISMENE

Thou hast a hot heart for chilling deeds.

ANTIGONE

I know that I please where I am most bound to please.

ISMENE

Aye, if thou canst; but thou wouldst what thou canst not.

ANTIGONE

Why, then, when my strength fails, I shall have done.

ISMENE

A hopeless quest should not be made at all.

ANTIGONE

If thus thou speakest, thou wilt have hatred from me, and will justly be subject to the lasting hatred of the dead. But leave me, and the folly that is mine alone, to suffer this dread thing; for I shall not suffer aught so dreadful as an ignoble death.

ISMENE

Go, then, if thou must; and of this be sure,—that, though thine errand is foolish, to thy dear ones thou art truly dear.

(*Exit* ANTIGONE *on the spectators' left.* ISMENE *retires into the palace by one of the two side-doors. When they have departed, the* CHORUS OF THEBAN ELDERS *enters.*)

CHORUS (*singing*)

strophe I

Beam of the sun, fairest light that ever dawned on Thebe of the seven gates, thou hast shone forth at last, eye of golden day, arisen above Dirce's streams! The warrior of the white shield, who came from Argos in his panoply, hath been stirred by thee to headlong flight, in swifter career;

LEADER OF THE CHORUS

systema I

who set forth against our land by reason of the vexed claims of Polyneices; and, like shrill-screaming eagle, he flew over into our land, in snow-white pinion sheathed, with an armèd throng, and with plumage of helms.

CHORUS

antistrophe I

He paused above our dwellings; he ravened around our sevenfold portals with spears athirst for blood; but he went hence, or ever his jaws were glutted with our gore, or the Fire-god's pine-fed flame had seized our crown of towers. So fierce was the noise of battle raised behind him, a thing too hard for him to conquer, as he wrestled with his dragon foe.

LEADER

systema 2

For Zeus utterly abhors the boasts of a proud tongue; and when he beheld them coming on in a great stream, in the haughty pride of clanging gold, he smote with brandished fire one who was now hasting to shou' victory at his goal upon our ramparts.

CHORUS

strophe 2

Swung down, he fell on the earth with a crash, torch in hand, he who so lately, in the frenzy of the mad onset, was raging against us with the blasts of his tempestuous hate. But those threats fared not as he hoped; and to other foes the mighty War-god dispensed their several dooms, dealing havoc around, a mighty helper at our need.

LEADER

systema 3

For seven captains at seven gates, matched against seven, left the tribute of their panoplies to Zeus who turns the battle; save those two of cruel fate, who, born of one sire and one mother, set against each other their twain conquering spears, and are sharers in a common death.

CHORUS

antistrophe 2

But since Victory of glorious name hath come to us, with joy responsive to the joy of Thebe whose chariots are many, let us enjoy forgetfulness after the late wars, and visit all the temples of the gods with night-long dance and song; and may Bacchus be our leader, whose dancing shakes the land of Thebe.

LEADER

systema 4

But lo, the king of the land comes yonder, Creon, son of Menoeceus, our new ruler by the new fortunes that the gods have given; what counsel is he pondering, that he hath proposed this special conference of elders, summoned by his general mandate?

(*Enter* CREON, *from the central doors of the palace, in the garb of king, with two attendants.*)

CREON

Sirs, the vessel of our State, after being tossed on wild waves, hath once more been safely steadied by the gods: and ye, out of all the folk, have been called apart by my summons, because I knew, first of all, how true and constant was your reverence for the royal power of Laius; how, again, when Oedipus was ruler of our land, and when he had perished, your steadfast loyalty still upheld their children. Since, then, his sons have fallen in one day by a twofold doom,—each smitten by the other, each stained with a brother's blood,—I now possess the throne and all its powers, by nearness of kinship to the dead.

No man can be fully known, in soul and spirit and mind, until he hath been seen versed in rule and law-giving. For if any, being supreme guide of the State, cleaves not to the best counsels, but, through some fear, keeps his lips locked, I hold, and have ever held, him most base; and if any makes a friend of more account than his fatherland, that man hath no place in my regard. For I—be Zeus my witness, who sees all things always—would not be silent if I saw ruin, instead of safety, coming to the citizens; nor would I ever deem the country's foe a friend to myself; remembering this, that our country is the ship that bears us safe, and that only while she prospers in our voyage can we make true friends.

Such are the rules by which I guard this city's greatness. And in accord with them is the edict which I have now published to the folk touching the sons of Oedipus;—that Eteocles, who hath fallen fighting for our city, in all renown of arms, shall be entombed, and crowned with every rite that follows the noblest dead to their rest. But for his brother, Polyneices,—who came back from exile, and sought to consume utterly with fire the city of his fathers and the shrines of his fathers' gods,—sought to taste of kindred blood, and to lead the remnant into slavery;—touching this man, it hath been proclaimed to our people that none shall grace him with sepulture or lament, but leave him unburied, a corpse for birds and dogs to eat, a ghastly sight of shame.

Such the spirit of my dealing; and never, by deed of mine, shall the wicked stand in honour before the just; but whoso hath good will to Thebes, he shall be honoured of me, in his life and in his death.

LEADER OF THE CHORUS

Such is thy pleasure, Creon, son of Menoeceus, touching this city's foe, and its friend; and thou hast power, I ween, to take what order thou wilt, both for the dead, and for all us who live.

CREON

See, then, that ye be guardians of the mandate.

LEADER

Lay the burden of this task on some younger man.

CREON

Nay, watchers of the corpse have been found.

LEADER

What, then, is this further charge that thou wouldst give?

CREON

That ye side not with the breakers of these commands.

LEADER

No man is so foolish that he is enamoured of death.

CREON

In sooth, that is the meed; yet lucre hath oft ruined men through their hopes.

(*A* GUARD *enters from the spectators' left.*)

GUARD

My liege, I will not say that I come breathless from speed, or that I have plied a nimble foot; for often did my thoughts make me pause, and wheel round in my path, to return. My mind was holding large discourse with me; 'Fool, why goest thou to thy certain doom?' 'Wretch, tarrying again? And if Creon hears this from another, must not thou smart for it?' So debating, I went on my way with lagging steps, and thus a short road was made long. At last, however, it carried the day that I should come hither—to thee; and, though my tale be nought, yet will I tell it; for I come with a good grip on one hope,—that I can suffer nothing but what is my fate.

CREON

And what is it that disquiets thee thus?

GUARD

I wish to tell thee first about myself—I did not do the deed—I did not see the doer—it were not right that I should come to any harm.

CREON

Thou hast a shrewd eye for thy mark; well dost thou fence thyself round against the blame; clearly thou hast some strange thing to tell.

GUARD

Aye, truly; dread news makes one pause long.

CREON

Then tell it, wilt thou, and so get thee gone?

GUARD

Well, this is it.—The corpse—some one hath just given it

burial, and gone away,—after sprinkling thirsty dust on the flesh, with such other rites as piety enjoins.

CREON

What sayest thou? What living man hath dared this deed?

GUARD

I know not; no stroke of pickaxe was seen there, no earth thrown up by mattock; the ground was hard and dry, unbroken, without track of wheels; the doer was one who had left no trace. And when the first day-watchman showed it to us, sore wonder fell on all. The dead man was veiled from us; not shut within a tomb, but lightly strewn with dust, as by the hand of one who shunned a curse. And no sign met the eye as though any beast of prey or any dog had come nigh to him, or torn him.

Then evil words flew fast and loud among us, guard accusing guard; and it would e'en have come to blows at last, nor was there any to hinder. Every man was the culprit, and no one was convicted, but all disclaimed knowledge of the deed. And we were ready to take red-hot iron in our hands;—to walk through fire;—to make oath by the gods that we had not done the deed,—that we were not privy to the planning or the doing.

At last, when all our searching was fruitless, one spake, who made us all bend our faces on the earth in fear; for we saw not how we could gainsay him, or escape mischance if we obeyed. His counsel was that this deed must be reported to thee, and not hidden. And this seemed best; and the lot doomed my hapless self to win this prize. So here I stand,—as unwelcome as unwilling, well I wot; for no man delights in the bearer of bad news.

LEADER

O king, my thoughts have long been whispering, can this deed, perchance, be e'en the work of gods?

CREON

Cease, ere thy words fill me utterly with wrath, lest thou be found at once an old man and foolish. For thou sayest what is not to be borne, in saying that the gods have care for this corpse. Was it for high reward of trusty service that they sought to hide his nakedness, who came to burn their pillared shrines and sacred treasures, to burn their land, and scatter its laws to the winds? Or dost thou behold the gods honouring the wicked? It cannot be. No! From the first there were certain in the town that muttered against me, chafing at this edict, wagging their heads in secret; and kept not their necks duly under the yoke, like men contented with my sway.

'Tis by them, well I know, that these have been beguiled and bribed to do this deed. Nothing so evil as money ever grew to be current among men. This lays cities low, this drives men from their homes, this trains and warps honest souls till they set themselves to works of shame; this still teaches folk to practise villainies, and to know every godless deed.

But all the men who wrought this thing for hire have made it sure that, soon or late, they shall pay the price. Now, as Zeus still hath my reverence, know this—I tell it thee on my oath:—If ye find not the very author of this burial, and produce him before mine eyes, death alone shall not be enough for you, till first, hung up alive, ye have revealed this outrage,—that henceforth ye may thieve with better knowledge whence lucre should be won, and learn that it is not well to love gain from every source. For thou wilt find that ill-gotten pelf brings more men to ruin than to weal.

GUARD

May I speak? Or shall I just turn and go?

CREON

Knowest thou not that even now thy voice offends?

GUARD

Is thy smart in the ears, or in the soul?

CREON

And why wouldst thou define the seat of my pain?

GUARD

The doer vexes thy mind, but I, thine ears.

CREON

Ah, thou art a born babbler, 'tis well seen.

GUARD

May be, but never the doer of this deed.

CREON

Yea, and more,—the seller of thy life for silver.

GUARD

Alas! 'Tis sad, truly, that he who judges should misjudge.

CREON

Let thy fancy play with 'judgment' as it will;—but, if ye show me not the doers of these things, ye shall avow that dastardly gains work sorrows.

(CREON *goes into the palace.*)

GUARD

Well, may he be found! so 'twere best. But, be he caught or be he not—fortune must settle that—truly thou wilt not see me here again. Saved, even now, beyond hope and thought, I owe the gods great thanks.

(*The* GUARD *goes out on the spectators' left.*)

CHORUS (*singing*)

strophe I

Wonders are many, and none is more wonderful than man; the power that crosses the white sea, driven by the stormy south-wind, making a path under surges that threaten to engulf him; and Earth, the eldest of the gods, the immortal, the unwearied, doth he wear. turning the soil with the offspring of horses, as the ploughs go to and fro from year to year.

antistrophe 1

And the light-hearted race of birds, and the tribes of savage beasts, and the sea-brood of the deep, he snares in the meshes of his woven toils, he leads captive, man excellent in wit. And he masters by his arts the beast whose lair is in the wilds, who roams the hills; he tames the horse of shaggy mane, he puts the yoke upon its neck, he tames the tireless mountain bull.

strophe 2

And speech, and wind-swift thought, and all the moods that mould a state, hath he taught himself; and how to flee the arrows of the frost, when 'tis hard lodging under the clear sky, and the arrows of the rushing rain; yea, he hath resource for all; without resource he meets nothing that must come: only against Death shall he call for aid in vain; but from baffling maladies he hath devised escapes.

antistrophe 2

Cunning beyond fancy's dream is the fertile skill which brings him, now to evil, now to good. When he honours the laws of the land, and that justice which he hath sworn by the gods to uphold, proudly stands his city: no city hath he who, for his rashness, dwells with sin. Never may he share my hearth, never think my thoughts, who doth these things!

(*Enter the* GUARD *on the spectators' left, leading in* ANTIGONE.)

LEADER OF THE CHORUS

What portent from the gods is this?—my soul is amazed. I know her—how can I deny that yon maiden is Antigone?

O hapless, and child of hapless sire,—of Oedipus! What means this? Thou, brought a prisoner?—thou, disloyal to the king's laws, and taken in folly?

GUARD

Here she is, the doer of the deed:—we caught this girl burying him:—but where is Creon?

(CREON *enters hurriedly from the palace.*)

LEADER

Lo, he comes forth again from the house, at our need.

CREON

What is it? What hath chanced, that makes my coming timely?

GUARD

O king, against nothing should men pledge their word; for the afterthought belies the first intent. I could have vowed that I should not soon be here again,—scared by thy threats, with which I had just been lashed: but,—since the joy that surprises and transcends our hopes is like in fulness to no other pleasure,—I have come, though 'tis in breach of my sworn oath, bringing this maid; who was taken showing grace to the dead. This time there was no casting of lots; no, this luck hath fallen to me, and to none else. And now, sire, take her thyself, question her, examine her, as thou wilt; but I have a right to free and final quittance of this trouble.

CREON

And thy prisoner here—how and whence hast thou taken her?

GUARD

She was burying the man; thou knowest all.

CREON

Dost thou mean what thou sayest? Dost thou speak aright?

GUARD

I saw her burying the corpse that thou hadst forbidden to bury. Is that plain and clear?

CREON

And how was she seen? how taken in the act?

GUARD

It befell on this wise. When we had come to the place,—with those dread menaces of thine upon us,—we swept away all the dust that covered the corpse, and bared the dank body well; and then sat us down on the brow of the hill, to windward, heedful that the smell from him should not strike us; every man was wide awake, and kept his neighbour alert with torrents of threats, if anyone should be careless of this task.

So went it, until the sun's bright orb stood in mid heaven, and the heat began to burn: and then suddenly a whirlwind lifted from the earth a storm of dust, a trouble in the sky, and filled the plain, marring all the leafage of its woods; and the wide air was choked therewith: we closed our eyes, and bore the plague from the gods.

And when, after a long while, this storm had passed, the maid was seen; and she cried aloud with the sharp cry of a bird in its bitterness,—even as when, within the empty nest, it sees the bed stripped of its nestlings. So she also, when she saw the corpse bare, lifted up a voice of wailing, and called down curses on the doers of that deed. And straightway she brought thirsty dust in her hands; and from a shapely ewer of bronze, held high, with thrice-poured drink-offering she crowned the dead.

We rushed forward when we saw it, and at once closed upon our quarry, who was in no wise dismayed. Then we taxed her with her past and present doings; and she stood not on denial of aught,—at once to my joy and to my pain. To have escaped from ills one's self is a great joy; but 'tis painful to bring friends to ill. Howbeit, all such things are of less account to me than mine own safety.

CREON

Thou—thou whose face is bent to earth—dost thou avow, or disavow, this deed?

ANTIGONE

I avow it; I make no denial.

CREON (*to* GUARD)

Thou canst betake thee whither thou wilt, free and clear of a grave charge.

(*Exit* GUARD)

(*To* ANTIGONE) Now, tell me thou—not in many words, but briefly—knewest thou that an edict had forbidden this?

ANTIGONE

I knew it: could I help it? It was public.

CREON

And thou didst indeed dare to transgress that law?

ANTIGONE

Yes; for it was not Zeus that had published me that edict; not such are the laws set among men by the Justice who dwells with the gods below; nor deemed I that thy decrees were of such force, that a mortal could override the unwritten and unfailing statutes of heaven. For their life is not of to-day or yesterday, but from all time, and no man knows when they were first put forth.

Not through dread of any human pride could I answer to the gods for breaking *these*. Die I must,—I knew that well (how should I not?)—even without thy edicts. But if I am to die before my time, I count that a gain: for when any one lives, as I do, compassed about with evils, can such an one find aught but gain in death?

So for me to meet this doom is trifling grief; but if I had suffered my mother's son to lie in death an unburied corpse, that would have grieved me; for this, I am not grieved. And if my present deeds are foolish in thy sight, it may be that a foolish judge arraigns my folly.

LEADER OF THE CHORUS

The maid shows herself passionate child of passionate sire, and knows not how to bend before troubles.

CREON

Yet I would have thee know that o'er-stubborn spirits are most often humbled; 'tis the stiffest iron, baked to hardness in the fire, that thou shalt oftenest see snapped and shivered; and I have known horses that show temper brought to order by a little curb; there is no room for pride, when thou art thy neighbour's slave.—This girl was already versed in insolence when she transgressed the laws that had been set forth; and, that done, lo, a second insult,—to vaunt of this, and exult in her deed.

Now verily I am no man, she is the man, if this victory shall rest with her, and bring no penalty. No! be she sister's child, or nearer to me in blood than any that worships Zeus at the altar of our house,—she and her kinsfolk shall not avoid a doom most dire; for indeed I charge that other with a like share in the plotting of this burial.

And summon her—for I saw her e'en now within,—raving, and not mistress of her wits. So oft, before the deed, the mind stands self-convicted in its treason, when folks are plotting mischief in the dark. But verily this, too, is hateful, —when one who hath been caught in wickedness then seeks to make the crime a glory.

ANTIGONE

Wouldst thou do more than take and slay me?

CREON

No more, indeed; having that, I have all.

ANTIGONE

Why then dost thou delay? In thy discourse there is nought that pleases me,—never may there be!—and so my words must needs be unpleasing to thee. And yet, for glory—whence could I have won a nobler, than by giving burial to mine own brother? All here would own that they thought it well, were not their lips sealed by fear. But royalty, blest in so much besides, hath the power to do and say what it will.

CREON

Thou differest from all these Thebans in that view.

ANTIGONE

These also share it; but they curb their tongues for thee.

CREON

And art thou not ashamed to act apart from them?

ANTIGONE

No; there is nothing shameful in piety to a brother.

CREON

Was it not a brother, too, that died in the opposite cause?

ANTIGONE

Brother by the same mother and the same sire.

CREON

Why, then, dost thou render a grace that is impious in his sight?

ANTIGONE

The dead man will not say that he so deems it.

CREON

Yea, if thou makest him but equal in honour with the wicked.

ANTIGONE

It was his brother, not his slave, that perished.

CREON

Wasting this land; while *he* fell as its champion.

ANTIGONE

Nevertheless, Hades desires these rites.

CREON

But the good desires not a like portion with the evil.

ANTIGONE

Who knows but this seems blameless in the world below?

CREON

A foe is never a friend—not even in death.

ANTIGONE

'Tis not my nature to join in hating, but in loving.

CREON

Pass, then, to the world of the dead, and, if thou must needs love, love them. While I live, no woman shall rule me.

(*Enter* ISMENE *from the house, led in by two attendants.*)

CHORUS (*chanting*)

Lo, yonder Ismene comes forth, shedding such tears as fond sisters weep; a cloud upon her brow casts its shadow over her darkly-flushing face, and breaks in rain on her fair cheek.

CREON

And thou, who, lurking like a viper in my house, wast secretly draining my life-blood, while I knew not that I was nurturing two pests, to rise against my throne—come, tell me now, wilt thou also confess thy part in this burial, or wilt thou forswear all knowledge of it?

ISMENE

I have done the deed,—if she allows my claim,—and share the burden of the charge.

ANTIGONE

Nay, justice will not suffer thee to do that: thou didst not consent to the deed, nor did I give thee part in it.

ISMENE

But, now that ills beset thee, I am not ashamed to sail the sea of trouble at thy side.

ANTIGONE

Whose was the deed, Hades and the dead are witnesses: a friend in words is not the friend that I love.

ISMENE

Nay, sister, reject me not, but let me die with thee, and duly honour the dead.

ANTIGONE

Share not thou my death, nor claim deeds to which thou hast not put thy hand: my death will suffice.

ISMENE

And what life is dear to me, bereft of thee?

ANTIGONE

Ask Creon; all thy care is for him.

ISMENE

Why vex me thus, when it avails thee nought?

ANTIGONE

Indeed, if I mock, 'tis with pain that I mock thee.

ISMENE

Tell me,—how can I serve thee, even now?

ANTIGONE

Save thyself: I grudge not thy escape.

ISMENE

Ah, woe is me! And shall I have no share in thy fate?

ANTIGONE

Thy choice was to live; mine, to die.

ISMENE

At least thy choice was not made without my protest.

ANTIGONE
One world approved thy wisdom; another, mine.

ISMENE
Howbeit, the offence is the same for both of us.

ANTIGONE
Be of good cheer; thou livest; but my life hath long been given to death, that so I might serve the dead.

CREON
Lo, one of these maidens hath newly shown herself foolish, as the other hath been since her life began.

ISMENE
Yea, O king, such reason as nature may have given abides not with the unfortunate, but goes astray.

CREON
Thine did, when thou chosest vile deeds with the vile.

ISMENE
What life could I endure, without her presence?

CREON
Nay, speak not of her 'presence'; she lives no more.

ISMENE
But wilt thou slay the betrothed of thine own son?

CREON
Nay, there are other fields for him to plough.

ISMENE
But there can never be such love as bound him to her.

CREON
I like not an evil wife for my son.

ANTIGONE
Haemon, beloved! How thy father wrongs thee!

CREON

Enough, enough of thee and of thy marriage!

LEADER OF THE CHORUS

Wilt thou indeed rob thy son of this maiden?

CREON

'Tis Death that shall stay these bridals for me.

LEADER

'Tis determined, it seems, that she shall die.

CREON

Determined, yes, for thee and for me.—(*To the two attendants*) No more delay—servants, take them within! Henceforth they must be women, and not range at large; for verily even the bold seek to fly, when they see Death now closing on their life.

(*Exeunt attendants, guarding* ANTIGONE *and* ISMENE.—CREON *remains.*)

CHORUS (*singing*)

strophe 1

Blest are they whose days have not tasted of evil. For when a house hath once been shaken from heaven, there the curse fails nevermore, passing from life to life of the race; even as, when the surge is driven over the darkness of the deep by the fierce breath of Thracian sea-winds, it rolls up the black sand from the depths, and there is a sullen roar from wind-vexed headlands that front the blows of the storm.

antistrophe 1

I see that from olden time the sorrows in the house of the Labdacidae are heaped upon the sorrows of the dead; and generation is not freed by generation, but some god strikes them down, and the race hath no deliverance.

For now that hope of which the light had been spread above the last root of the house of Oedipus—that hope, in turn, is brought low—by the blood-stained dust due to the gods infernal, and by folly in speech, and frenzy at the heart.

strophe 2

Thy power, O Zeus, what human trespass can limit? That power which neither Sleep, the all-ensnaring, nor the untiring months of the gods can master; but thou, a ruler to whom time brings not old age, dwellest in the dazzling splendour of Olympus.

And through the future, near and far, as through the past, shall this law hold good: Nothing that is vast enters into the life of mortals without a curse.

antistrophe 2

For that hope whose wanderings are so wide is to many men a comfort, but to many a false lure of giddy desires, and the disappointment comes on one who knoweth nought till he burn his foot against the hot fire.

For with wisdom hath some one given forth the famous saying, that evil seems good, soon or late, to him whose mind the god draws to mischief; and but for the briefest space doth he fare free of woe.

LEADER OF THE CHORUS

But lo, Haemon, the last of thy sons;—comes he grieving for the doom of his promised bride, Antigone, and bitter for the baffled hope of his marriage?

(*Enter* HAEMON)

CREON

We shall know soon, better than seers could tell us.—My son, hearing the fixed doom of thy betrothed, art thou come, in rage against thy father? Or have I thy good will, act how I may?

HAEMON

Father, I am thine; and thou, in thy wisdom, tracest for me rules which I shall follow. No marriage shall be deemed by me a greater gain than thy good guidance.

CREON

Yea, this, my son, should be thy heart's fixed law,—in all things to obey thy father's will. 'Tis for this that men pray to see dutiful children grow up around them in their homes, —that such may requite their father's foe with evil, and honour, as their father doth, his friend. But he who begets unprofitable children—what shall we say that he hath sown, but troubles for himself, and much triumph for his foes? Then do not thou, my son, at pleasure's beck, dethrone thy reason for a woman's sake; knowing that this is a joy that soon grows cold in clasping arms,—an evil woman to share thy bed and thy home. For what wound could strike deeper than a false friend? Nay, with loathing, and as if she were thine enemy, let this girl go to find a husband in the house of Hades. For since I have taken her, alone of all the city, in open disobedience, I will not make myself a liar to my people—I will slay her.

So let her appeal as she will to the majesty of kindred blood: If I am to nurture mine own kindred in naughtiness, needs must I bear with it in aliens. He who does his duty in his own household will be found righteous in the State also. But if any one transgresses, and does violence to the laws, or thinks to dictate to his rulers, such an one can win no praise from me. No, whomsoever the city may appoint, that man must be obeyed, in little things and great, in just things and unjust; and I should feel sure that one who thus obeys would be a good ruler no less than a good subject, and in the storm of spears would stand his ground where he was set, loyal and dauntless at his comrade's side.

But disobedience is the worst of evils. This it is that ruins cities; this makes homes desolate; by this, the ranks of allies are broken into headlong rout; but, of the lives whose course is fair, the greater part owes safety to obedience. Therefore we must support the cause of order, and in no wise suffer a woman to worst us. Better to fall from power, if we must, by a man's hand; then we should not be called weaker than a woman.

LEADER

To us, unless our years have stolen our wit, thou seemest to say wisely what thou sayest.

HAEMON

Father, the gods implant reason in men, the highest of all things that we call our own. Not mine the skill—far from me be the quest!—to say wherein thou speakest not aright; and yet another man, too, might have some useful thought. At least, it is my natural office to watch, on thy behalf, all that men say, or do, or find to blame. For the dread of thy frown forbids the citizen to speak such words as would offend thine ear; but I can hear these murmurs in the dark, these moanings of the city for this maiden; 'no woman,' they say, 'ever merited her doom less,—none ever was to die so shamefully for deeds so glorious as hers; who, when her own brother had fallen in bloody strife, would not leave him unburied, to be devoured by carrion dogs, or by any bird:—deserves not *she* the meed of golden honour?'

Such is the darkling rumour that spreads in secret. For me, my father, no treasure is so precious as thy welfare. What, indeed, is a nobler ornament for children than a prospering sire's fair fame, or for sire than son's? Wear not, then, one mood only in thyself; think not that thy word, and thine alone, must be right. For if any man thinks that he alone is wise,—that in speech, or in mind, he hath no peer,—such a soul, when laid open, is ever found empty.

No, though a man be wise, 'tis no shame for him to learn

many things, and to bend in season. Seest thou, beside the wintry torrent's course, how the trees that yield to it save every twig, while the stiff-necked perish root and branch? And even thus he who keeps the sheet of his sail taut, and never slackens it, upsets his boat, and finishes his voyage with keel uppermost.

Nay, forego thy wrath; permit thyself to change. For if I, a younger man, may offer my thought, it were far best, I ween, that men should be all-wise by nature; but, otherwise —and oft the scale inclines not so—'tis good also to learn from those who speak aright.

LEADER

Sire, 'tis meet that thou shouldest profit by his words, if he speaks aught in season, and thou, Haemon, by thy father's; for on both parts there hath been wise speech.

CREON

Men of my age—are we indeed to be schooled, then, by men of his?

HAEMON

In nothing that is not right; but if I am young, thou shouldest look to my merits, not to my years.

CREON

Is it a merit to honour the unruly?

HAEMON

I could wish no one to show respect for evil-doers.

CREON

Then is not she tainted with that malady?

HAEMON

Our Theban folk, with one voice, denies it.

CREON

Shall Thebes prescribe to me how I must rule?

HAEMON

See, there thou hast spoken like a youth indeed.

CREON

Am I to rule this land by other judgment than mine own?

HAEMON

That is no city which belongs to one man.

CREON

Is not the city held to be the ruler's?

HAEMON

Thou wouldst make a good monarch of a desert.

CREON

This boy, it seems, is the woman's champion.

HAEMON

If thou art a woman; indeed, my care is for thee.

CREON

Shameless, at open feud with thy father!

HAEMON

Nay, I see thee offending against justice.

CREON

Do I offend, when I respect mine own prerogatives?

HAEMON

Thou dost not respect them, when thou tramplest on the gods' honours.

CREON

O dastard nature, yielding place to woman!

HAEMON

Thou wilt never find me yield to baseness.

CREON

All thy words, at least, plead for that girl.

HAEMON

And for thee, and for me, and for the gods below.

CREON

Thou canst never marry her, on this side the grave.

HAEMON

Then she must die, and in death destroy another.

CREON

How! doth thy boldness run to open threats?

HAEMON

What threat is it, to combat vain resolves?

CREON

Thou shalt rue thy witless teaching of wisdom.

HAEMON

Wert thou not my father, I would have called thee unwise.

CREON

Thou woman's slave, use not wheedling speech with me.

HAEMON

Thou wouldest speak, and then hear no reply?

CREON

Sayest thou so? Now, by the heaven above us—be sure of it—thou shalt smart for taunting me in this opprobrious strain. Bring forth that hated thing, that she may die forthwith in his presence—before his eyes—at her bridegroom's side!

HAEMON

No, not at my side—never think it—shall she perish; nor shalt thou ever set eyes more upon my face:—rave, then, with such friends as can endure thee.

(*Exit* HAEMON)

LEADER

The man is gone, O king, in angry haste; a youthful mind, when stung, is fierce.

CREON

Let him do, or dream, more than man—good speed to him! —But he shall not save these two girls from their doom.

LEADER

Dost thou indeed purpose to slay both?

CREON

Not her whose hands are pure: thou sayest well.

LEADER

And by what doom mean'st thou to slay the other?

CREON

I will take her where the path is loneliest, and hide her, living, in a rocky vault, with so much food set forth as piety prescribes, that the city may avoid a public stain. And there, praying to Hades, the only god whom she worships, perchance she will obtain release from death; or else will learn, at last, though late, that it is lost labour to revere the dead.

(CREON *goes into the palace.*)

CHORUS (*singing*)

strophe

Love, unconquered in the fight, Love, who makest havoc of wealth, who keepest thy vigil on the soft cheek of a maiden; thou roamest over the sea, and among the homes of dwellers in the wilds; no immortal can escape thee, nor any among men whose life is for a day; and he to whom thou hast come is mad.

antistrophe

The just themselves have their minds warped by thee to wrong, for their ruin: 'tis thou that hast stirred up this present strife of kinsmen; victorious is the love-kindling light from the eyes of the fair bride; it is a power enthroned in sway beside the eternal laws; for there the goddess Aphrodite is working her unconquerable will.

(ANTIGONE *is led out of the palace by two of* CREON'S *attendants who are about to conduct her to her doom.*)

But now I also am carried beyond the bounds of loyalty, and can no more keep back the streaming tears, when I see Antigone thus passing to the bridal chamber where all are laid to rest.

(*The following lines between* ANTIGONE *and the* CHORUS *are chanted responsively.*)

ANTIGONE

strophe I

See me, citizens of my fatherland, setting forth on my last way, looking my last on the sunlight that is for me no more; no, Hades who gives sleep to all leads me living to Acheron's shore; who have had no portion in the chant that brings the bride, nor hath any song been mine for the crowning of bridals; whom the lord of the Dark Lake shall wed.

CHORUS

systema I

Glorious, therefore, and with praise, thou departest to that deep place of the dead: wasting sickness hath not smitten thee; thou hast not found the wages of the sword; no, mistress of thine own fate, and still alive thou shalt pass to Hades, as no other of mortal kind hath passed.

ANTIGONE

antistrophe I

I have heard in other days how dread a doom befell our Phrygian guest, the daughter of Tantalus, on the

Sipylian heights; how, like clinging ivy, the growth of stone subdued her; and the rains fail not, as men tell, from her wasting form, nor fails the snow, while beneath her weeping lids the tears bedew her bosom; and most like to hers is the fate that brings me to my rest.

CHORUS

systema 2

Yet she was a goddess, thou knowest, and born of gods; we are mortals, and of mortal race. But 'tis great renown for a woman who hath perished that she should have shared the doom of the godlike, in her life, and afterward in death.

ANTIGONE

strophe 2

Ah, I am mocked! In the name of our fathers' gods, can ye not wait till I am gone,—must ye taunt me to my face, O my city, and ye, her wealthy sons? Ah, fount of Dirce, and thou holy ground of Thebe whose chariots are many; ye, at least, will bear me witness, in what sort, unwept of friends, and by what laws I pass to the rock-closed prison of my strange tomb, ah me unhappy! who have no home on the earth or in the shades, no home with the living or with the dead.

CHORUS

strophe 3

Thou hast rushed forward to the utmost verge of daring; and against that throne where Justice sits on high thou hast fallen, my daughter, with a grievous fall. But in this ordeal thou art paying, haply, for thy father's sin.

ANTIGONE

antistrophe 2

Thou hast touched on my bitterest thought,—awaking the ever-new lament for my sire and for all the doom given to us, the famed house of Labdacus. Alas for the horrors of the mother's bed! alas for the wretched mother's slumber at the side of her own son,—and my sire! From what manner of parents did I take my miserable being! And to them I go thus, accursed, unwed, to share their home. Alas, my brother, ill-starred in thy marriage, in thy death thou hast undone my life!

CHORUS

antistrophe 3

Reverent action claims a certain praise for reverence; but an offence against power cannot be brooked by him who hath power in his keeping. Thy self-willed temper hath wrought thy ruin.

ANTIGONE

epode

Unwept, unfriended, without marriage-song, I am led forth in my sorrow on this journey that can be delayed no more. No longer, hapless one, may I behold yon day-star's sacred eye; but for my fate no tear is shed, no friend makes moan.

(CREON *enters from the palace.*)

CREON

Know ye not that songs and wailings before death would never cease, if it profited to utter them? Away with her—away! And when ye have enclosed her, according to my word, in her vaulted grave, leave her alone, forlorn—whether she wishes to die, or to live a buried life in such a home. Our hands are clean as touching this maiden. But this is certain—she shall be deprived of her sojourn in the light.

ANTIGONE

Tomb, bridal-chamber, eternal prison in the caverned rock, whither I go to find mine own, those many who have perished, and whom Persephone hath received among the dead! Last of all shall I pass thither, and far most miserably of all, before the term of my life is spent. But I cherish good hope that my coming will be welcome to my father, and pleasant to thee, my mother, and welcome, brother, to thee; for, when ye died, with mine own hands I washed and dressed you, and poured drink-offerings at your graves; and now, Polyneices, 'tis for tending thy corpse that I win such recompense as this.

And yet I honoured thee, as the wise will deem, rightly. Never, had I been a mother of children, or if a husband had been mouldering in death, would I have taken this task upon me in the city's despite. What law, ye ask, is my warrant for that word? The husband lost, another might have been found, and child from another, to replace the first-born; but, father and mother hidden with Hades, no brother's life could ever bloom for me again. Such was the law whereby I held thee first in honour; but Creon deemed me guilty of error therein, and of outrage, ah brother mine! And now he leads me thus, a captive in his hands; no bridal bed, no bridal song hath been mine, no joy of marriage, no portion in the nurture of children; but thus, forlorn of friends, unhappy one, I go living to the vaults of death.

And what law of heaven have I transgressed? Why, hapless one, should I look to the gods any more,—what ally should I invoke,—when by piety I have earned the name of impious? Nay, then, if these things are pleasing to the gods, when I have suffered my doom, I shall come to know my sin; but if the sin is with my judges, I could wish them no fuller measure of evil than they, on their part, mete wrongfully to me.

CHORUS

Still the same tempest of the soul vexes this maiden with the same fierce gusts.

CREON

Then for this shall her guards have cause to rue their slowness.

ANTIGONE

Ah me! that word hath come very near to death.

CREON

I can cheer thee with no hope that this doom is not thus to be fulfilled.

ANTIGONE

O city of my fathers in the land of Thebe! O ye gods, eldest of our race!—they lead me hence—now, now—they tarry not! Behold me, princes of Thebes, the last daughter of the house of your kings,—see what I suffer, and from whom, because I feared to cast away the fear of Heaven!

(ANTIGONE *is led away by the guards.*)

CHORUS (*singing*)

strophe I

Even thus endured Danae in her beauty to change the light of day for brass-bound walls; and in that chamber, secret as the grave, she was held close prisoner; yet was she of a proud lineage, O my daughter, and charged with the keeping of the seed of Zeus, that fell in the golden rain.

But dreadful is the mysterious power of fate; there is no deliverance from it by wealth or by war, by fenced city, or dark, sea-beaten ships.

antistrophe I

And bonds tamed the son of Dryas, swift to wrath, that king of the Edonians; so paid he for his frenzied taunts, when, by the will of Dionysus, he was pent in a rocky prison. There the fierce exuberance of his madness slowly passed away. That man learned to know the god, whom in his frenzy he had provoked with mockeries; for he had sought to quell the god-possessed women, and the Bacchanalian fire; and he angered the Muses that love the flute.

strophe 2

And by the waters of the Dark Rocks, the waters of the twofold sea, are the shores of Bosporus, and Thracian Salmydessus; where Ares, neighbour to the city, saw the accurst, blinding wound dealt to the two sons of Phineus by his fierce wife,—the wound that brought darkness to those vengeance-craving orbs, smitten with her bloody hands, smitten with her shuttle for a dagger.

antistrophe 2

Pining in their misery, they bewailed their cruel doom, those sons of a mother hapless in her marriage; but she traced her descent from the ancient line of the Erechtheidae; and in far-distant caves she was nursed amid her father's storms, that child of Boreas, swift as a steed over the steep hills, a daughter of gods; yet upon her also the gray Fates bore hard, my daughter.

(*Enter* TEIRESIAS, *led by a Boy, on the spectators' right.*)

TEIRESIAS

Princes of Thebes, we have come with linked steps, both served by the eyes of one; for thus, by a guide's help, the blind must walk.

CREON

And what, aged Teiresias, are thy tidings?

TEIRESIAS

I will tell thee; and do thou hearken to the seer.

CREON

Indeed, it has not been my wont to slight thy counsel.

TEIRESIAS

Therefore didst thou steer our city's course aright.

CREON

I have felt. and can attest, thy benefits.

TEIRESIAS

Mark that now, once more, thou standest on fate's fine edge.

CREON

What means this? How I shudder at thy message!

TEIRESIAS

Thou wilt learn, when thou hearest the warnings of mine art. As I took my place on mine old seat of augury, where all birds have been wont to gather within my ken, I heard a strange voice among them; they were screaming with dire, feverish rage, that drowned their language in a jargon; and I knew that they were rending each other with their talons, murderously; the whirr of wings told no doubtful tale.

Forthwith, in fear, I essayed burnt-sacrifice on a duly kindled altar; but from my offerings the Fire-god showed no flame; a dank moisture, oozing from the thigh-flesh, trickled forth upon the embers, and smoked, and sputtered; the gall was scattered to the air; and the streaming thighs lay bared of the fat that had been wrapped round them.

Such was the failure of the rites by which I vainly asked a sign, as from this boy I learned; for he is my guide, as I am guide to others. And 'tis thy counsel that hath brought this sickness on our State. For the altars of our city and of our hearths have been tainted, one and all, by birds and dogs, with carrion from the hapless corpse, the son of Oedipus; and therefore the gods no more accept prayer and sacrifice at our hands, or the flame of meat-offering; nor doth any bird give a clear sign by its shrill cry, for they have tasted the fatness of a slain man's blood.

Think, then, on these things, my son. All men are liable to err; but when an error hath been made, that man is no longer witless or unblest who heals the ill into which he hath fallen, and remains not stubborn.

Self-will, we know, incurs the charge of folly. Nay, allow the claim of the dead; stab not the fallen; what prowess is it to slay the slain anew? I have sought thy good, and for thy good I speak: and never is it sweeter to learn from a good counsellor than when he counsels for thine own gain.

CREON

Old man, ye all shoot your shafts at me, as archers at the butts;—ye must needs practise on me with seer-craft also;—aye, the seer-tribe hath long trafficked in me, and made me their merchandise. Gain your gains, drive your trade, if ye list, in the silver-gold of Sardis and the gold of India; but ye shall not hide that man in the grave,—no, though the eagles of Zeus should bear the carrion morsels to their Master's throne—no, not for dread of that defilement will I suffer his burial:—for well I know that no mortal can defile the gods.—But, aged Teiresias, the wisest fall with a shameful fall, when they clothe shameful thoughts in fair words, for lucre's sake.

TEIRESIAS

Alas! Doth any man know, doth any consider . . .

CREON

Whereof? What general truth dost thou announce?

TEIRESIAS

How precious, above all wealth, is good counsel.

CREON

As folly, I think, is the worst mischief.

TEIRESIAS

Yet thou are tainted with that distemper.

CREON

I would not answer the seer with a taunt.

TEIRESIAS

But thou dost, in saying that I prophesy falsely.

CREON

Well, the prophet-tribe was ever fond of money.

TEIRESIAS

And the race bred of tyrants loves base gain.

CREON

Knowest thou that thy speech is spoken of thy king?

TEIRESIAS

I know it; for through me thou hast saved Thebes.

CREON

Thou art a wise seer; but thou lovest evil deeds.

TEIRESIAS

Thou wilt rouse me to utter the dread secret in my soul.

CREON

Out with it!—Only speak it not for gain.

TEIRESIAS

Indeed, methinks, I shall not,—as touching thee.

CREON

Know that thou shalt not trade on my resolve.

TEIRESIAS

Then know thou—aye, know it well—that thou shalt not live through many more courses of the sun's swift chariot, ere one begotten of thine own loins shall have been given by thee, a corpse for corpses; because thou hast thrust children of the sunlight to the shades, and ruthlessly lodged a living soul in the grave; but keepest in this world one who belongs to the gods infernal, a corpse unburied, unhonoured, all unhallowed. In such thou hast no part, nor have the gods above, but this is a violence done to them by thee. Therefore the avenging destroyers lie in wait for thee, the Furies of Hades and of the gods, that thou mayest be taken in these same ills.

And mark well if I speak these things as a hireling. A time not long to be delayed shall awaken the wailing of men and of women in thy house. And a tumult of hatred against thee stirs all the cities whose mangled sons had the burial-rite from dogs, or from wild beasts, or from some winged bird that bore a polluting breath to each city that contains the hearths of the dead.

Such arrows for thy heart—since thou provokest me—have I launched at thee, archer-like, in my anger,—sure arrows, of which thou shalt not escape the smart.—Boy, lead me home, that he may spend his rage on younger men, and learn to keep a tongue more temperate, and to bear within his breast a better mind than now he bears.

(*The Boy leads* TEIRESIAS *out.*)

LEADER OF THE CHORUS

The man hath gone, O King, with dread prophecies. And, since the hair on this head, once dark, hath been white, I know that he hath never been a false prophet to our city.

CREON

I, too, know it well, and am troubled in soul. 'Tis dire to yield; but, by resistance, to smite my pride with ruin—this, too, is a dire choice.

LEADER

Son of Menoeceus, it behoves thee to take wise counsel.

CREON

What should I do, then? Speak, and I will obey.

LEADER

Go thou, and free the maiden from her rocky chamber, and make a tomb for the unburied dead.

CREON

And this is thy counsel? Thou wouldst have me yield?

LEADER

Yea, King, and with all speed; for swift harms from the gods cut short the folly of men.

CREON

Ah me, 'tis hard, but I resign my cherished resolve,—I obey. We must not wage a vain war with destiny.

LEADER

Go, thou, and do these things; leave them not to others.

CREON

Even as I am I'll go:—on, on, my servants, each and all of you,—take axes in your hands, and hasten to the ground that ye see yonder! Since our judgment hath taken this turn, I will be present to unloose her, as I myself bound her. My heart misgives me, 'tis best to keep the established laws, even to life's end.

(CREON *and his servants hasten out on the spectators' left.*)

CHORUS (*singing*)

strophe I

O thou of many names, glory of the Cadmeian bride, offspring of loud-thundering Zeus! thou who watchest over famed Italia, and reignest, where all guests are welcomed, in the sheltered plain of Eleusinian Deo! O Bacchus, dweller in Thebe, mother-city of Bacchants, by the softly-gliding stream of Ismenus, on the soil where the fierce dragon's teeth were sown!

antistrophe I

Thou hast been seen where torch-flames glare through smoke, above the crests of the twin peaks, where move the Corycian nymphs, thy votaries, hard by Castalia's stream.

Thou comest from the ivy-mantled slopes of Nysa's hills, and from the shore green with many-clustered vines, while thy name is lifted up on strains of more than mortal power, as thou visitest the ways of Thebe:

strophe 2

Thebe, of all cities, thou holdest first in honour, thou, and thy mother whom the lightning smote; and now, when all our people is captive to a violent plague, come thou with healing feet over the Parnassian height, or over the moaning strait!

antistrophe 2

O thou with whom the stars rejoice as they move, the stars whose breath is fire; O master of the voices of the night; son begotten of Zeus; appear, O king, with thine attendant Thyiads, who in night-long frenzy dance before thee, the giver of good gifts, Iacchus!

(*Enter* MESSENGER, *on the spectators' left.*)

MESSENGER

Dwellers by the house of Cadmus and of Amphion, there is no estate of mortal life that I would ever praise or blame as settled. Fortune raises and Fortune humbles the lucky or unlucky from day to day, and no one can prophesy to men concerning those things which are established. For Creon was blest once, as I count bliss; he had saved this land of Cadmus from its foes; he was clothed with sole dominion in the land; he reigned, the glorious sire of princely children. And now all hath been lost. For when a man hath forfeited his pleasures, I count him not as living,—I hold him but a breathing corpse. Heap up riches in thy house, if thou wilt; live in kingly state; yet, if there be no gladness therewith, I would not give the shadow of a vapour for all the rest, compared with joy.

LEADER OF THE CHORUS

And what is this new grief that thou hast to tell for our princes?

MESSENGER

Death; and the living are guilty for the dead.

LEADER

And who is the slayer? Who the stricken? Speak.

MESSENGER

Haemon hath perished; his blood hath been shed by no stranger.

LEADER

By his father's hand, or by his own?

MESSENGER

By his own, in wrath with his sire for the murder.

LEADER

O prophet, how true, then, hast thou proved thy word!

MESSENGER

These things stand thus; ye must consider of the rest.

LEADER

Lo, I see the hapless Eurydice, Creon's wife, approaching; she comes from the house by chance, haply,—or because she knows the tidings of her son.

(*Enter* EURYDICE *from the palace.*)

EURYDICE

People of Thebes, I heard your words as I was going forth, to salute the goddess Pallas with my prayers. Even as I was loosing the fastenings of the gate, to open it, the message of a household woe smote on mine ear: I sank back, terror-stricken, into the arms of my handmaids, and my senses fled. But say again what the tidings were; I shall hear them as one who is no stranger to sorrow.

MESSENGER

Dear lady, I will witness of what I saw, and will leave no word of the truth untold. Why, indeed, should I soothe thee with words in which I must presently be found false? Truth is ever best.—I attended thy lord as his guide to the furthest part of the plain, where the body of Polyneices, torn by dogs, still lay unpitied. We prayed the goddess of the roads, and Pluto, in mercy to restrain their wrath; we washed the dead with holy washing; and with freshly-plucked boughs we solemnly burned such relics as there were. We raised a high mound of his native earth; and then we turned away to enter the maiden's nuptial chamber with rocky couch, the caverned mansion of the bride of Death. And, from afar off, one of us heard a voice of loud wailing at that bride's unhallowed bower; and came to tell our master Creon.

And as the king drew nearer, doubtful sounds of a bitter cry floated around him! he groaned, and said in accents of anguish, 'Wretched that I am, can my foreboding be true? Am I going on the wofullest way that ever I went? My son's voice greets me.—Go, my servants,—haste ye nearer, and when ye have reached the tomb, pass through the gap, where the stones have been wrenched away, to the cell's very mouth,—and look, and see if 'tis Haemon's voice that I know, or if mine ear is cheated by the gods.'

This search, at our despairing master's word, we went to make; and in the furthest part of the tomb we descried *her* hanging by the neck, slung by a thread-wrought halter of fine linen: while *he* was embracing her with arms thrown around her waist,—bewailing the loss of his bride who is with the dead, and his father's deeds, and his own ill-starred love.

But his father, when he saw him, cried aloud with a dread cry and went in, and called to him with a voice of wailing:—'Unhappy, what a deed hast thou done! What thought hath come to thee? What manner of mischance hath marred thy reason? Come forth, my child! I pray thee—I implore!' But the boy glared at him with fierce eyes, spat in his face, and, without a word of answer, drew his cross-hilted sword:—as his father rushed forth in flight, he missed his aim;—then, hapless one, wroth with himself, he straightway leaned with all his weight against his sword, and drove it, half its length, into his side; and, while sense lingered, he clasped the maiden to his faint embrace, and, as he gasped, sent forth on her pale cheek the swift stream of the oozing blood.

Corpse enfolding corpse he lies; he hath won his nuptial rites, poor youth, not here, yet in the halls of Death; and he hath witnessed to mankind that, of all curses which cleave to man, ill counsel is the sovereign curse.

(EURYDICE *retires into the house.*)

LEADER

What wouldst thou augur from this? The lady hath turned back, and is gone, without a word, good or evil.

MESSENGER

I, too, am startled; yet I nourish the hope that, at these sore tidings of her son, she cannot deign to give her sorrow public vent, but in the privacy of the house will set her handmaids to mourn the household grief. For she is not untaught of discretion, that she should err.

LEADER

I know not; but to me, at least, a strained silence seems to portend peril, no less than vain abundance of lament.

MESSENGER

Well, I will enter the house, and learn whether indeed she is not hiding some repressed purpose in the depths of a passionate heart. Yea, thou sayest well: excess of silence, too, may have a perilous meaning.

(*The* MESSENGER *goes into the palace. Enter* CREON, *on the spectators' left, with attendants, carrying the shrouded body of* HAEMON *on a bier. The following lines between* CREON *and the* CHORUS *are chanted responsively.*)

CHORUS

Lo, yonder the king himself draws near, bearing that
which tells too clear a tale,—the work of no stranger's
madness,—if we may say it,—but of his own misdeeds.

CREON

strophe 1

Woe for the sins of a darkened soul, stubborn sins, fraught with death! Ah, ye behold us, the sire who hath slain, the son who hath perished! Woe is me, for the wretched blindness of my counsels! Alas, my son, thou hast died in thy youth, by a timeless doom, woe is me! —thy spirit hath fled,—not by thy folly, but by mine own!

CHORUS

strophe 2

Ah me, how all too late thou seemest to see the right!

CREON

Ah me, I have learned the bitter lesson! But then, methinks, oh then, some god smote me from above with crushing weight, and hurled me into ways of cruelty, woe is me,—overthrowing and trampling on my joy! Woe, woe, for the troublous toils of men!

(*Enter* MESSENGER *from the house.*)

MESSENGER

Sire, thou hast come, methinks, as one whose hands are not empty, but who hath store laid up besides; thou bearest yonder burden with thee; and thou art soon to look upon the woes within thy house.

CREON

And what worse ill is yet to follow upon ills?

MESSENGER

Thy queen hath died, true mother of yon corpse—ah, hapless lady!—by blows newly dealt.

CREON

antistrophe 1

Oh Hades, all-receiving, whom no sacrifice can appease! Hast thou, then, no mercy for me? O thou herald of evil, bitter tidings, what word dost thou utter? Alas, I was already as dead, and thou hast smitten me anew! What sayest thou, my son? What is this new message that thou bringest—woe, woe is me!—of a wife's doom, — of slaughter heaped on slaughter?

CHORUS

Thou canst behold: 'tis no longer hidden within.

(*The doors of the palace are opened, and the corpse of* EURYDICE *is disclosed.*)

CREON

antistrophe 2

Ah me,—yonder I behold a new, a second woe! What destiny, ah what, can yet await me? I have but now raised my son in my arms,—and there, again, I see a corpse before me! Alas, alas, unhappy mother! Alas, my child!

MESSENGER

There, at the altar, self-stabbed with a keen knife, she suffered her darkening eyes to close, when she had wailed for the noble fate of Megareus who died before, and then for his fate who lies there,—and when, with her last breath, she had invoked evil fortunes upon thee, the slayer of thy sons.

CREON

strophe 3

Woe, woe! I thrill with dread. Is there none to strike me to the heart with two-edged sword?—O miserable that I am, and steeped in miserable anguish!

MESSENGER

Yea, both this son's doom, and that other's, were laid to thy charge by her whose corpse thou seest.

CREON

And what was the manner of the violent deed by which she passed away?

MESSENGER

Her own hand struck her to the heart, when she had learned her son's sorely lamented fate.

CREON

strophe 4

Ah me, this guilt can never be fixed on any other of mortal kind, for my acquittal! I, even I, was thy slayer, wretched that I am—I own the truth. Lead me away, O my servants, lead me hence with all speed, whose life is but as death!

CHORUS

Thy counsels are good, if there can be good with ills; briefest is best, when trouble is in our path.

CREON

antistrophe 3

Oh, let it come, let it appear, that fairest of fates for me, that brings my last day,—aye, best fate of all! Oh, let it come, that I may never look upon to-morrow's light.

CHORUS

These things are in the future; present tasks claim our care: the ordering of the future rests where it should rest.

CREON

All my desires, at least, were summed in that prayer.

CHORUS

Pray thou no more; for mortals have no escape from destined woe.

CREON

antistrophe 4

Lead me away, I pray you; a rash, foolish man; who have slain thee, ah my son, unwittingly, and thee, too, my wife—unhappy that I am! I know not which way

I should bend my gaze, or where I should seek support; for all is amiss with that which is in my hands,—and yonder, again, a crushing fate hath leapt upon my head.

(*As* CREON *is being conducted into the palace, the* LEADER OF THE CHORUS *speaks the closing verses.*)

LEADER

Wisdom is the supreme part of happiness; and reverence towards the gods must be inviolate. Great words of prideful men are ever punished with great blows, and, in old age, teach the chastened to be wise.

ALCESTIS

by

EURIPIDES

Characters in the Play

Apollo
Death
Chorus of Old Men
A Woman Servant
Alcestis, *the Queen, wife of* Admetus
Admetus, *King of Thessaly*
Eumelus, *their child*
Heracles
Pheres, *father of* Admetus
A Man Servant

INTRODUCTION

THE *Alcestis* is the earliest of the plays of Euripides which we now possess. Presented in 438 B.C., it constituted the fourth play in a tetralogy which the poet had entered in competition for the tragic award of that year. Contrary to the usual practice which demanded that the fourth member of the tetralogy be a Satyr-play, Euripides has placed the *Alcestis* in this position, for which by its very character as a "tragi-comedy" it is peculiarly suited. Although on the whole the play is tragic in tone, it is rendered somewhat lighter, first by the part which the slightly drunken Heracles plays in the action, and finally by the happy resolution of the plot.

Possibly a folk-tale of wide currency was the original source for the legend upon which Euripides drew in writing his play. The version which he knew, and which had been interpreted by an earlier tragic poet, Phrynichus, contained the story of Admetus, king of Thessaly. Apollo, so the legend runs, had incurred the displeasure of his father Zeus, had been banished from Olympus, and condemned to serve under a mortal master for a stated period of time. He came to Thessaly and dwelt with Admetus, an exemplary king. As Apollo's term of service was drawing to a close, it became known that Admetus was doomed to an early death. Apollo, desiring to reward him for his kindness and apparent excellence of character, prevailed upon the Fates to spare him from his premature death. The Fates agreed, on condition that Admetus could procure a substitute who would be willing to die in his place. Admetus approached his father, mother, friends and kin, in his effort to find such a substitute, but all refused his request. Finally it was Alcestis, his devoted wife, who undertook the service. The play opens on the day when she is to die.

Euripides in the *Alcestis* has taken a human problem and stated it in such striking terms of character and situation that its point cannot be missed. Pheres in his way illuminates the question at issue by his uncompromising condemnation of his son, Admetus. Alcestis has a more important function since her character throws that of her husband into higher relief. She herself meets her end with fortitude, breaking just enough at the very last moment so that her portrayal becomes convincing. She manages, however, to be calm and matter-of-fact, in striking contrast to Admetus when in his egotism and sentimentality he begins to lose control of himself. As the play advances a sharper and sharper light is thrown upon him. In the last analysis, the actual means by which Alcestis is restored and the part which Heracles plays here, which in turn cannot be divorced from his conventional rôle as a brawling character in straight comedy, are irrelevant so far as the central significance of the play is concerned. This significance lies in the study of self-sacrifice and its implications. There is nothing but praise for Alcestis' act, yet the further problem is raised: what happens to the individual who accepts the benefits of a sacrifice made by another? Admetus at the end of the play has had the veil torn from his eyes, and he realizes at last the extent of his own vileness. With a sure hand Euripides has communicated his meaning.

ALCESTIS

(SCENE:—*At Pherae, outside the Palace of* ADMETUS, *King of Thessaly. The centre of the scene represents a portico with columns and a large double-door. To the left are the women's quarters, to the right the guest rooms. The centre doors of the Palace slowly open inwards, and Apollo comes out. In his left hand he carries a large unstrung golden bow. He moves slowly and majestically, turns, and raises his right hand in salutation to the Palace.*)

APOLLO

DWELLING of Admetus, wherein I, a God, deigned to accept the food of serfs!

The cause was Zeus. He struck Asclepius, my son, full in the breast with a bolt of thunder, and laid him dead. Then in wild rage I slew the Cyclopes who forge the fire of Zeus. To atone for this my Father forced me to labour as a hireling for a mortal man; and I came to this country, and tended oxen for my host. To this hour I have protected him and his. I, who am just, chanced on the son of Pheres, a just man, whom I have saved from Death by tricking the Fates. The Goddesses pledged me their faith Admetus should escape immediate death if, in exchange, another corpse were given to the Under-Gods.

One by one he tested all his friends, and even his father and the old mother who had brought him forth—and found none that would die for him and never more behold the light of day, save only his wife. Now, her spirit waiting to break loose, she droops upon his arm within the house; this is the day when she must die and render up her life.

But I must leave this Palace's dear roof, for fear pollution soil me in the house.

See! Death, Lord of All the Dead, now comes to lead her to the house of Hades! Most punctually he comes! How well he marked the day she had to die!

(*From the right comes* DEATH, *with a drawn sword in his hand. He moves stealthily towards the Palace; then sees* APOLLO *and halts abruptly. The two Deities confront each other.*)

DEATH

Ha! Phoebus! You! Before this Palace! Lawlessly would you grasp, abolish the rights of the Lower Gods! Did you not beguile the Fates and snatch Admetus from the grave? Does not that suffice? Now, once again, you have armed your hand with the bow, to guard the daughter of Pelias who must die in her husband's stead!

APOLLO

Fear not! I hold for right, and proffer you just words.

DEATH

If you hold for right, why then your bow?

APOLLO

My custom is ever to carry it.

DEATH

Yes! And you use it unjustly to aid this house!

APOLLO

I grieve for a friend's woe.

DEATH

So you would rob me of a second body?

APOLLO

Not by force I won the other.

DEATH

Why, then, is he in the world and not below the ground?

APOLLO

In his stead he gives his wife—whom you have come to take.

DEATH

And shall take—to the Underworld below the earth!

APOLLO

Take her, and go! I know not if I can persuade you . . .

DEATH

Not to kill her I must kill? I am appointed to that task.

APOLLO

No, no! But to delay death for those about to die.

DEATH

I hear your words and guess your wish!

APOLLO

May not Alcestis live to old age?

DEATH

No! I also prize my rights!

APOLLO

Yet at most you win one life.

DEATH

They who die young yield me a greater prize.

APOLLO

If she dies old, the burial will be richer.

DEATH

Phoebus, that argument favours the rich.

APOLLO

What! Are you witty unawares?

DEATH

The rich would gladly pay to die old

APOLLO

So you will not grant me this favour?

DEATH

Not I! You know my nature.

APOLLO

Yes! Hateful to men and a horror to the gods!

DEATH

You cannot always have more than your due.

APOLLO

Yet you shall change, most cruel though you are! For a man comes to the dwelling of Pheres, sent by Eurystheus to fetch a horse-drawn chariot from the harsh-wintered lands of Thrace; and he shall be a guest in the house of Admetus, and by force shall he tear this woman from you. Thus shall you gain no thanks from us, and yet you shall do this thing —and my hatred be upon you!

(APOLLO *goes out.* DEATH *gazes after him derisively.*)

DEATH

Talk all you will, you will get no more of me! The woman shall go down to the dwelling of Hades.

Now must I go to consecrate her for the sacrifice with this sword; for when once this blade has shorn the victim's hair, then he is sacred to the Lower Gods!

(DEATH *enters the Palace by the open main door. The* CHORUS *enters from the right. They are the Elders or Notables of the city, and therefore move slowly, leaning upon their staffs.*)

LEADER OF THE CHORUS (*chanting*)

Why is there no sound outside the Palace? Why is the dwelling of Admetus silent? Not a friend here to tell me if I must weep for a dead Queen or whether she lives and looks upon the light, Alcestis, the daughter of Pelias, whom among all women I hold the best wife to her spouse!

CHORUS (*singing*)

Is a sob to be heard?
Or the beating of hands
In the house?
The lament for her end?
Not one,
Not one of her servants
Stands at the gate!

Ah! to roll back the wave of our woe,
O Healer,
Appear!

FIRST SEMI-CHORUS

Were she dead
They had not been silent.

SECOND SEMI-CHORUS

She is but a dead body!

FIRST SEMI-CHORUS

Yet she has not departed the house.

SECOND SEMI-CHORUS

Ah! Let me not boast!
Why do you cling to hope?

FIRST SEMI-CHORUS

Would Admetus bury her solitary,
Make a grave alone for a wife so dear?

CHORUS

At the gate I see not
The lustral water from the spring
Which stands at the gates of the dead!
No shorn tress in the portal
Laid in lament for the dead!
The young women beat not their hands!

SECOND SEMI-CHORUS

Yet to-day is the day appointed. . . .

FIRST SEMI-CHORUS

Ah! What have you said?

SECOND SEMI-CHORUS

When she must descend under earth!

FIRST SEMI-CHORUS

You have pierced my soul!
You have pierced my mind!

SECOND SEMI-CHORUS

He that for long
Has been held in esteem
Must weep when the good are destroyed.

CHORUS

No!
There is no place on earth
To send forth a suppliant ship—
Not to Lycia,
Not to Ammon's waterless shrine—
To save her from death!
The dreadful doom is at hand.
To what laden altar of what God
Shall I turn my steps?

He alone—
If the light yet shone for his eye—
Asclepius, Phoebus's son,
Could have led her back
From the land of shadows,
From the gates of Hades.
For he raised the dead
Ere the Zeus-driven shaft
Slew him with thunder fire. . . .
But now
What hope can I hold for her life?

LEADER (*chanting*)

The King has fulfilled
Every rite;
The altars of all the Gods
Drip with the blood of slain beasts:
Nothing, nothing avails.

(*From the women's quarters in the left wing of the Palace comes a woman in tears. She is not a slave, but one of the personal attendants on the Queen.*)

But now from the house comes one of her women servants, all in tears. What now shall I learn? (*To the weeping Servant*) It is well to weep when our lords are in sorrow—but tell us, we would know, is she alive, is she dead?

SERVANT

You may say she is both alive and dead.

LEADER

How can the same man be dead and yet behold the light?

SERVANT

She gasps, she is on the verge of death.

LEADER

Ah, unhappy man! For such a husband what loss is such a wife!

SERVANT

The King will not know his loss until he suffers it.

LEADER

Then there is no hope that her life may be saved?

SERVANT

The fated day constrains her.

LEADER

Are all things befitting prepared for her?

SERVANT

The robes in which her lord will bury her are ready.

LEADER

Then let her know that she dies gloriously, the best of women beneath the sun by far!

SERVANT

How should she not be the best! Who shall deny it? What should the best among women be? How better might a woman hold faith to her lord than gladly to die for him? This the whole city knows, but you will marvel when you hear what she has done within the house. When she knew that the last of her days was come she bathed her white body in river water, she took garments and gems from her rooms of cedar wood, and clad herself nobly; then, standing before the hearth-shrine, she uttered this prayer:

'O Goddess, since now I must descend beneath the earth, for the last time I make supplication to you: and entreat you to protect my motherless children. Wed my son to a fair bride, and my daughter to a noble husband. Let not my children die untimely, as I their mother am destroyed, but grant that they live out happy lives with good fortune in their own land!'

To every altar in Admetus's house she went, hung them with garlands, offered prayer, cut myrtle boughs—unweeping, unlamenting; nor did the coming doom change the bright colour of her face.

Then to her marriage-room she went, flung herself down upon her bed, and wept, and said:

'O my marriage-bed, wherein I loosed my virgin girdle to him for whom I die! Farewell! I have no hatred for you. Only me you lose. Because I held my faith to you and to my lord—I must die. Another woman shall possess you, not more chaste indeed than I, more fortunate perhaps.'

She fell upon her knees and kissed it, and all the bed was damp with the tide of tears which flooded to her eyes. And when she was fulfilled of many tears, drooping she rose from her bed and made as if to go, and many times she turned to go and many times turned back, and flung herself once more upon the bed.

Her children clung to their mother's dress, and wept; and she clasped them in her arms and kissed them turn by turn, as a dying woman.

All the servants in the house wept with compassion for their Queen. But she held out her hand to each, and there was none so base to whom she did not speak, and who did not reply again.

Such is the misery in Admetus's house. If he had died, he would be nothing now; and, having escaped, he suffers an agony he will never forget.

LEADER

And does Admetus lament this woe—since he must be robbed of so noble a woman?

SERVANT

He weeps, and clasps in his arms his dear bedfellow, and cries to her not to abandon him, asking impossible things. For she pines, and is wasted by sickness. She falls away, a frail burden on his arm; and yet, though faintly she still breathes, still strives to look upon the sunlight. which she shall never see hereafter—since now for the last time she looks upon the orb and splendour of the sun!

I go, and shall announce that you are here; for all men are not so well-minded to their lords as loyally to stand near them in misfortunes, but you for long have been a friend to both my lords.

(*She goes back into the women's quarters of the Palace. The* CHORUS *now begins to sing.*)

FIRST SEMI-CHORUS

O Zeus,
What end to these woes?

What escape from the Fate
Which oppresses our lords?

SECOND SEMI-CHORUS

Will none come forth?
Must I shear my hair?
Must we wrap ourselves
In black mourning folds?

FIRST SEMI-CHORUS

It is certain, O friends, it is certain!
But still let us cry to the Gods;
Very great is the power of the Gods.

CHORUS

O King, O Healer,
Seek out appeasement
To Admetus's agony!
Grant this, Oh, grant it!
Once before did you find it;
Now once more
Be the Releaser from death.
The Restrainer of blood-drenched Hades!

SECOND SEMI-CHORUS

Alas!
O son of Pheres.
What ills shall you suffer
Being robbed of your spouse!

FIRST SEMI-CHORUS

At sight of such woes
Shall we cut our throats?
Shall we slip
A dangling noose round our necks?

CHORUS

See! See!
She comes
From the house with her lord!

Cry out, Oh, lament.
O land of Pherae,
For the best of women
Fades away in her doom
Under the earth,
To dark Hades!

(*From the central door of the Palace comes a splendid but tragical procession. Preceded by the royal guards,* ADMETUS *enters, supporting* ALCESTIS. *The two children, a boy and a girl, cling to their mother's dress. There is a train of attendants and waiting women, who bring a low throne for the fainting* ALCESTIS.)

LEADER OF THE CHORUS (*chanting*)

Never shall I say that we ought to rejoice in marriage, but rather weep; this have I seen from of old and now I look upon the fate of the King, who loses the best of wives, and henceforth until the end his life shall be intolerable.

ALCESTIS (*chanting*)

Sun, and you, light of day,
Vast whirlings of swift cloud!

ADMETUS

The sun looks upon you and me, both of us miserable, who have wrought nothing against the Gods to deserve death.

ALCESTIS (*chanting*)

O Earth, O roof-tree of my home,
Bridal-bed of my country, Iolcus!

ADMETUS

Rouse up, O unhappy one, and do not leave me! Call upon the mighty Gods to pity!

ALCESTIS

(*starting up and gazing wildly in terror, chanting*)

I see the two-oared boat,
I see the boat on the lake!
And Charon,
Ferryman of the Dead,
Calls to me, his hand on the oar:
'Why linger? Hasten! You delay me!'
Angrily he urges me.

ADMETUS

Alas! How bitter to me is that ferrying of which you speak! O my unhappy one, how we suffer!

ALCESTIS (*chanting*)

He drags me, he drags me away—
Do you not see?—
To the House of the Dead,
The Winged One
Glaring under dark brows,
Hades!—
What is it you do?
Set me free!—
What a path must I travel,
O most hapless of women!

ADMETUS

O piteous to those that love you, above all to me and to these children who sorrow in this common grief!

ALCESTIS (*chanting*)

Loose me, Oh, loose me now;
Lay me down;
All strength is gone from my feet.

(*She falls back in the throne.*)

Hades draws near!
Dark night falls on my eyes,

My children, my children,
Never more, Oh, never more
Shall your mother be yours!
O children, farewell,
Live happy in the light of day.

ADMETUS (*chanting*)

Alas! I hear this unhappy speech, and for me it is worse than all death. Ah! By the Gods, do not abandon me! Ah! By our children, whom you leave motherless, take heart! If you die, I become as nothing; in you we have our life and death; we revere your love.

ALCESTIS (*recovering herself*)

Admetus, you see the things I suffer; and now before I die I mean to tell you what I wish.

To show you honour and—at the cost of my life—that you may still behold the light, I die; and yet I might have lived and wedded any in Thessaly I chose, and dwelt with happiness in a royal home. But, torn from you, I would not live with fatherless children, nor have I hoarded up those gifts of youth in which I found delight. Yet he who begot you, she who brought you forth, abandoned you when it had been beautiful in them to die, beautiful to die with dignity to save their son! They had no child but you, no hope if you were dead that other children might be born to them. Thus I should have lived my life out, and you too, and you would not lament as now, made solitary from your wife, that you must rear our children motherless!

But these things are a God's doing and are thus.

Well! Do not forget this gift, for I shall ask—not a recompense, since nothing is more precious than life, but—only what is just, as you yourself will say, since if you have not lost your senses you must love these children no less than I. Let them be masters in my house; marry not again, and set a stepmother over them, a woman harsher than I, who in her jealousy will lift her hand against my children and yours. Ah! not this, let not this be, I entreat you! The new stepmother hates the first wife's children, the viper itself is not more cruel. The son indeed finds a strong rampart in his father—but you, my daughter, how shall you live your virgin life out in happiness? How will you fare with your father's new wife? Ah! Let her not cast evil report upon you and thus wreck your marriage in the height of your youth! You will have no mother, O my child, to give you in marriage, to comfort you in childbed when none is tenderer than a mother!

And I must die. Not to-morrow, nor to-morrow's morrow comes this misfortune on me, but even now I shall be named with those that are no more. Farewell! Live happy! You, my husband, may boast you had the best of wives; and you, my children, that you lost the best of mothers!

(*She falls back.*)

LEADER

Take heart! I do not hesitate to speak for him. This he will do, unless he has lost his senses.

ADMETUS

It shall be so, it shall be! Have no fear! And since I held you living as my wife, so, when dead, you only shall be called my wife, and in your place no bride of Thessaly shall salute me hers; no other woman is noble enough for that, no other indeed so beautiful of face. My children shall suffice me; I pray the Gods I may enjoy them, since you we have not enjoyed.

I shall wear mourning for you, O my wife, not for one year but all my days, abhorring the woman who bore me, hating my father—for they loved me in words, not deeds. But you—to save my life you give the dearest thing you have! Should I not weep then, losing such a wife as you?

I shall make an end of merry drinking parties, and of flower-crowned feasts and of the music which possessed my house. Never again shall I touch the lyre, never again shall

I raise my spirits to sing to the Libyan flute—for you have taken from me all my joy. Your image, carven by the skilled hands of artists, shall be laid in our marriage-bed; I shall clasp it, and my hands shall cling to it and I shall speak your name and so, not having you, shall think I have my dear wife in my arms—a cold delight, I know, but it will lighten the burden of my days. Often you will gladden me, appearing in my dreams; for sweet it is to look on those we love in dreams, however brief the night.

Ah! If I had the tongue and song of Orpheus so that I might charm Demeter's Daughter or her Lord, and snatch you back from Hades, I would go down to hell; and neither Pluto's dog nor Charon, Leader of the Dead, should hinder me until I had brought your life back to the light!

At least await me there whenever I shall die, and prepare the house where you will dwell with me. I shall lay a solemn charge upon these children to stretch me in the same cedar shroud with you, and lay my side against your side; for even in death let me not be separate from you, you who alone were faithful to me!

LEADER (*to* ADMETUS)

And I also will keep this sad mourning with you, as a friend with a friend; for she is worthy of it.

ALCESTIS

O my children, you have heard your father say that never will he set another wife over you and never thus insult me.

ADMETUS

Again I say it, and will perform it too!

ALCESTIS (*placing the children's hands in his*)

Then take these children from my hand.

ADMETUS

I take them—dear gifts from a dear hand.

ALCESTIS

Now you must be the mother for me to my children

ADMETUS

It must be so, since they are robbed of you.

ALCESTIS

O children, I should have lived my life out—and I go to the Underworld.

ADMETUS

Alas! What shall *I* do, left alone by you?

ALCESTIS

Time will console you. The dead are nothing.

ADMETUS

Take me with you, by the Gods! Take me to the Underworld!

ALCESTIS

It is enough that I should die—for you.

ADMETUS

O Fate, what a wife you steal from me!

ALCESTIS (*growing faint*)

My dimmed eyes are heavily oppressed.

ADMETUS

O woman, I am lost if you leave me!

ALCESTIS

You may say of me that I am nothing.

ADMETUS

Lift up your head! Do not abandon your children!

ALCESTIS

Ah! Indeed it is unwillingly—but, farewell, my children!

ADMETUS

Look at them, look. . . .

ALCESTIS

I am nothing.

ADMETUS

What are you doing? Are you leaving me?

ALCESTIS (*falling back dead*)

Farewell.

ADMETUS (*staring at the body*)

Wretch that I am, I am lost!

LEADER

She is gone! The wife of Admetus is no more.

EUMELUS (*chanting*)

Ah! Misery!
Mother has gone,
Gone to the Underworld!
She lives no more,
O my Father,
In the sunlight.
O sad one,
You have left us
To live motherless!

See, Oh, see her eyelids
And her drooping hands!
Mother, Mother,
Hearken to me, listen,
I beseech you!
I—I—Mother!—
I am calling to you,
Your little bird fallen upon your face!

ADMETUS

She hears not, she sees not. You and I are smitten by a dread calamity.

EUMELUS (*chanting*)

Father, I am a child,
And I am left
Like a lonely ship

By the mother I loved.
Oh! The cruel things I suffer!
And you, little sister,
Suffer with me.

O my Father,
Vain, vain was your wedding,
You did not walk with her
To the end of old age.
She died first;
And your death, O Mother,
Destroys our house.

LEADER

Admetus, you must endure this calamity. You are not the first and will not be the last to lose a noble wife. We all are doomed to die.

ADMETUS

I know it.

Not unawares did this woe swoop down on me; for long it has gnawed at me.

But, since I shall ordain the funeral rites for this dead body, you must be there, and meanwhile let a threnody re-echo to the implacable God of the Underworld. And all you men of Thessaly whom I rule—I order you to share the mourning for this woman with severed hair and black-robed garb. You who yoke the four-horsed chariot and the swift single horses, cut the mane from their necks with your steel.

Let there be no noise of flutes or lyre within the city until twelve moons are fulfilled. Never shall I bury another body so dear to me, never one that has loved me better. From me she deserves all honour, since she alone would die for me!

(*The body of* ALCESTIS *is carried solemnly into the Palace, followed by* ADMETUS, *with bowed head, holding one of his children by each hand. When all have entered, the great doors are quietly shut.*)

Chorus (*singing*)

strophe 1

O Daughter of Pelias,
Hail to you in the house of Hades,
In the sunless home where you shall dwell!
Let Hades, the dark-haired God,
Let the old man, Leader of the Dead,
Who sits at the oar and helm,
Know you:
Far, far off is the best of women
Borne beyond the flood of Acheron
In the two-oared boat!

antistrophe 1

Often shall the Muses' servants
Sing of you to the seven-toned
Lyre-shell of the mountain-tortoise,
And praise you with mourning songs at Sparta
When the circling season
Brings back the month Carneius
Under the nightlong upraised moon,
And in bright glad Athens.
Such a theme do you leave by your death
For the music of singers!

strophe 2

Ah! That I had the power
To bring you back to the light
From the dark halls of Hades,
And from the waves of Cocytus
With the oar of the river of hell!
Oh, you only,
O dearest of women,
You only dared give your life
For the life of your lord in Hades!
Light rest the earth above you,
O woman.

If your lord choose another bridal-bed
He shall be hateful to me
As to your own children.

antistrophe 2

When his mother
And the old father that begot him
Would not give their bodies to the earth
For their son's sake,
They dared not deliver him—O cruel!
Though their heads were grey.
But you,
In your lively youth,
Died for him, and are gone from the light!
Ah! might I be joined
With a wife so dear!
But in life such fortune is rare.
How happy were my days with her!

(*From the left* HERACLES *enters. He is black-bearded and of great physical strength; he wears a lion-skin over his shoulders and carries a large club.*)

HERACLES (*with a gesture of salutation*)

Friends, dwellers in the lands of Pherae, do I find Admetus in his home?

LEADER OF THE CHORUS

The son of Pheres is in his home, O Heracles. But, tell us, what brings you to the land of Thessaly and to the city of Pherae?

HERACLES

I have a task I must achieve for Eurystheus of Tiryns.

LEADER

Where do you go? To what quest are you yoked?

HERACLES

The quest of the four-horsed chariot of Diomedes, the Thracian.

LEADER

But how will you achieve it? Do you know this stranger?

HERACLES

No, I have never been to the land of the Bistones.

LEADER

You cannot obtain the horses without a struggle.

HERACLES

I cannot renounce my labours.

LEADER

You must kill to return, or you will remain there dead.

HERACLES

It will not be the first contest I have risked.

LEADER

And if you conquer the King will you gain anything?

HERACLES

I shall bring back his foals to the lord of Tiryns.

LEADER

It is not easy to thrust the bit into their jaws.

HERACLES

Only if they breathe fire from their nostrils!

LEADER

But they tear men with their swift jaws.

HERACLES

You speak of the food of wild mountain beasts, not of horses.

LEADER

You may see their mangers foul with blood.

HERACLES

Of what father does the breeder boast himself the son?

LEADER

Of Ares, the lord of the gold-rich shield of Thrace!

HERACLES

In this task once more you remind me of my fate, which is ever upon harsh steep ways, since I must join battle with the sons of Ares—first with Lycaon, then with Cycnus, and now in this third contest I am come to match myself with these steeds and their master!

LEADER

But see, the lord of this land, Admetus himself, comes from the house!

(*The central doors of the Palace have opened, and* ADMETUS *comes slowly on the Stage, preceded and followed by guards and attendants. The King has put off all symbols of royalty, and is dressed in black. His long hair is clipped close to his head.* ADMETUS *dissembles his grief throughout this scene, in obedience to the laws of hospitality, which were particularly reverenced in Thessaly.*)

ADMETUS

Hail! Son of Zeus and of the blood of Perseus!

HERACLES

And hail to you, Admetus, lord of the Thessalians!

ADMETUS

May it be so! I know your friendship well.

HERACLES

What means this shorn hair, this mourning robe?

ADMETUS

To-day I must bury a dead body.

HERACLES

May a God avert harm from your children!

ADMETUS

The children I have begotten are alive in the house.

HERACLES

Your father was ripe for death—if it is he has gone?

ADMETUS

He lives—and she who brought me forth, O Heracles.

HERACLES

Your wife—Alcestis—she is not dead?

ADMETUS (*evasively*)

Of her I might make a double answer.

HERACLES

Do you mean that she is dead or alive?

ADMETUS (*ambiguously*)

She is and is not—and for this I grieve.

HERACLES (*perplexed*)

I am no wiser—you speak obscurely.

ADMETUS

Did you not know the fate which must befall her?

HERACLES

I know she submitted to die for you.

ADMETUS

How then can she be alive, having consented to this?

HERACLES

Ah! Do not weep for your wife till that time comes.

ADMETUS

Those who are about to die are dead, and the dead are nothing.

HERACLES

Men hold that to be and not to be are different things.

ADMETUS

You hold for one, Heracles, and I for the other.

HERACLES

Whom, then, do you mourn? Which of your friends is dead?

ADMETUS
A woman. We spoke of her just now.

HERACLES (*mistaking his meaning*)
A stranger? Or one born of your kin?

ADMETUS
A stranger, but one related to this house.

HERACLES
But how, then, did she chance to die in your house?

ADMETUS
When her father died she was sheltered here.

HERACLES
Alas! Would I had not found you in this grief, Admetus!

ADMETUS
What plan are you weaving with those words?

HERACLES
I shall go to the hearth of another friend.

ADMETUS
Not so, O King! This wrong must not be.

HERACLES (*hesitating*)
The coming of a guest is troublesome to those who mourn.

ADMETUS (*decisively*)
The dead are dead. Enter my house.

HERACLES
But it is shameful to feast among weeping friends.

ADMETUS
We shall put you in the guest-rooms, which are far apart.

HERACLES
Let me go, and I will give you a thousand thanks.

ADMETUS

No, you shall not go to another man's hearth. (*To a servant*) Guide him, and open for him the guest-rooms apart from the house. (HERACLES *enters the Palace by the guests' door; when he has gone in,* ADMETUS *turns to the other servants*) Close the inner door of the courtyard; it is unseemly that guests rejoicing at table should hear lamentations, and be saddened.

(*The attendants go into the Palace.*)

LEADER

What are you about? When such a calamity has fallen upon you, Admetus, have you the heart to entertain a guest? Are you mad?

ADMETUS

And if I had driven away a guest who came to my house and city, would you have praised me more? No, indeed! My misfortune would have been no less, and I inhospitable. One more ill would have been added to those I have if my house were called inhospitable. I myself find him the best of hosts when I enter the thirsty land of Argos.

LEADER

But why did you hide from him the fate that has befallen, if the man came as a friend, as you say?

ADMETUS

Never would he have entered my house if he had guessed my misfortune.

To some, I know, I shall appear senseless in doing this, and they will blame me; but my roof knows not to reject or insult a guest.

(*He goes into the Palace, as the* CHORUS *begins its song.*)

CHORUS (*singing*)

strophe I

O house of a bountiful lord,
Ever open to many guests,

The God of Pytho,
Apollo of the beautiful lyre,
Deigned to dwell in you
And to live a shepherd in your lands!
On the slope of the hillsides
He played melodies of mating
On the Pipes of Pan to his herds.

antistrophe 1

And the dappled lynxes fed with them
In joy at your singing;
From the wooded vale of Orthrys
Came a yellow troop of lions;
To the sound of your lyre, O Phoebus,
Danced the dappled fawn
Moving on light feet
Beyond the high-crested pines,
Charmed by your sweet singing.

strophe 2

He dwells in a home most rich in flocks
By the lovely moving Boebian lake.
At the dark stabling-place of the Sun
He takes the sky of the Molossians
As a bourne to his ploughing of fields,
To the soils of his plains;
He bears sway
As far as the harbourless
Coast of the Aegean Sea,
As far as Pelion.

antistrophe 2

Even to-day he opened his house
And received a guest,
Though his eyelids were wet
With tears wept by the corpse
Of a dear bedfellow dead in the house.
For the noble spirit is proclaimed by honour;

All wisdom lies with the good.
I admire him:
And in my soul I know
The devout man shall have joy.

(*The funeral procession of* ALCESTIS *enters from the door of the women's quarters. The body, carried on a bier by men servants, is followed by* ADMETUS *and his two children. Behind them comes a train of attendants and servants carrying the funeral offerings. All are in mourning.* ADMETUS *addresses the* CHORUS.)

ADMETUS

O friendly presence of you men of Pherae! Now that the body is prepared, and the servants bear it on high to the tomb and the fire, do you, as is fitting, salute the dead as she goes forth on her last journey.

(PHERES, *the father of* ADMETUS, *enters, followed by attendants bearing funeral offerings.*)

LEADER OF THE CHORUS

But I see your father, tottering with an old man's walk, and his followers bearing in their hands for your wife garments as an offering to the dead.

PHERES

My son, I have come to share your sorrow, for the wife you have lost was indeed noble and virtuous—none can deny it. But these things must be endured, however intolerable they may be.

Take these garments, and let her descend under the earth. Her body must be honoured, for she died to save your life, my son; she has not made me childless, nor left me to be destroyed without you in my hapless old age; and she has given glorious fame to all women by daring so noble a deed! (*He lifts his hand in salutation to the body of* ALCESTIS.) O woman, who saved my son, who raised me up when I had fallen, hail! Be happy in the halls of Hades! I declare it—such marriages are profitable to mankind; otherwise, it is foolish to marry.

ADMETUS (*furiously*)

It was not my wish that you should come to this burial, and I deny that your presence is that of a friend! She shall never wear these garments of yours; she needs not your gifts for her burial. You should have grieved when I was about to die; but you stood aside, and now do you come to wail over a corpse when you, an old man, allowed a young woman to die?

Were you in very truth father of this body of mine? Did she, who claims to be and is called my mother, bring me forth? Or was I bred of a slave's seed and secretly brought to your wife's breast? You have proved what you are when it comes to the test, and therefore I am not your begotten son; or you surpass all men in cowardice, for, being at the very verge and end of life, you had neither courage nor will to die for your son. But this you left to a woman, a stranger, whom alone I hold as my father and my mother!

Yet it had been a beautiful deed in you to die for your son, and short indeed was the time left you to live. She and I would have lived out our lives, and I should not now be here alone lamenting my misery.

You enjoyed all that a happy man can enjoy—you passed the flower of your age as a king, and in me your son you had an heir to your dominion; you would not have died childless, leaving an orphaned house to be plundered by strangers. You will not say that you abandoned me to death because I dishonoured your old age, for above all I was respectful to you—and this is the gratitude I have from you and my mother!

Beget more sons, and quickly, to cherish your old age and wrap you in a shroud when dead and lay your body out in state! This hand of mine shall not inter you. I am dead to you. I look upon the light of day because another saved me—I say I am her son, and will cherish her old age!

Vainly do old men pray for death, regretting their age and the long span of life. If death draws near, none wants to die, and age is no more a burden to him.

LEADER

Admetus! The present misfortune is enough. Do not provoke your father's spirit.

(ADMETUS *turns angrily to depart, but* PHERES *prevents him.*)

PHERES

My son, do you think you are pursuing some hireling Lydian or Phrygian with your taunts? Do you know I am a Thessalian, a free man lawfully begotten by a Thessalian father? You are over-insolent, and you shall not leave thus, after wounding me with your boyish insults. I indeed begot you, and bred you up to be lord of this land, but I am not bound to die for you. It is not a law of our ancestors or of Hellas that the fathers should die for the children! You were born to live your own life, whether miserable or fortunate; and what is due to you from me you have. You rule over many men, and I shall leave you many wide fields even as I received them from my own father. How, then, have I wronged you? Of what have I robbed you? Do not die for me, any more than I die for you. You love to look upon the light of day—do you think your father hates it? I tell myself that we are a long time underground and that life is short, but sweet.

But you—you strove shamelessly not to die, and you are alive, you shirked your fate by killing her! And you call me a coward, you, the worst of cowards, surpassed by a woman who died for you, pretty boy? And now you insult those who should be dear to you, when they refuse to die for a coward like you!

Be silent! Learn that if you love your life, so do others. If you utter insults, you shall hear many, and true ones too!

LEADER

These insults and those that went before suffice. Old man, cease to revile your son.

ADMETUS (*to* PHERES)

Speak on! I shall refute you. If the truth wounds you when you hear it you should not have wronged me.

PHERES

I should have wronged you far more if I had died for you.

ADMETUS

It is the same then to die an old man and in the flower of life?

PHERES

We should live one life, not two.

ADMETUS

May you live longer than God!

PHERES

Do you curse your parents when they have done you no wrong?

ADMETUS

I see you are in love with long life.

PHERES

But you are not carrying her dead body in place of your own?

ADMETUS

It is the proof of your cowardice, O worst of men.

PHERES

You cannot say she died for me!

ADMETUS

Alas! May you one day need my help.

PHERES

Woo many women, so that more may die for you.

ADMETUS

To your shame be it—you who dared not die.

PHERES

Sweet is the daylight of the Gods, very sweet.

ADMETUS

Your spirit is mean, not a man's.

PHERES

Would you laugh to carry an old man's body to the grave?

ADMETUS

You will die infamous, whenever you die.

PHERES

It will matter little enough to me to hear ill of myself when I am dead!

ADMETUS

Alas! Alas! How full of impudence is old age!

PHERES

She was not impudent, but foolish.

ADMETUS

Go! Leave me to bury her body.

PHERES (*turning away*)

I go. You, her murderer, will bury her—but soon you must render an account to her relatives. Acastus is not a man if he fails to avenge his sister's blood on you!

(PHERES *goes out by the way he entered, followed by his attendants.* ADMETUS *gazes angrily after him.*)

ADMETUS

Go with a curse, you, and she who dwells with you! Grow old, as you ought, childless though you have a child. You shall never return to this house. And if I could renounce your hearth as my father's by heralds, I would do it. But we—since this sorrow must be endured—let us go, and set her body on the funeral pyre.

(*The Procession moves slowly along the stage, and is joined by the* CHORUS. *As they pass, the* LEADER *salutes the body of* ALCESTIS.)

LEADER (*chanting*)

Alas! Alas! You who suffer for your courage, O noblest and best of women, hail! May Hermes of the Dead, may Hades, greet you kindly. If there are rewards for the dead, may you share them as you sit by the bride of the Lord of the Dead!

(*The Procession has filed out. A servant in mourning hurries out from the guests' quarters.*)

SERVANT

Many guests from every land, I know, have come to the Palace of Admetus, and I have set food before them, but never one worse than this guest have I welcomed to the hearth.

First, though he saw our Lord was in mourning, he entered, and dared to pass through the gates. Then, knowing our misfortune, he did not soberly accept what was offered him, but if anything was not served to him he ordered us to bring it. In both hands he took a cup of ivy-wood, and drank the unmixed wine of the dark grape-mother, until he was encompassed and heated with the flame of wine. He crowned his head with myrtle sprays, howling discordant songs. There was he caring nothing for Admetus's misery, and we servants weeping for our Queen; and yet we hid our tear-laden eyes from the guest, for so Admetus had commanded.

And now in the Palace I must entertain this stranger, some villainous thief and brigand, while she, the Queen I mourn, has gone from the house unfollowed, unsaluted, she who was as a mother to me and all us servants, for she sheltered us from a myriad troubles by softening her husband's wrath.

Am I not right, then, to hate this stranger, who came to us in the midst of sorrow?

(HERACLES *comes from the Palace. He is drunkenly merry, with a myrtle wreath on his head, and a large cup and wine-skin in his hands. He staggers a little.*)

HERACLES

Hey, you! Why so solemn and anxious? A servant should not be sullen with guests, but greet them with a cheerful heart.

You see before you a man who is your lord's friend, and you greet him with a gloomy, frowning face, because of your zeal about a strange woman's death. Come here, and let me make you a little wiser!

(*With drunken gravity*) Know the nature of human life? Don't think you do. You couldn't. Listen to me. All mortals must die. Isn't one who knows if he'll be alive to-morrow morning. Who knows where Fortune will lead? Nobody can teach it. Nobody learn it by rules. So, rejoice in what you hear, and learn from me! Drink! Count each day as it comes as Life—and leave the rest to Fortune. Above all, honour the Love Goddess, sweetest of all the Gods to mortal men, a kindly goddess! Put all the rest aside. Trust in what I say, if you think I speak truth—as I believe. Get rid of this gloom, rise superior to Fortune. Crown yourself with flowers and drink with me, won't you? I know the regular clink of the wine-cup will row you from darkness and gloom to another haven. Mortals should think mortal thoughts. To all solemn and frowning men, life I say is not life, but a disaster.

SERVANT

We know all that, but what we endure here to-day is far indeed from gladness and laughter.

HERACLES

But the dead woman was a stranger. Lament not overmuch, then, for the Lords of this Palace are still alive.

SERVANT

How, alive? Do you not know the misery of this house?

HERACLES

Your lord did not lie to me?

SERVANT

He goes too far in hospitality!

HERACLES

But why should I suffer for a stranger's death?

SERVANT

It touches this house only too nearly.

HERACLES

Did he hide some misfortune from me?

SERVANT

Go in peace! The miseries of our lords concern us.

HERACLES

That speech does not imply mourning for a stranger!

SERVANT

No, or I should not have been disgusted to see you drinking.

HERACLES

Have I then been basely treated by my host?

SERVANT

You did not come to this house at a welcome hour. We are in mourning. You see my head is shaved and the black garments I wear.

HERACLES

But who, then, is dead? One of the children? The old father?

SERVANT

O stranger, Admetus no longer has a wife.

HERACLES

What! And yet I was received in this way?

SERVANT

He was ashamed to send you away from his house.

HERACLES

O hapless one! What a wife you have lost!

SERVANT

Not she alone, but all of us are lost.

HERACLES (*now completely sobered*)

I felt there was something when I saw his tear-wet eyes, his shaven head, his distracted look. But he persuaded me he was taking the body of a stranger to the grave. Against my will I entered these gates, and drank in the home of this generous man—and he in such grief! And shall I drink at such a time with garlands of flowers on my head? You, why did you not tell me that such misery had come upon this house? Where is he burying her? Where shall I find him?

SERVANT

Beside the straight road which leads to Larissa you will see a tomb of polished stone outside the walls.

(*Returns to the servants' quarters*)

HERACLES

O heart of me, much-enduring heart, O right arm, now indeed must you show what son was born to Zeus by Alcmena, the Tirynthian, daughter of Electryon! For I must save this dead woman, and bring back Alcestis to this house as a grace to Admetus.

I shall watch for Death, the black-robed Lord of the Dead, and I know I shall find him near the tomb, drinking the blood of the sacrifices. If I can leap upon him from an ambush, seize him, grasp him in my arms, no power in the world shall tear his bruised sides from me until he has yielded up this woman. If I miss my prey, if he does not come near the bleeding sacrifice, I will go down to Kore and her lord in their sunless dwelling, and I will make my entreaty to them, and I know they will give me Alcestis to bring back to the hands of the host who welcomed me, who did not repulse me from his house, though he was smitten with a heavy woe which most nobly he hid from me! Where would be a warmer welcome in Thessaly or in all the dwellings of Hellas?

He shall not say he was generous to an ingrate!

(HERACLES *goes out. Presently* ADMETUS *and his attendants, followed by the* CHORUS, *return from the burial of* ALCESTIS.)

ADMETUS (*chanting*)

Alas!

Hateful approach, hateful sight of my widowed house! Oh me! Oh me! Alas! Whither shall I go? Where rest? What can I say? What refrain from saying? Why can I not die? Indeed my mother bore me for a hapless fate. I envy the dead, I long to be with them, theirs are the dwellings where I would be. Without pleasure I look upon the light of day and set my feet upon the earth—so precious a hostage has Death taken from me to deliver unto Hades!

CHORUS

(*chanting responsively with* ADMETUS)

Go forward,
Enter your house.

ADMETUS

Alas!

CHORUS

Your grief deserves our tears.

ADMETUS

O Gods!

CHORUS

I know you have entered into sorrow.

ADMETUS

Woe! Woe!

CHORUS

Yet you bring no aid to the dead.

ADMETUS

Oh me! Oh me!

CHORUS

Heavy shall it be for you
Never to look again
On the face of the woman you love.

ADMETUS

You bring to my mind the grief that breaks my heart. What sorrow is worse for a man than the loss of such a woman? I would I had never married, never shared my house with her. I envy the wifeless and the childless. They live but one life—what is suffering to them? But the sickness of children, bridal-beds ravished by Death—dreadful! when we might be wifeless and childless to the end.

CHORUS

Chance, dreadful Chance, has stricken you.

ADMETUS

Alas!

CHORUS

But you set no limit to your grief.

ADMETUS

Ah! Gods!

CHORUS

A heavy burden to bear, and yet . . .

ADMETUS

Woe! Woe!

CHORUS

Courage! You are not the first to lose . . .

ADMETUS

Oh me! Oh me!

CHORUS

A wife.
Different men
Fate crushes with different blows.

ADMETUS

O long grief and mourning for those beloved under the earth!

Why did you stay me from casting myself into the hollow grave to lie down for ever in death by the best of women? Two lives, not one, had then been seized by Hades, most faithful one to the other; and together we should have crossed the lake of the Underworld.

CHORUS

A son most worthy of tears
Was lost to one of my house,
Yet, childless, he suffered with courage,
Though the white was thick in his hair
And his days were far-spent!

ADMETUS

O visage of my house! How shall I enter you? How shall I dwell in you, now that Fate has turned its face from me? How great is the change! Once, of old, I entered my house with marriage-songs and the torches of Pelion, holding a loved woman by the hand, followed by a merry crowd shouting good wishes to her who is dead and to me, because we had joined our lives, being both noble and born of noble lines. To-day, in place of marriage-songs are lamentations; instead of white garments I am clad in mourning, to return to my house and a solitary bed.

CHORUS

Grief has fallen upon you
In the midst of a happy life
Untouched by misfortune.
But your life and your spirit are safe.
She is dead,
She has left your love.
Is this so new?
Ere now many men
Death has severed from wives.

ADMETUS (*speaking*)

O friends, whatsoever may be thought by others, to me it seems that my wife's fate is happier than mine. Now, no pain ever shall touch her again; she has reached the noble end of all her sufferings. But I, I who should have died, I have escaped my fate, only to drag out a wretched life. Only now do I perceive it.

How shall I summon strength to enter this house? Whom shall I greet? Who will greet me in joy at my coming? Whither shall I turn my steps? I shall be driven forth by solitude when I see my bed widowed of my wife, empty the chairs on which she sat, a dusty floor beneath my roof, my children falling at my knees and calling for their mother, and the servants lamenting for the noble lady lost from the house!

Such will be my life within the house. Without, I shall be driven from marriage-feasts and gatherings of the women of Thessaly. I shall not endure to look upon my wife's friends. Those who hate me will say: 'See how he lives in shame, the man who dared not die, the coward who gave his wife to Hades in his stead! Is that a man? He hates his parents, yet he himself refused to die!'

This evil fame I have added to my other sorrows. O my friends, what then avails it that I live, if I must live in misery and shame?

(*He covers his head with his robe, and crouches in abject misery on the steps of his Palace.*)

CHORUS (*singing*)

strophe 1

I have lived with the Muses
And on lofty heights:
Many doctrines have I learned;
But Fate is above us all.
Nothing avails against Fate—
Neither the Thracian tablets
Marked with Orphic symbols,
Nor the herbs given by Phoebus
To the children of Asclepius
To heal men of their sickness.

antistrophe 1

None can come near to her altars,
None worship her statues;
She regards not our sacrifice.
O sacred goddess,
Bear no more hardly upon me
Than in days overpast!
With a gesture Zeus judges,
But the sentence is yours.
Hard iron yields to your strength;
Your fierce will knows not gentleness.

strophe 2

And the Goddess has bound you
Ineluctably in the gyves of her hands.
Yield.
Can your tears give life to the dead?
For the sons of the Gods
Swoon in the shadow of Death.

Dear was she in our midst,
Dear still among the dead,
For the noblest of women was she
Who lay in your bed.

antistrophe 2

Ah!
Let the grave of your spouse
Be no more counted as a tomb,
But revered as the Gods,
And greeted by all who pass by!
The wanderer shall turn from his path,
Saying: 'She died for her lord;
A blessed spirit she is now.
Hail, O sacred lady, be our friend!'
Thus shall men speak of her.

(ADMETUS *is still crouched on the Palace steps, when* HERACLES *enters from the side, leading a veiled woman.*)

LEADER OF THE CHORUS

But see! The son of Alcmena, as I think, comes to your house.

(ADMETUS *uncovers his head, and faces the new-comer.*)

HERACLES

Admetus, a man should speak freely to his friends, and not keep reproaches silent in his heart. Since I was near you in your misfortune, I should have wished to show myself your friend. But you did not tell me the dead body was your wife's, and you took me into your house as if you were in mourning only for a stranger. And I put a garland of flowers upon my head, and poured wine-offerings to the Gods, when your house was filled with lamentation. I blame you, yes, I blame you for this—but I will not upbraid you in your misfortune.

Why I turned back and am here, I shall tell you. Take

and keep this woman for me until I have slain the King of the Bistones and return here with the horses of Thrace. If ill happens to me—may I return safely!—I give her to you to serve in your house.

With much striving I won her to my hands. On my way I found public games, worthy of athletes, and I have brought back this woman whom I won as the prize of victory. The winners of the easy tests had horses; heads of cattle were given to those who won in boxing and wrestling. Then came a woman as a prize. Since I was present, it would have been shameful for me to miss this glorious gain. Therefore, as I said, you must take care of this woman, whom I bring to you, not as one stolen but as the prize of my efforts. Perhaps in time you will approve of what I do.

ADMETUS

Not from disdain, nor to treat you as a foe, did I conceal my wife's fate from you. But if you had turned aside to another man's hearth, one more grief had been added to my sorrow. It was enough that I should weep my woe.

This woman—O King, I beg it may be thus—enjoin some other Thessalian, one who is not in sorrow, to guard her. In Pherae there are many to welcome you. Do not remind me of my grief. Seeing her in my house, I could not restrain my tears. Add not a further anguish to my pain, for what I suffer is too great. And then—where could I harbour a young woman in my house? For she is young—I see by her clothes and jewels. Could she live with the men under my roof? How, then, could she remain chaste, if she moved to and fro among the young men? Heracles, it is not easy to restrain the young. . . . I am thinking of your interests. . . . Must I take her to my dead wife's room? How could I endure her to enter that bed? I fear a double reproach—from my people, who would accuse me of betraying my saviour to slip into another woman's bed, and from my dead wife, who deserves my respect, for which I must take care.

O woman, whosoever you may be, you have the form of Alcestis, and your body is like hers.

Ah! By all the Gods, take her from my sight! Do not insult a broken man. When I look upon her—she seems my wife—my heart is torn asunder—tears flow from my eyes. Miserable creature that I am, now I taste the bitterness of my sorrow.

LEADER

I do not praise this meeting; but, whatever happens, we must accept the gifts of the Gods.

HERACLES

Oh, that I might bring your wife back into the light of day from the dwelling of the Under-Gods, as a gift of grace to you!

ADMETUS

I know you would wish this—but to what end? The dead cannot return to the light of day.

HERACLES

Do not exaggerate, but bear this with decorum.

ADMETUS

Easier to advise than bear the test.

HERACLES

How will it aid you to lament for ever?

ADMETUS

I know—but my love whirls me away.

HERACLES

Love for the dead leads us to tears.

ADMETUS

I am overwhelmed beyond words.

HERACLES

You have lost a good wife—who denies it?

ADMETUS

So that for me there is no more pleasure in life.

HERACLES

Time will heal this open wound.

ADMETUS

You might say Time, if Time were death!

HERACLES

Another woman, a new marriage, shall console you.

ADMETUS

Oh, hush! What have you said? A thing unbelievable!

HERACLES

What! You will not marry? Your bed will remain widowed?

ADMETUS

No other woman shall ever lie at my side.

HERACLES

Do you think that avails the dead?

ADMETUS

Wherever she may be, I must do her honour.

HERACLES

I praise you—but men will call you mad.

ADMETUS

Yet never more shall I be called a bridegroom.

HERACLES

I praise your faithful love to your wife.

ADMETUS

May I die if I betray her even when dead!

HERACLES (*offering him the veiled woman's hand*)

Receive her then into your noble house.

ADMETUS
No, by Zeus who begot you, no!

HERACLES
Yet you will do wrong if you do not take her.

ADMETUS
If I do it, remorse will tear my heart.

HERACLES
Yield—perhaps it will be a good thing for you.

ADMETUS
Ah! If only you had not won her in the contest!

HERACLES
But I conquered—and you conquered with me.

ADMETUS
It is true—but let the woman go hence.

HERACLES
She shall go, if she must. But first—ought she to go?

ADMETUS
She must—unless it would anger you.

HERACLES
There is good reason for my zeal.

ADMETUS
You have conquered then—but not for my pleasure.

HERACLES
One day you will praise me for it—be persuaded.

ADMETUS (*to his attendants*)
Lead her in, since she must be received in this house

HERACLES
No, I cannot leave such a woman to servants.

ADMETUS

Then lead her in yourself, if you wish.

HERACLES

I must leave her in your hands.

ADMETUS

I must not touch her—let her go into the house.

HERACLES

I trust only in your right hand.

ADMETUS

O King, you force me to this against my will.

HERACLES

Put forth your hand and take this woman.

ADMETUS (*turning aside his head*)

It is held out.

HERACLES

As if you were cutting off a Gorgon's head! Do you hold her?

ADMETUS

Yes.

HERACLES

Then keep her. You shall not deny that the son of Zeus is a grateful guest. (*Takes off the veil and shows* ALCESTIS.) Look at her, and see if she is not like your wife. And may joy put an end to all your sorrow!

ADMETUS (*drops her hand and starts back*)

O Gods! What am I to say? Unhoped-for wonder! Do I really look upon my wife? Or am I snared in the mockery of a God?

HERACLES

No, you look upon your wife indeed.

ADMETUS

Beware! May it not be some phantom from the Underworld?

HERACLES

Do not think your guest a sorcerer.

ADMETUS

But do I indeed look upon the wife I buried?

HERACLES

Yes—but I do not wonder at your mistrust.

ADMETUS

Can I touch, speak to her, as my living wife?

HERACLES

Speak to her—you have all you desired.

ADMETUS (*taking* ALCESTIS *in his arms*)

O face and body of the dearest of women! I have you once more, when I thought I should never see you again!

HERACLES

You have her—may the envy of the Gods be averted from you!

ADMETUS

O noble son of greatest Zeus, fortune be yours, and may your Father guard you! But how did you bring her back from the Underworld to the light of day?

HERACLES

By fighting with the spirit who was her master.

ADMETUS

Then did you contend with Death?

HERACLES

I hid by the tomb and leaped upon him.

ADMETUS

But why is she speechless?

HERACLES

You may not hear her voice until she is purified from her consecration to the Lower Gods, and until the third dawn has risen. Lead her in.

And you, Admetus, show as ever a good man's welcome to your guests.

Farewell! I go to fulfil the task set me by the King, the son of Sthenelus.

ADMETUS

Stay with us, and share our hearth.

HERACLES

That may be hereafter, but now I must be gone in haste.

(HERACLES *departs.*)

ADMETUS (*gazing after him*)

Good fortune to you, and come back here! (*To the* CHORUS) In all the city and in the four quarters of Thessaly let there be choruses to rejoice at this good fortune, and let the altars smoke with the flesh of oxen in sacrifice! To-day we have changed the past for a better life. I am happy.

(*He leads* ALCESTIS *into the Palace.*)

CHORUS (*singing*)

Spirits have many shapes,
Many strange things are performed by the Gods.
The expected does not always happen,
And God makes a way for the unexpected.
So ends this action.

MEDEA

by

EURIPIDES

Characters in the Play

Nurse of Medea
Attendant on her Children
Medea
Chorus of Corinthian Women
Creon, *King of Corinth*
Jason
Aegeus, *King of Athens*
Messenger
The two Sons of Jason and Medea

INTRODUCTION

In the *Medea*, produced in 431 B.C., seven years after the *Alcestis*, Euripides has turned to the familiar and romantic myth of the Argonauts. Jason had been ordered by his wicked uncle, Pelias, to procure the golden fleece owned and jealously guarded by Aeetes, king of far-off Colchis. He therefore gathered a band of Greek heroes and demi-gods, built the Argo, the first ship of Greece, and sailed on the expedition which was intended to prove fatal to its commander. Jason gained possession of the fleece, but only through the assistance of the Colchian princess, Medea, who had fallen deeply in love with him. She was endowed with the supernatural powers of a sorceress, which she did not scruple to use on Jason's behalf, and she left her native land with Jason, after having deceived her father and slain her brother that Jason might succeed in his quest. Back in the court of Pelias, the usurping king of Iolcos, where Jason held the rightful claim to the throne, Medea acted again to abet her lord. On this occasion, she contrived the death of Pelias, but Jason was unable to place himself in power. The ill-starred pair, with the two sons who had been born to them, fled in exile to Corinth. It is here that the action of our play commences, and the situation at the very opening foreshadows in intensity the remainder of the play, for Jason has deserted Medea, and has wedded the daughter of Creon, the king of Corinth.

Euripides in the course of the tragedy submits his two leading characters to a penetrating psychological analysis. Jason is portrayed as a supreme egotist, who resents being under such great obligation as he is to Medea, yet who has not been unwilling to accept the benefits which have accrued to him through Medea's crimes. There may be a certain slight degree of genuineness in his defense, that he is marrying the Corinthian princess in order to consolidate not only his own position in their new home, but also that of Medea and their children. In contrast, Medea has but a single guiding passion, and that is her love for Jason. She committed every crime for Jason, because she loved him and desired to bind him closer to herself. And now that he has abandoned her, all the intensity of her love has changed violently into an intensity of hate and a desire for revenge. The means she employs are horrifying. By killing Creon and his daughter, through her gifts of the poisoned robe and chaplet, and by slaying her own children, Medea renders Jason abjectly desolate. The depth of her passion for vengeance is intensified when pathetically overwhelmed by love for her children she momentarily weakens in her resolve to kill them. Her final act therefore is presented with redoubled force.

Critics have been troubled by the dramatic function of the scene in which Aegeus appears and offers an ultimate refuge for Medea. The scene may be more integral to the play than these critics have suspected because in it the childlessness of Aegeus seems to suggest to Medea that her revenge take the form of killing her children, in order that Jason may suffer in like fashion. The playwright has also been censured because he permits Medea to escape in the dragon-chariot at the end. Perhaps an answer may lie in the fact that, horrible though Medea's acts are, still she commands a modicum of sympathy, for Jason's injustice to her has driven her to these extremes, and by allowing her to escape the poet partially justifies her deeds. Furthermore, Euripides may have been influenced by the existence of a cult of Medea's children at Corinth, and may have resolved his play so that it would accord with the traditions of the cult. Whatever may be the explanation of these supposed flaws, the play itself does display almost unrivalled psychological and emotional power. Ultimately, the abortive alliance between Jason and Medea has destroyed them both.

MEDEA

(SCENE:—*Before* MEDEA'S *house in Corinth, near the palace of* CREON. *The* NURSE *enters from the house.*)

NURSE

AH! WOULD to Heaven the good ship Argo ne'er had sped its course to the Colchian land through the misty blue Symplegades, nor ever in the glens of Pelion the pine been felled to furnish with oars the chieftain's hands, who went to fetch the golden fleece for Pelias; for then would my own mistress Medea never have sailed to the turrets of Iolcos, her soul with love for Jason smitten, nor would she have beguiled the daughters of Pelias to slay their father and come to live here in the land of Corinth with her husband and children, where her exile found favour with the citizens to whose land she had come, and in all things of her own accord was she at one with Jason, the greatest safeguard this when wife and husband do agree; but now their love is all turned to hate, and tenderest ties are weak. For Jason hath betrayed his own children and my mistress dear for the love of a royal bride, for he hath wedded the daughter of Creon, lord of this land. While Medea, his hapless wife, thus scorned, appeals to the oaths he swore, recalls the strong pledge his right hand gave, and bids heaven be witness what requital she is finding from Jason. And here she lies fasting, yielding her body to her grief, wasting away in tears ever since she learnt that she was wronged by her husband, never lifting her eye nor raising her face from off the ground; and she lends as deaf an ear to her friend's warning as if she were a rock or ocean billow, save when she turns her snow-white neck aside and softly to herself bemoans her father dear, her country and her home, which she gave up to come hither with the man who now holds her in dishonour. She, poor lady, hath by sad experience learnt how good a thing it is never to quit one's native land. And she hates her children now and feels no joy at seeing them; I fear she may contrive some untoward scheme; for her mood is dangerous nor will she brook her cruel treatment; full well I know her, and I much do dread that she will plunge the keen sword through their hearts, stealing without a word into the chamber where their marriage couch is spread, or else that she will slay the prince and bridegroom too, and so find some calamity still more grievous than the present; for dreadful is her wrath; verily the man that doth incur her hate will have no easy task to raise o'er her a song of triumph. Lo! where her sons come hither from their childish sports; little they reck of their mother's woes, for the soul of the young is no friend to sorrow.

(*The* ATTENDANT *leads in* MEDEA'S *children.*)

ATTENDANT

Why dost thou, so long my lady's own handmaid, stand here at the gate alone, loudly lamenting to thyself the piteous tale? how comes it that Medea will have thee leave her to herself?

NURSE

Old man, attendant on the sons of Jason, our masters' fortunes when they go awry make good slaves grieve and touch their hearts. Oh! I have come to such a pitch of grief that there stole a yearning wish upon me to come forth hither and proclaim to heaven and earth my mistress's hard fate.

ATTENDANT

What! has not the poor lady ceased yet from her lamentation?

NURSE

Would I were as thou art! the mischief is but now beginning; it has not reached its climax yet.

ATTENDANT

O foolish one, if I may call my mistress such a name; how little she recks of evils yet more recent!

NURSE

What mean'st, old man? grudge not to tell me.

ATTENDANT

'Tis naught; I do repent me even of the words I have spoken.

NURSE

Nay, by thy beard I conjure thee, hide it not from thy fellow-slave; I will be silent, if need be, on that text.

ATTENDANT

I heard one say, pretending not to listen as I approached the place where our greybeards sit playing draughts near Pirene's sacred spring, that Creon, the ruler of this land, is bent on driving these children and their mother from the boundaries of Corinth; but I know not whether the news is to be relied upon, and would fain it were not.

NURSE

What! will Jason brook such treatment of his sons, even though he be at variance with their mother?

ATTENDANT

Old ties give way to new; he bears no longer any love to this family.

NURSE

Undone, it seems, are we, if to old woes fresh ones we add, ere we have drained the former to the dregs.

ATTENDANT

Hold thou thy peace, say not a word of this; 'tis no time for our mistress to learn hereof.

NURSE

O children, do ye hear how your father feels towards you? Perdition catch him, but no! he is my master still; yet is he proved a very traitor to his nearest and dearest.

ATTENDANT

And who 'mongst men is not? Art learning only now, that every single man cares for himself more than for his neighbour, some from honest motives, others for mere gain's sake? seeing that to indulge his passion their father has ceased to love these children.

NURSE

Go, children, within the house; all will be well. Do thou keep them as far away as may be, and bring them not near their mother in her evil hour. For ere this have I seen her eyeing them savagely, as though she were minded to do them some hurt, and well I know she will not cease from her fury till she have pounced on some victim. At least may she turn her hand against her foes, and not against her friends.

MEDEA (*chanting within*)

Ah, me! a wretched suffering woman I! O would that I could die!

NURSE (*chanting*)

'Tis as I said, my dear children; wild fancies stir your mother's heart, wild fury goads her on. Into the house without delay, come not near her eye, approach her not, beware her savage mood, the fell tempest of her reckless heart. In, in with what speed ye may. For 'tis plain she will soon redouble her fury; that cry is but the herald of the gathering storm-cloud whose lightning soon will flash; what will her proud restless soul, in the anguish of despair, be guilty of?

(*The* ATTENDANT *takes the children into the house.*)

MEDEA (*chanting within*)

Ah, me! the agony I have suffered, deep enough to call for these laments! Curse you and your father too, ye children damned, sons of a doomed mother! Ruin seize the whole family!

NURSE (*chanting*)

Ah me! ah me! the pity of it! Why, pray, do thy children share their father's crime? Why hatest thou them? Woe is you, poor children, how do I grieve for you lest ye suffer some outrage! Strange are the tempers of princes, and maybe because they seldom have to obey, and mostly lord it over others, change they their moods with difficulty. 'Tis better then to have been trained to live on equal terms. Be it mine to reach old age, not in proud pomp, but in security! Moderation wins the day first as a better word for men to use, and likewise it is far the best course for them to pursue; but greatness that doth o'erreach itself, brings no blessing to mortal men; but pays a penalty of greater ruin whenever fortune is wroth with a family.

(*The* CHORUS *enters. The following lines between the* NURSE, CHORUS, *and* MEDEA *are sung.*)

CHORUS

I heard the voice, uplifted loud, of our poor Colchian lady, nor yet is she quiet; speak, aged dame, for as I stood by the house with double gates I heard a voice of weeping from within, and I do grieve, lady, for the sorrows of this house, for it hath won my love.

NURSE

'Tis a house no more; all that is passed away long since; a royal bride keeps Jason at her side, while our mistress pines away in her bower, finding no comfort for her soul in aught her friends can say.

MEDEA (*within*)

Oh, oh! Would that Heaven's levin bolt would cleave this head in twain! What gain is life to me? Woe, woe is me! O, to die and win release, quitting this loathed existence!

CHORUS

Didst hear, O Zeus, thou earth, and thou, O light, the piteous note of woe the hapless wife is uttering? How shall a yearning for that insatiate resting-place ever hasten for thee, poor reckless one, the end that death alone can bring? Never pray for that. And if thy lord prefers a fresh love, be not angered with him for that; Zeus will judge 'twixt thee and him herein. Then mourn not for thy husband's loss too much, nor waste thyself away.

MEDEA (*within*)

Great Themis, and husband of Themis, behold what I am suffering now, though I did bind that accursed one, my husband, by strong oaths to me! O, to see him and his bride some day brought to utter destruction, they and their house with them, for that they presume to wrong me thus unprovoked. O my father, my country, that I have left to my shame, after slaying my own brother.

NURSE

Do ye hear her words, how loudly she adjures Themis, oft invoked, and Zeus, whom men regard as keeper of their oaths? On no mere trifle surely will our mistress spend her rage.

CHORUS

Would that she would come forth for us to see, and listen to the words of counsel we might give, if haply she might lay aside the fierce fury of her wrath, and her temper stern. Never be my zeal at any rate denied my friends! But go thou and bring her hither outside the house, and tell her this our friendly thought; haste thee ere she do some mischief to those inside the house, for this sorrow of hers is mounting high.

NURSE

This will I do; but I doubt whether I shall persuade my mistress; still willingly will I undertake this trouble for you; albeit, she glares upon her servants with the look of a lioness with cubs, whenso anyone draws nigh to speak to her. Wert thou to call the men of old time rude uncultured boors thou wouldst not err, seeing that they devised their hymns for festive occasions, for banquets, and to grace the board, a pleasure to catch the ear, shed o'er our life, but no man hath found a way to allay hated grief by music and the minstrel's varied strain, whence arise slaughters and fell strokes of fate to o'erthrow the homes of men. And yet this were surely a gain, to heal men's wounds by music's spell, but why tune they their idle song where rich banquets are spread? For of itself doth the rich banquet, set before them, afford to men delight.

CHORUS

I heard a bitter cry of lamentation! loudly, bitterly she calls on the traitor of her marriage bed, her perfidious spouse; by grievous wrongs oppressed she invokes Themis, bride of Zeus, witness of oaths, who brought her unto Hellas, the land that fronts the strand of Asia, o'er the sea by night through ocean's boundless gate.

(*As the* CHORUS *finishes its song,* MEDEA *enters from the house.*)

MEDEA

From the house I have come forth, Corinthian ladies, for fear lest you be blaming me; for well I know that amongst men many by showing pride have gotten them an ill name and a reputation for indifference, both those who shun men's gaze and those who move amid the stranger crowd, and likewise they who choose a quiet walk in life. For there is no just discernment in the eyes of men, for they, or ever they have surely learnt their neighbour's heart, loathe him at first sight, though never wronged by him; and so a stranger most of all should adopt a city's views; nor do I commend that citizen, who, in the stubbornness of his heart, from churlishness resents the city's will.

But on me hath fallen this unforeseen disaster, and sapped my life; ruined I am, and long to resign the boon of existence, kind friends, and die. For he who was all the world to me, as well thou knowest, hath turned out the worst of men, my own husband. Of all things that have life and sense we women are the most hapless creatures; first must we buy a husband at a great price, and o'er ourselves a tyrant set which is an evil worse than the first; and herein lies the most important issue, whether our choice be good or bad. For divorce is not honourable to women, nor can we disown our lords. Next must the wife, coming as she does to ways and customs new, since she hath not learnt the lesson in her home, have a diviner's eye to see how best to treat the partner of her life. If haply we perform these tasks with thoroughness and tact, and the husband live with us, without resenting the yoke, our life is a happy one; if not, 'twere best to die. But when a man is vexed with what he finds indoors, he goeth forth and rids his soul of its disgust, betaking him to some friend or comrade of like age; whilst we must needs regard his single self.

And yet they say we live secure at home, while they are at the wars, with their sorry reasoning, for I would gladly take my stand in battle array three times o'er, than once give birth. But enough! this language suits not thee as it does me; thou hast a city here, a father's house, some joy in life, and friends to share thy thoughts, but I am destitute, without a city, and therefore scorned by my husband, a captive I from a foreign shore, with no mother, brother, or kinsman in whom to find a new haven of refuge from this calamity. Wherefore this one boon and only this I wish to win from thee,—thy silence, if haply I can some way or means devise to avenge me on my husband for this cruel treatment, and on the man who gave to him his daughter, and on her who is his wife. For though a woman be timorous enough in all else, and as regards courage, a coward at the mere sight of steel, yet in the moment she finds her honour wronged, no heart is filled with deadlier thoughts than hers.

LEADER OF THE CHORUS

This will I do; for thou wilt be taking a just vengeance on thy husband, Medea. That thou shouldst mourn thy lot surprises me not. But lo! I see Creon, king of this land coming hither, to announce some new resolve.

(CREON *enters, with his retinue.*)

CREON

Hark thee, Medea, I bid thee take those sullen looks and angry thoughts against thy husband forth from this land in exile, and with thee take both thy children and that without delay, for I am judge in this sentence, and I will not return unto my house till I banish thee beyond the borders of the land.

MEDEA

Ah, me! now is utter destruction come upon me, unhappy that I am! For my enemies are bearing down on me full sail, nor have I any landing-place to come at in my trouble. Yet for all my wretched plight I will ask thee, Creon, wherefore dost thou drive me from the land?

CREON

I fear thee,—no longer need I veil my dread 'neath words,—lest thou devise against my child some cureless ill. Many things contribute to this fear of mine; thou art a witch by nature, expert in countless sorceries, and thou art chafing for the loss of thy husband's affection. I hear, too, so they tell me, that thou dost threaten the father of the bride, her husband, and herself with some mischief; wherefore I will take precautions ere our troubles come. For 'tis better for me to incur thy hatred now, lady, than to soften my heart and bitterly repent it hereafter.

MEDEA

Alas! this is not now the first time, but oft before, O Creon, hath my reputation injured me and caused sore mischief. Wherefore whoso is wise in his generation ought never to have his children taught to be too clever; for besides the reputation they get for idleness, they purchase bitter odium from the citizens. For if thou shouldst import new learning amongst dullards, thou wilt be thought a useless trifler, void of knowledge; while if thy fame in the city o'ertops that of the pretenders to cunning knowledge, thou wilt win their dislike. I too myself share in this ill-luck. Some think me clever and hate me, others say I am too reserved, and some the very reverse; others find me hard to please and not so very clever after all. Be that as it may, thou dost fear me lest I bring on thee something to mar thy harmony. Fear me not, Creon, my position scarce is such that I should seek to quarrel with princes. Why should I, for how hast thou injured me? Thou hast betrothed thy daughter where thy fancy prompted thee. No, 'tis my husband I hate, though I doubt not thou hast acted wisely herein. And now I grudge not thy prosperity; betroth thy child, good luck to thee, but let me abide in this land, for though I have been wronged I will be still and yield to my superiors.

CREON

Thy words are soft to hear, but much I dread lest thou art devising some mischief in thy heart, and less than ever do I trust thee now; for a cunning woman, and man likewise, is easier to guard against when quick-tempered than when taciturn. Nay, begone at once! speak me no speeches, for this is decreed, nor hast thou any art whereby thou shalt abide amongst us, since thou hatest me.

MEDEA

O, say not so! by thy knees and by thy daughter newly-wed, I do implore!

CREON

Thou wastest words; thou wilt never persuade me.

MEDEA

What, wilt thou banish me, and to my prayers no pity yield?

CREON

I will, for I love not thee above my own family.

MEDEA

O my country! what fond memories I have of thee in this hour!

CREON

Yea, for I myself love my city best of all things save my children.

MEDEA

Ah me! ah me! to mortal man how dread a scourge is love!

CREON

That, I deem, is according to the turn our fortunes take.

MEDEA

O Zeus! let not the author of these my troubles escape thee.

CREON

Begone, thou silly woman, and free me from my toil.

MEDEA

The toil is mine, no lack of it.

CREON

Soon wilt thou be thrust out forcibly by the hand of servants.

MEDEA

Not that, not that, I do entreat thee, Creon!

CREON

Thou wilt cause disturbance yet, it seems.

MEDEA

I will begone; I ask thee not this boon to grant.

CREON

Why then this violence? why dost thou not depart?

MEDEA

Suffer me to abide this single day and devise some plan for the manner of my exile, and means of living for my children, since their father cares not to provide his babes therewith. Then pity them; thou too hast children of thine own; thou needs must have a kindly heart. For my own lot I care naught, though I an exile am, but for those babes I weep, that they should learn what sorrow means.

CREON

Mine is a nature anything but harsh; full oft by showing pity have I suffered shipwreck; and now albeit I clearly see my error, yet shalt thou gain this request, lady; but I do forewarn thee, if to-morrow's rising sun shall find thee and thy children within the borders of this land, thou diest; my word is spoken and it will not lie. So now, if abide thou must, stay this one day only, for in it thou canst not do any of the fearful deeds I dread.

(CREON *and his retinue go out.*)

CHORUS (*chanting*)

Ah! poor lady, woe is thee! Alas, for thy sorrows! Whither wilt thou turn? What protection, what home or country to save thee from thy troubles wilt thou find? O Medea, in what a hopeless sea of misery heaven hath plunged thee!

MEDEA

On all sides sorrow pens me in. Who shall gainsay this? But all is not yet lost! think not so. Still there are troubles in store for the new bride, and for her bridegroom no light toil. Dost think I would ever have fawned on yonder man, unless to gain some end or form some scheme? Nay, I would not so much as have spoken to him or touched him with my hand. But he has in folly so far stepped in that, though he might have checked my plot by banishing me from the land, he hath allowed me to abide this day, in which I will lay low in death three of my enemies—a father and his daughter and my husband too. Now, though I have many ways to compass their death, I am not sure, friends, which I am to try first. Shall I set fire to the bridal mansion, or plunge the whetted sword through their hearts, softly stealing into the chamber where their couch is spread? One thing stands in my way. If I am caught making my way into the chamber, intent on my design, I shall be put to death and cause my foes to mock. 'Twere best to take the shortest way—the way we women are most skilled in—by poison to destroy them. Well, suppose them dead; what city will receive me? What friendly host will give me a shelter in his land, a home secure, and save my soul alive? None. So I will wait yet a little while in case some tower of defence rise up for me; then will I proceed to this bloody deed in crafty silence; but if some unexpected mischance drive me forth, I will with mine own hand seize the sword, e'en though I die for it, and slay them, and go forth on my bold path of daring. By that dread queen whom I revere before all others and have chosen to share my task, by Hecate who dwells within my inmost chamber, not one of them shall wound my heart and rue it not. Bitter and sad will I make their marriage for them; bitter shall be the wooing of it, bitter my exile from the land. Up, then, Medea, spare not the secrets of thy art in plotting and devising; on to the danger. Now comes a struggle needing courage. Dost see what thou art suffering? 'Tis not for thee to be a laughing-stock to the race of Sisyphus by reason of this wedding of Jason, sprung, as thou art, from a noble sire, and of the Sun-god's race. Thou hast cunning; and, more than this, we women, though by nature little apt for virtuous deeds, are most expert to fashion any mischief.

CHORUS (*singing*)

strophe 1

Back to their source the holy rivers turn their tide. Order and the universe are being reversed. 'Tis men whose counsels are treacherous, whose oath by heaven is no longer sure. Rumour shall bring a change o'er my life, bringing it into good repute. Honour's dawn is breaking for woman's sex; no more shall the foul tongue of slander fix upon us.

antistrophe 1

The songs of the poets of old shall cease to make our faithlessness their theme. Phoebus, lord of minstrelsy, hath not implanted in our mind the gift of heavenly song, else had I sung an answering strain to the race of males, for time's long chapter affords many a theme on their sex as well as ours.

strophe 2

With mind distraught didst thou thy father's house desert on thy voyage betwixt ocean's twin rocks, and on a foreign strand thou dwellest, thy bed left husbandless, poor lady, and thou an exile from the land, dishonoured, persecuted.

antistrophe 2

Gone is the grace that oaths once had. Through all the breadth of Hellas honour is found no more; to heaven hath it sped away. For thee no father's house is open, woe is thee! to be a haven from the troublous storm, while o'er thy home is set another queen, the bride that is preferred to thee.

(*As the* CHORUS *finishes its song,* JASON *enters, alone.* MEDEA *comes out of the house.*)

JASON

It is not now I first remark, but oft ere this, how unruly a pest is a harsh temper. For instance, thou, hadst thou but patiently endured the will of thy superiors, mightest have remained here in this land and house, but now for thy idle words wilt thou be banished. Thy words are naught to me. Cease not to call Jason basest of men; but for those words thou hast spoken against our rulers, count it all gain that exile is thy only punishment. I ever tried to check the outbursts of the angry monarch, and would have had thee stay, but thou wouldst not forego thy silly rage, always reviling our rulers, and so thou wilt be banished. Yet even after all this I weary not of my goodwill, but am come with thus much forethought, lady, that thou mayst not be destitute nor want for aught, when, with thy sons, thou art cast out. Many an evil doth exile bring in its train with it; for even though thou hatest me, never will I harbour hard thoughts of thee.

MEDEA

Thou craven villain (for that is the only name my tongue can find for thee, a foul reproach on thy unmanliness), comest thou to me, thou, most hated foe of gods, of me, and of all mankind? 'Tis no proof of courage or hardihood to confront thy friends after injuring them, but that worst of all human diseases—loss of shame. Yet hast thou done well to come; for I shall ease my soul by reviling thee, and thou wilt be vexed at my recital. I will begin at the very beginning. I saved thy life, as every Hellene knows who sailed with thee aboard the good ship Argo, when thou wert sent to tame and yoke fire-breathing bulls, and to sow the deadly tilth. Yea, and I slew the dragon which guarded the golden fleece, keeping sleepless watch o'er it with many a wreathed coil, and I raised for thee a beacon of deliverance. Father and home of my free will I left and came with thee to Iolcos, 'neath Pelion's hills, for my love was stronger than my prudence. Next I caused the death of Pelias by a doom most grievous, even by his own children's hand, beguiling them of all their fear. All this have I done for thee, thou traitor! and thou hast cast me over, taking to thyself another wife, though children have been born to us. Hadst thou been childless still, I could have pardoned thy desire for this new union. Gone is now the trust I put in oaths. I cannot even understand whether thou thinkest that the gods of old no longer rule, or that fresh decrees are now in vogue amongst mankind, for thy conscience must tell thee thou hast not kept faith with me. Ah! poor right hand, which thou didst often grasp. These knees thou didst embrace! All in vain, I suffered a traitor to touch me! How short of my hopes I am fallen! But come, I will deal with thee as though thou wert my friend. Yet what kindness can I expect from one so base as thee? But yet I will do it, for my questioning will show thee yet more base. Whither can I turn me now? to my father's house, to my own country, which I for thee deserted to come hither? to the hapless daughters of Pelias? A glad welcome, I trow, would they give me in their home, whose father's death I compassed! My case stands even thus: I am become the bitter foe to those of mine own home, and those whom I need ne'er have wronged I have made mine enemies to pleasure thee. Wherefore to reward me for this thou hast made me doubly blest in the eyes of many a wife in Hellas; and in thee I own a peerless, trusty lord. O woe is me, if indeed I am to be cast forth an exile from the land, without one friend; one lone woman with her babes forlorn! Yea, a fine reproach to thee in thy bridal hour, that thy children and the wife who saved thy life are beggars and vagabonds! O Zeus! why hast thou granted unto man clear signs to know the sham in gold, while on man's brow no brand is stamped whereby to gauge the villain's heart?

LEADER OF THE CHORUS

There is a something terrible and past all cure, when quarrels arise 'twixt those who are near and dear.

JASON

Needs must I now, it seems, turn orator, and, like a good helmsman on a ship with close-reefed sails, weather that wearisome tongue of thine. Now, I believe, since thou wilt exaggerate thy favours, that to Cypris alone of gods or men I owe the safety of my voyage. Thou hast a subtle wit enough; yet were it a hateful thing for me to say that the Love-god constrained thee by his resistless shaft to save my life. However, I will not reckon this too nicely; 'twas kindly done, however thou didst serve me. Yet for my safety hast thou received more than ever thou gavest, as I will show. First, thou dwellest in Hellas, instead of thy barbarian land, and hast learnt what justice means and how to live by law, not by the dictates of brute force; and all the Hellenes recognize thy cleverness, and thou hast gained a name; whereas, if thou hadst dwelt upon the confines of the earth, no tongue had mentioned thee. Give me no gold within my halls, nor skill to sing a fairer strain than ever Orpheus sang, unless therewith my fame be spread abroad! So much I say to thee about my own toils, for 'twas thou didst challenge me to this retort. As for the taunts thou urgest against my marriage with the princess, I will prove to thee, first, that I am prudent herein, next chastened in my love, and last a powerful friend to thee and to thy sons; only hold thy peace. Since I have here withdrawn from Iolcos with many a hopeless trouble at my back, what happier device could I, an exile, frame than marriage with the daughter of the king? 'Tis not because I loathe thee for my wife—the thought that rankles in thy heart; 'tis not because I am smitten with desire for a new bride, nor yet that I am eager to vie with others in begetting many children, for those we have are quite enough, and I do not complain. Nay, 'tis that we—and this is most important—may dwell in comfort, instead of suffering want (for well I know that every whilom friend avoids the poor), and that I might rear my sons as doth befit my house; further, that I might be the father of brothers for the children thou hast borne, and raise these to the same high rank, uniting the family in one,—to my lasting bliss. Thou, indeed, hast no need of more children, but me it profits to help my present family by that which is to be. Have I miscarried here? Not even thou wouldest say so unless a rival's charms rankled in thy bosom. No, but you women have such strange ideas, that you think all is well so long as your married life runs smooth; but if some mischance occur to ruffle your love, all that was good and lovely erst you reckon as your foes. Yea, men should have begotten children from some other source, no female race existing; thus would no evil ever have fallen on mankind.

LEADER

This speech, O Jason, hast thou with specious art arranged; but yet I think—albeit in speaking I am indiscreet—that thou hast sinned in thy betrayal of thy wife.

MEDEA

No doubt I differ from the mass of men on many points; for, to my mind, whoso hath skill to fence with words in an unjust cause, incurs the heaviest penalty; for such an one, confident that he can cast a decent veil of words o'er his injustice, dares to practise it; and yet he is not so very clever after all. So do not thou put forth thy specious pleas and clever words to me now, for one word of mine will lay thee low. Hadst thou not had a villain's heart, thou shouldst have gained my consent, then made this match, instead of hiding it from those who loved thee.

JASON

Thou wouldest have lent me ready aid, no doubt, in this proposal, if I had told thee of my marriage, seeing that not even now canst thou restrain thy soul's hot fury.

MEDEA

This was not what restrained thee; but thine eye was turned towards old age, and a foreign wife began to appear a shame to thee.

JASON

Be well assured of this: 'twas not for the woman's sake I wedded the king's daughter, my present wife; but, as I have already told thee, I wished to insure thy safety and to be the father of royal sons bound by blood to my own children—a bulwark to our house.

MEDEA

May that prosperity, whose end is woe, ne'er be mine, nor such wealth as would ever sting my heart!

JASON

Change that prayer as I will teach thee, and thou wilt show more wisdom. Never let happiness appear in sorrow's guise, nor, when thy fortune smiles, pretend she frowns!

MEDEA

Mock on; thou hast a place of refuge; I am alone, an exile soon to be.

JASON

Thy own free choice was this; blame no one else.

MEDEA

What did I do? Marry, then betray thee?

JASON

Against the king thou didst invoke an impious curse.

MEDEA

On thy house too maybe I bring the curse.

JASON

Know this, I will no further dispute this point with thee. But, if thou wilt of my fortune somewhat take for the children or thyself to help thy exile, say on; for I am ready to grant it with ungrudging hand, yea and to send tokens to my friends elsewhere who shall treat thee well. If thou refuse this offer, thou wilt do a foolish deed, but if thou cease from anger the greater will be thy gain.

MEDEA

I will have naught to do with friends of thine, naught will I receive of thee, offer it not to me; a villain's gifts can bring no blessing.

JASON

At least I call the gods to witness, that I am ready in all things to serve thee and thy children, but thou dost scorn my favours and thrustest thy friends stubbornly away; wherefore thy lot will be more bitter still.

MEDEA

Away! By love for thy young bride entrapped, too long thou lingerest outside her chamber; go wed, for, if God will, thou shalt have such a marriage as thou wouldst fain refuse.

(JASON *goes out.*)

CHORUS (*singing*)

strophe I

When in excess and past all limits Love doth come, he brings not glory or repute to man; but if the Cyprian queen in moderate might approach, no goddess is so full of charm as she. Never, O never, lady mine, discharge at me from thy golden bow a shaft invincible, in passion's venom dipped.

antistrophe 1

On me may chastity, heaven's fairest gift, look with a favouring eye; never may Cypris, goddess dread, fasten on me a temper to dispute, or restless jealousy, smiting my soul with mad desire for unlawful love, but may she hallow peaceful married life and shrewdly decide whom each of us shall wed.

strophe 2

O my country, O my own dear home! God grant I may never be an outcast from my city, leading that cruel helpless life, whose every day is misery. Ere that may I this life complete and yield to death, ay, death; for there is no misery that doth surpass the loss of fatherland.

antistrophe 2

I have seen with mine eyes, nor from the lips of others have I the lesson learnt; no city, not one friend doth pity thee in this awful woe. May he perish and find no favour, whoso hath not in him honour for his friends, freely unlocking his heart to them. Never shall he be friend of mine.

(MEDEA *has been seated in despair on her door-step during the choral song.* AEGEUS *and his attendants enter.*)

AEGEUS

All hail, Medea! no man knoweth fairer prelude to the greeting of friends than this.

MEDEA

All hail to thee likewise, Aegeus, son of wise Pandion. Whence comest thou to this land?

AEGEUS

From Phoebus' ancient oracle.

MEDEA

What took thee on thy travels to the prophetic centre of the earth?

AEGEUS

The wish to ask how I might raise up seed unto myself.

MEDEA

Pray tell me, hast thou till now dragged on a childless life?

AEGEUS

I have no child owing to the visitation of some god.

MEDEA

Hast thou a wife, or hast thou never known the married state?

AEGEUS

I have a wife joined to me in wedlock's bond.

MEDEA

What said Phoebus to thee as to children?

AEGEUS

Words too subtle for man to comprehend.

MEDEA

Surely I may learn the god's answer?

AEGEUS

Most assuredly, for it is just thy subtle wit it needs.

MEDEA

What said the god? speak, if I may hear it.

AEGEUS

He bade me "not loose the wineskin's pendent neck."

MEDEA

Till when? what must thou do first, what country visit?

AEGEUS

Till I to my native home return.

MEDEA

What object hast thou in sailing to this land?

AEGEUS

O'er Troezen's realm is Pittheus king.

MEDEA

Pelops' son, a man devout they say.

AEGEUS

To him I fain would impart the oracle of the god.

MEDEA

The man is shrewd and versed in such-like lore.

AEGEUS

Aye, and to me the dearest of all my warrior friends.

MEDEA

Good luck to thee! success to all thy wishes!

AEGEUS

But why that downcast eye, that wasted cheek?

MEDEA

O Aegeus, my husband has proved most evil.

AEGEUS

What meanest thou? explain to me clearly the cause of thy despondency.

MEDEA

Jason is wronging me though I have given him no cause.

AEGEUS

What hath he done? tell me more clearly.

MEDEA

He is taking another wife to succeed me as mistress of his house.

AEGEUS

Can he have brought himself to such a dastard deed?

MEDEA

Be assured thereof; I, whom he loved of yore, am in dishonour now.

AEGEUS

Hath he found a new love? or does he loathe thy bed?

MEDEA

Much in love is he! A traitor to his friend is he become.

AEGEUS

Enough! if he is a villain as thou sayest.

MEDEA

The alliance he is so much enamoured of is with a princess.

AEGEUS

Who gives his daughter to him? go on, I pray.

MEDEA

Creon, who is lord of this land of Corinth.

AEGEUS

Lady, I can well pardon thy grief.

MEDEA

I am undone, and more than that, am banished from the land.

AEGEUS

By whom? fresh woe this word of thine unfolds.

MEDEA

Creon drives me forth in exile from Corinth.

AEGEUS

Doth Jason allow it? This too I blame him for.

MEDEA

Not in words, but he will not stand out against it. O, I implore thee by this beard and by thy knees, in suppliant posture, pity, O pity my sorrows; do not see me cast forth forlorn, but receive me in thy country, to a seat within thy halls. So may thy wish by heaven's grace be crowned with a full harvest of offspring, and may thy life close in happiness! Thou knowest not the rare good luck thou findest here, for I will make thy childlessness to cease and cause thee to beget fair issue; so potent are the spells I know.

AEGEUS

Lady, on many grounds I am most fain to grant thee this thy boon, first for the gods' sake, next for the children whom thou dost promise I shall beget; for in respect of this I am completely lost. 'Tis thus with me; if e'er thou reach my land, I will attempt to champion thee as I am bound to do. Only one warning I do give thee first, lady; I will not from this land bear thee away, yet if of thyself thou reach my halls, there shalt thou bide in safety and I will never yield thee up to any man. But from this land escape without my aid, for I have no wish to incur the blame of my allies as well.

MEDEA

It shall be even so; but wouldst thou pledge thy word to this, I should in all be well content with thee.

AEGEUS

Surely thou dost trust me? or is there aught that troubles thee?

MEDEA

Thee I trust; but Pelias' house and Creon are my foes. Wherefore, if thou art bound by an oath, thou wilt not give me up to them when they come to drag me from the land, but, having entered into a compact and sworn by heaven as well, thou wilt become my friend and disregard their overtures. Weak is any aid of mine, whilst they have wealth and a princely house.

AEGEUS

Lady, thy words show much foresight, so if this is thy will, I do not refuse. For I shall feel secure and safe if I have some pretext to offer to thy foes, and thy case too the firmer stands. Now name thy gods.

MEDEA

Swear by the plain of Earth, by Helios my father's sire, and, in one comprehensive oath, by all the race of gods.

AEGEUS

What shall I swear to do, from what refrain? Tell me that.

MEDEA

Swear that thou wilt never of thyself expel me from thy land, nor, whilst life is thine, permit any other, one of my foes maybe, to hale me thence if so he will.

AEGEUS

By Earth I swear, by the Sun-god's holy beam and by all the host of heaven that I will stand fast to the terms I hear thee make.

MEDEA

'Tis enough. If thou shouldst break this oath, what curse dost thou invoke upon thyself?

AEGEUS

Whate'er betides the impious.

MEDEA

Go in peace; all is well, and I with what speed I may, will to thy city come, when I have wrought my purpose and obtained my wish.

(AEGEUS *and his retinue depart.*)

CHORUS (*chanting*)

May Maia's princely son go with thee on thy way to bring thee to thy home, and mayest thou attain that on which thy soul is set so firmly, for to my mind thou seemest a generous man, O Aegeus.

MEDEA

O Zeus, and Justice, child of Zeus, and Sun-god's light, now will I triumph o'er my foes, kind friends; on victory's road have I set forth; good hope have I of wreaking vengeance on those I hate. For where we were in most distress this stranger hath appeared, to be a haven in my counsels; to him will we make fast the cables of our ship when we come to the town and citadel of Pallas. But now will I explain to thee my plans in full; do not expect to hear a pleasant tale. A servant of mine will I to Jason send and crave an interview; then when he comes I will address him with soft words, say, "this pleases me," and, "that is well," even the marriage with the princess, which my treacherous lord is celebrating, and add "it suits us both, 'twas well thought out"; then will I entreat that here my children may abide, not that I mean to leave them in a hostile land for foes to flout, but that I may slay the king's daughter by guile. For I will send them with gifts in their hands, carrying them unto the bride to save them from banishment, a robe of finest woof and a chaplet of gold. And if these ornaments she take and put them on, miserably shall she die, and likewise everyone who touches her; with such fell poisons will I smear my gifts. And here I quit this theme; but I shudder at the deed I must do next; for I will slay the children I have borne; there is none shall take them from my toils; and when I have utterly confounded Jason's house I will leave the land, escaping punishment for my dear children's murder, after my most unholy deed. For I cannot endure the taunts of enemies, kind friends; enough! what gain is life to me? I have no country, home, or refuge left. O, I did wrong, that hour I left my father's home, persuaded by that Hellene's words, who now shall pay the penalty, so help me God. Never shall he see again alive the children I bore to him, nor from his new bride shall he beget issue, for she must die a hideous death, slain by my drugs. Let no one deem me a poor weak woman who sits with folded hands, but of another mould, dangerous to foes and well-disposed to friends; for they win the fairest fame who live their life like me.

LEADER OF THE CHORUS

Since thou hast imparted this design to me, I bid thee hold thy hand, both from a wish to serve thee and because I would uphold the laws men make.

MEDEA

It cannot but be so; thy words I pardon since thou art not in the same sorry plight that I am.

LEADER

O lady, wilt thou steel thyself to slay thy children twain?

MEDEA

I will, for that will stab my husband to the heart.

LEADER

It may, but thou wilt be the saddest wife alive.

MEDEA

No matter; wasted is every word that comes 'twixt now and then. Ho! (*The* NURSE *enters in answer to her call.*) Thou, go call me Jason hither, for thee I do employ on every mission of trust. No word divulge of all my purpose, as thou art to thy mistress loyal and likewise of my sex.

(*The* NURSE *goes out.*)

CHORUS (*singing*)

strophe 1

Sons of Erechtheus, heroes happy from of yore, children of the blessed gods, fed on wisdom's glorious food in a holy land ne'er pillaged by its foes, ye who move with sprightly step through a climate ever bright and clear, where, as legend tells, the Muses nine, Pieria's holy maids, were brought to birth by Harmonia with the golden hair.

antistrophe 1

And poets sing how Cypris drawing water from the streams of fair-flowing Cephissus breathes o'er the land a gentle breeze of balmy winds, and ever as she crowns her tresses with a garland of sweet rose-buds sends forth the Loves to sit by wisdom's side, to take a part in every excellence.

strophe 2

How then shall the city of sacred streams, the land that welcomes those it loves, receive thee, the murderess of thy children, thee whose presence with others is a pollution? Think on the murder of thy children, consider the bloody deed thou takest on thee. Nay, by thy knees we, one and all, implore thee, slay not thy babes.

antistrophe 2

Where shall hand or heart find hardihood enough in wreaking such a fearsome deed upon thy sons? How wilt thou look upon thy babes, and still without a tear retain thy bloody purpose? Thou canst not, when they fall at thy feet for mercy, steel thy heart and dip in their blood thy hand.

(JASON *enters.*)

JASON

I am come at thy bidding, for e'en though thy hate for me is bitter thou shalt not fail in this small boon, but I will hear what new request thou hast to make of me, lady.

MEDEA

Jason, I crave thy pardon for the words I spoke, and well thou mayest brook my burst of passion, for ere now we twain have shared much love. For I have reasoned with my soul and railed upon me thus, "Ah! poor heart! why am I thus distraught, why so angered 'gainst all good advice, why have I come to hate the rulers of the land, my husband too, who does the best for me he can, in wedding with a princess and rearing for my children noble brothers? Shall I not cease to fret? What possesses me, when heaven its best doth offer? Have I not my children to consider? do I forget that we are fugitives, in need of friends?" When I had thought all this I saw how foolish I had been, how senselessly enraged. So now I do commend thee and think thee most wise in forming this connection for us; but I was mad, I who should have shared in these designs, helped on thy plans, and lent my aid to bring about the match, only too pleased to wait upon thy bride. But what we are, we are, we women, evil I will not say; wherefore thou shouldst not sink to our sorry level nor with our weapons meet our childishness.

I yield and do confess that I was wrong then, but now have I come to a better mind. Come hither, my children, come, leave the house, step forth, and with me greet and bid farewell to your father, be reconciled from all past bitterness unto your friends, as now your mother is; for we have made a truce and anger is no more.

(*The* ATTENDANT *comes out of the house with the children.*)

Take his right hand; ah me! my sad fate! when I reflect, as now, upon the hidden future. O my children, since there awaits you even thus a long, long life, stretch forth the hand to take a fond farewell. Ah me! how new to tears am I, how full of fear! For now that I have at last released me from my quarrel with your father, I let the tear-drops stream adown my tender cheek.

LEADER OF THE CHORUS

From my eyes too bursts forth the copious tear; O, may no greater ill than the present e'er befall!

JASON

Lady, I praise this conduct, not that I blame what is past; for it is but natural to the female sex to vent their spleen against a husband when he trafficks in other marriages besides his own. But thy heart is changed to wiser schemes and thou art determined on the better course, late though it be; this is acting like a woman of sober sense. And for you, my sons, hath your father provided with all good heed a sure refuge, by God's grace; for ye, I trow, shall with your brothers share hereafter the foremost rank in this Corinthian realm. Only grow up, for all the rest your sire and whoso of the gods is kind to us is bringing to pass. May I see you reach man's full estate, high o'er the heads of those I hate! But thou, lady, why with fresh tears dost thou thine eyelids wet, turning away thy wan cheek, with no welcome for these my happy tidings?

MEDEA

'Tis naught; upon these children my thoughts were turned.

JASON

Then take heart; for I will see that it is well with them.

MEDEA

I will do so; nor will I doubt thy word; woman is a weak creature, ever given to tears.

JASON

Why prithee, unhappy one, dost moan o'er these children?

MEDEA

I gave them birth; and when thou didst pray long life for them, pity entered into my soul to think that these things must be. But the reason of thy coming hither to speak with me is partly told, the rest will I now mention. Since it is the pleasure of the rulers of the land to banish me, and well I know 'twere best for me to stand not in the way of thee or of the rulers by dwelling here, enemy as I am thought unto their house, forth from this land in exile am I going, but these children,—that they may know thy fostering hand, beg Creon to remit their banishment.

JASON

I doubt whether I can persuade him, yet must I attempt it.

MEDEA

At least do thou bid thy wife ask her sire this boon, to remit the exile of the children from this land.

JASON

Yea, that will I; and her methinks I shall persuade, since she is a woman like the rest.

MEDEA

I too will aid thee in this task, for by the children's hand I will send to her gifts that far surpass in beauty, I well know, aught that now is seen 'mongst men, a robe of finest tissue and a chaplet of chased gold. But one of my attendants must haste and bring the ornaments hither. (*A servant goes into the house.*) Happy shall she be not once alone but ten thousandfold, for in thee she wins the noblest soul to share her love, and gets these gifts as well which on a day my father's sire, the Sun-god, bestowed on his descendants. (*The servant returns and hands the gifts to the children.*) My children, take in your hands these wedding gifts, and bear them as an offering to the royal maid, the happy bride; for verily the gifts she shall receive are not to be scorned.

JASON

But why so rashly rob thyself of these gifts? Dost think a royal palace wants for robes or gold? Keep them, nor give them to another. For well I know that if my lady hold me in esteem, she will set my price above all wealth.

MEDEA

Say not so; 'tis said that gifts tempt even gods; and o'er men's minds gold holds more potent sway than countless words. Fortune smiles upon thy bride, and heaven now doth swell her triumph; youth is hers and princely power; yet to save my children from exile I would barter life, not dross alone. Children, when we are come to the rich palace, pray your father's new bride, my mistress, with suppliant voice to save you from exile, offering her these ornaments the while; for it is most needful that she receive the gifts in her own hand. Now go and linger not; may ye succeed and to your mother bring back the glad tidings she fain would hear!

(JASON, *the* ATTENDANT, *and the children go out together.*)

CHORUS (*singing*)

strophe I

Gone, gone is every hope I had that the children yet might live; forth to their doom they now proceed. The hapless bride will take, ay, take the golden crown that is to be her ruin; with her own hand will she lift and place upon her golden locks the garniture of death.

antistrophe I

Its grace and sheen divine will tempt her to put on the robe and crown of gold, and in that act will she deck herself to be a bride amid the dead. Such is the snare whereinto she will fall, such is the deadly doom that waits the hapless maid, nor shall she from the curse escape.

strophe 2

And thou, poor wretch, who to thy sorrow art wedding a king's daughter, little thinkest of the doom thou art bringing on thy children's life, or of the cruel death that waits thy bride. Woe is thee! how art thou fallen from thy high estate!

antistrophe 2

Next do I bewail thy sorrows, O mother hapless in thy children, thou who wilt slay thy babes because thou hast a rival, the babes thy husband hath deserted impiously to join him to another bride.

(*The* ATTENDANT *enters with the children.*)

ATTENDANT

Thy children, lady, are from exile freed, and gladly did the royal bride accept thy gifts in her own hands, and so thy children made their peace with her.

MEDEA

Ah!

ATTENDANT

Why art so disquieted in thy prosperous hour? Why turnest thou thy cheek away, and hast no welcome for my glad news?

MEDEA

Ah me!

ATTENDANT

These groans but ill accord with the news I bring.

MEDEA

Ah me! once more I say.

ATTENDANT

Have I unwittingly announced some evil tidings? Have I erred in thinking my news was good?

MEDEA

Thy news is as it is; I blame thee not.

ATTENDANT

Then why this downcast eye, these floods of tears?

MEDEA

Old friend, needs must I weep; for the gods and I with fell intent devised these schemes.

ATTENDANT

Be of good cheer; thou too of a surety shalt by thy sons yet be brought home again.

MEDEA

Ere that shall I bring others to their home, ah! woe is me!

ATTENDANT

'Thou art not the only mother from thy children reft. Bear patiently thy troubles as a mortal must.

MEDEA

I will obey; go thou within the house and make the day's provision for the children. (*The* ATTENDANT *enters the house.* MEDEA *turns to the children.*) O my babes, my babes, ye have still a city and a home, where far from me and my sad lot you will live your lives, reft of your mother for ever; while I must to another land in banishment, or ever I have had my joy of you, or lived to see you happy, or ever I have graced your marriage couch, your bride, your bridal bower, or lifted high the wedding torch. Ah me! a victim of my own self-will. So it was all in vain I reared you, O my sons; in vain did suffer, racked with anguish, enduring the cruel pangs of childbirth. 'Fore Heaven I once had hope, poor me! high hope of ye that you would nurse me in my age and deck my corpse with loving hands, a boon we mortals covet; but now is my sweet fancy dead and gone; for I must lose you both and in bitterness and sorrow drag through life.

And ye shall never with fond eyes see your mother more, for o'er your life there comes a change. Ah me! ah me! why do ye look at me so, my children? why smile that last sweet smile? Ah me! what am I to do? My heart gives way when I behold my children's laughing eyes. O, I cannot; farewell to all my former schemes; I will take the children from the land, the babes I bore. Why should I wound their sire by wounding them, and get me a twofold measure of sorrow? No, no, I will not do it. Farewell my scheming! And yet what possesses me? Can I consent to let those foes of mine escape from punishment, and incur their mockery? I must face this deed. Out upon my craven heart! to think that I should even have let the soft words escape my soul. Into the house, children! (*The children go into the house.*) And whoso feels he must not be present at my sacrifice, must see to it himself; I will not spoil my handiwork. Ah! ah! do not, my heart, O do not do this deed! Let the children go, unhappy one, spare the babes! For if they live, they will cheer thee in our exile there. Nay, by the fiends of hell's abyss, never, never will I hand my children over to their foes to mock and flout. Die they must in any case, and since 'tis so, why I, the mother who bore them, will give the fatal blow. In any case their doom is fixed and there is no escape. Already the crown is on her head, the robe is round her, and she is dying, the royal bride; that do I know full well. But now since I have a piteous path to tread, and yet more piteous still the path I send my children on, fain would I say farewell to them. (*The children come out at her call. She takes them in her arms.*) O my babes, my babes, let your mother kiss your hands. Ah! hands I love so well, O lips most dear to me! O noble form and features of my children, I wish ye joy, but in that other land, for here your father robs you of your home. O the sweet embrace, the soft young cheek, the fragrant breath! my children! Go, leave me; I cannot bear to longer look upon ye; my sorrow wins the day. At last I understand the awful deed I am to do; but passion, that cause of direst woes to mortal man, hath triumphed o'er my sober thoughts.

(*She goes into the house with the children.*)

CHORUS (*chanting*)

Oft ere now have I pursued subtler themes and have faced graver issues than woman's sex should seek to probe; but then e'en we aspire to culture, which dwells with us to teach us wisdom; I say not all; for small is the class amongst women—(one maybe shalt thou find 'mid many)—that is not incapable of wisdom. And amongst mortals I do assert that they who are wholly without experience and have never had children far surpass in happiness those who are parents. The childless, because they have never proved whether children grow up to be a blessing or curse to men are removed from all share in many troubles; whilst those who have a sweet race of children growing up in their houses do wear away, as I perceive, their whole life through; first with the thought how they may train them up in virtue, next how they shall leave their sons the means to live; and after all this 'tis far from clear whether on good or bad children they bestow their toil. But one last crowning woe for every mortal man I now will name; suppose that they have found sufficient means to live, and seen their children grow to man's estate and walk in virtue's path, still if fortune so befall, comes Death and bears the children's bodies off to Hades. Can it be any profit to the gods to heap upon us mortal men beside our other woes this further grief for children lost, a grief surpassing all?

(MEDEA *comes out of the house.*)

MEDEA

Kind friends, long have I waited expectantly to know how things would at the palace chance. And lo! I see one of

Jason's servants coming hither, whose hurried gasps for breath proclaim him the bearer of some fresh tidings.

(*A* MESSENGER *rushes in.*)

MESSENGER

Fly, fly, Medea! who hast wrought an awful deed, transgressing every law; nor leave behind or sea-borne bark or car that scours the plain.

MEDEA

Why, what hath chanced that calls for such a flight of mine?

MESSENGER

The princess is dead, a moment gone, and Creon too, her sire, slain by those drugs of thine.

MEDEA

Tidings most fair are thine! Henceforth shalt thou be ranked amongst my friends and benefactors.

MESSENGER

Ha! What? Art sane? Art not distraught, lady, who hearest with joy the outrage to our royal house done, and art not at the horrid tale afraid?

MEDEA

Somewhat have I, too, to say in answer to thy words. Be not so hasty, friend, but tell the manner of their death, for thou wouldst give me double joy, if so they perished miserably.

MESSENGER

When the children twain whom thou didst bear came with their father and entered the palace of the bride, right glad were we thralls who had shared thy griefs, for instantly from ear to ear a rumour spread that thou and thy lord had made up your former quarrel. One kissed thy children's hands, another their golden hair, while I for very joy went with them in person to the women's chambers. Our mistress, whom now we do revere in thy room, cast a longing glance at Jason, ere she saw thy children twain; but then she veiled her eyes and turned her blanching cheek away, disgusted at their coming; but thy husband tried to check his young bride's angry humour with these words: "O, be not angered 'gainst thy friends; cease from wrath and turn once more thy face this way, counting as friends whomso thy husband counts, and accept these gifts, and for my sake crave thy sire to remit these children's exile." Soon as she saw the ornaments, no longer she held out, but yielded to her lord in all; and ere the father and his sons were far from the palace gone, she took the broidered robe and put it on, and set the golden crown about her tresses, arranging her hair at her bright mirror, with many a happy smile at her breathless counterfeit. Then rising from her seat she passed across the chamber, tripping lightly on her fair white foot, exulting in the gift, with many a glance at her uplifted ankle. When lo! a scene of awful horror did ensue. In a moment she turned pale, reeled backwards, trembling in every limb, and sinks upon a seat scarce soon enough to save herself from falling to the ground. An aged dame, one of her company, thinking belike it was a fit from Pan or some god sent, raised a cry of prayer, till from her mouth she saw the foam-flakes issue, her eyeballs rolling in their sockets, and all the blood her face desert; then did she raise a loud scream far different from her former cry. Forthwith one handmaid rushed to her father's house, another to her new bridegroom to tell his bride's sad fate, and the whole house echoed with their running to and fro. By this time would a quick walker have made the turn in a course of six plethra and reached the goal, when she with one awful shriek awoke, poor sufferer, from her speechless trance and oped her closed eyes, for against her a twofold anguish was warring. The chaplet of gold about her head was sending forth a wondrous stream of ravening flame, while the fine raiment, thy children's gift, was preying on the hapless maiden's fair white flesh; and she starts from her seat in a blaze and seeks to fly, shaking her hair and head this way and that, to cast the crown therefrom; but the gold held firm to its fastenings, and the flame, as she shook her locks, blazed forth the more with double fury. Then to the earth she sinks, by the cruel blow o'ercome; past all recognition now save to a father's eye; for her eyes had lost their tranquil gaze, her face no more its natural look preserved, and from the crown of her head blood and fire in mingled stream ran down; and from her bones the flesh kept peeling off beneath the gnawing of those secret drugs, e'en as when the pine-tree weeps its tears of pitch, a fearsome sight to see. And all were afraid to touch the corpse, for we were warned by what had chanced. Anon came her hapless father unto the house, all unwitting of her doom, and stumbles o'er the dead, and loud he cried, and folding his arms about her kissed her, with words like these the while, "O my poor, poor child, which of the gods hath destroyed thee thus foully? Who is robbing me of thee, old as I am and ripe for death? O my child, alas! would I could die with thee!" He ceased his sad lament, and would have raised his aged frame, but found himself held fast by the fine-spun robe as ivy that clings to the branches of the bay, and then ensued a fearful struggle. He strove to rise, but she still held him back; and if ever he pulled with all his might, from off his bones his aged flesh he tore. At last he gave it up, and breathed forth his soul in awful suffering; for he could no longer master the pain. So there they lie, daughter and aged sire, dead side by side, a grievous sight that calls for tears. And as for thee, I leave thee out of my consideration, for thyself must discover a means to escape punishment. Not now for the first time I think this human life a shadow; yea, and without shrinking I will say that they amongst men who pretend to wisdom and expend deep thought on words do incur a serious charge of folly; for amongst mortals no man is happy; wealth may pour in and make one luckier than another, but none can happy be.

(*The* MESSENGER *departs.*)

LEADER OF THE CHORUS

This day the deity, it seems, will mass on Jason, as he well deserves, a heavy load of evils. Woe is thee, daughter of Creon! We pity thy sad fate, gone as thou art to Hades' halls as the price of thy marriage with Jason.

MEDEA

My friends, I am resolved upon the deed; at once will I slay my children and then leave this land, without delaying long enough to hand them over to some more savage hand to butcher. Needs must they die in any case; and since they must, I will slay them—I, the mother that bare them. O heart of mine, steel thyself! Why do I hesitate to do the awful deed that must be done? Come, take the sword, thou wretched hand of mine! Take it, and advance to the post whence starts thy life of sorrow! Away with cowardice! Give not one thought to thy babes, how dear they are or how thou art their mother. This one brief day forget thy children dear, and after that lament; for though thou wilt slay them yet they were thy darlings still, and I am a lady of sorrows.

(MEDEA *enters the house.*)

CHORUS (*chanting*)

O earth, O sun whose beam illumines all, look, look upon this lost woman, ere she stretch forth her murderous hand upon her sons for blood; for lo! these are scions of thy own golden seed, and the blood of gods is in danger of being shed by man. O light, from Zeus proceeding, stay her, hold her hand, forth from the house chase this fell bloody fiend by demons led. Vainly wasted were the throes thy children cost thee; vainly hast thou borne, it seems, sweet babes, O thou who hast left behind thee that passage through the blue Symplegades, that strangers justly hate. Ah! hapless one, why doth fierce anger thy soul assail? Why in its place is fell murder growing up? For grievous unto mortal men are pollutions that come of kindred blood poured on the earth, woes to suit each crime hurled from heaven on the murderer's house.

FIRST SON (*within*)

Ah, me; what can I do? Whither fly to escape my mother's blows?

SECOND SON (*within*)

I know not, sweet brother mine; we are lost.

CHORUS (*chanting*)

Didst hear, didst hear the children's cry? O lady, born to sorrow, victim of an evil fate! Shall I enter the house? For the children's sake I am resolved to ward off the murder.

FIRST SON (*within*)

Yea, by heaven I adjure you; help, your aid is needed.

SECOND SON (*within*)

Even now the toils of the sword are closing round us.

CHORUS (*chanting*)

O hapless mother, surely thou hast a heart of stone or steel to slay the offspring of thy womb by such a murderous doom. Of all the wives of yore I know but one who laid her hand upon her children dear, even Ino, whom the gods did madden in the day that the wife of Zeus drove her wandering from her home. But she, poor sufferer, flung herself into the sea because of the foul murder of her children, leaping o'er the wave-beat cliff, and in her death was she united to her children twain. Can there be any deed of horror left to follow this? Woe for the wooing of women fraught with disaster! What sorrows hast thou caused for men ere now!

(JASON *and his attendants enter.*)

JASON

Ladies, stationed near this house, pray tell me is the author of these hideous deeds, Medea, still within, or hath she fled from hence? For she must hide beneath the earth or soar on wings towards heaven's vault, if she would avoid the vengeance of the royal house. Is she so sure she will escape herself unpunished from this house, when she hath slain the rulers of the land? But enough of this! I am forgetting her children. As for her, those whom she hath wronged will do the like by her; but I am come to save the children's life, lest the victim's kin visit their wrath on me, in vengeance for the murder foul, wrought by my children's mother.

LEADER OF THE CHORUS

Unhappy man, thou knowest not the full extent of thy misery, else had thou never said those words.

JASON

How now? Can she want to kill me too?

LEADER

Thy sons are dead; slain by their own mother's hand.

JASON

O God! what sayest thou? Woman, thou hast sealed my doom.

LEADER

Thy children are no more; be sure of this.

JASON

Where slew she them; within the palace or outside?

LEADER

Throw wide the doors and see thy children's murdered corpses.

JASON

Haste, ye slaves, loose the bolts, undo the fastenings, that I may see the sight of twofold woe, my murdered sons and her, whose blood in vengeance I will shed.

(MEDEA *appears above the house, on a chariot drawn by dragons; the children's corpses are beside her.*)

MEDEA

Why shake those doors and attempt to loose their bolts, in quest of the dead and me their murderess? From such toil desist. If thou wouldst aught with me, say on, if so thou wilt; but never shalt thou lay hand on me, so swift the steeds the sun, my father's sire, to me doth give to save me from the hand of my foes.

JASON

Accursed woman! by gods, by me and all mankind abhorred as never woman was, who hadst the heart to stab thy babes, thou their mother, leaving me undone and childless; this hast thou done and still dost gaze upon the sun and earth after this deed most impious. Curses on thee! I now perceive what then I missed in the day I brought thee, fraught with doom, from thy home in a barbarian land to dwell in Hellas, traitress to thy sire and to the land that nurtured thee. On me the gods have hurled the curse that dogged thy steps, for thou didst slay thy brother at his hearth ere thou cam'st aboard our fair ship, Argo. Such was the outset of thy life of crime; then didst thou wed with me, and having borne me sons to glut thy passion's lust, thou now hast slain them. Not one amongst the wives of Hellas e'er had dared this deed; yet before them all I chose thee for my wife, wedding a foe to be my doom, no woman, but a lioness fiercer than Tyrrhene Scylla in nature.

But with reproaches heaped a thousandfold I cannot wound thee, so brazen is thy nature. Perish, vile sorceress, murderess of thy babes! Whilst I must mourn my luckless fate, for I shall ne'er enjoy my new-found bride, nor shall I have the children, whom I bred and reared, alive to say the last farewell to me; nay, I have lost them.

MEDEA

To this thy speech I could have made a long reply, but Father Zeus knows well all I have done for thee, and the treatment thou hast given me. Yet thou wert not ordained to scorn my love and lead a life of joy in mockery of me, nor was thy royal bride nor Creon, who gave thee a second wife, to thrust me from this land and rue it not. Wherefore, if thou wilt, call me e'en a lioness, and Scylla, whose home is in the Tyrrhene land; for I in turn have wrung thy heart, as well I might.

JASON

Thou, too, art grieved thyself, and sharest in my sorrow.

MEDEA

Be well assured I am; but it relieves my pain to know thou canst not mock at me.

JASON

O my children, how vile a mother ye have found!

MEDEA

My sons, your father's feeble lust has been your ruin!

JASON

'Twas not my hand, at any rate, that slew them.

MEDEA

No, but thy foul treatment of me, and thy new marriage.

JASON

Didst think that marriage cause enough to murder them?

MEDEA

Dost think a woman counts this a trifling injury?

JASON

So she be self-restrained; but in thy eyes all is evil.

MEDEA

Thy sons are dead and gone. That will stab thy heart.

JASON

They live, methinks, to bring a curse upon thy head.

MEDEA

The gods know, whoso of them began this troublous coil.

JASON

Indeed, they know that hateful heart of thine.

MEDEA

Thou art as hateful. I am aweary of thy bitter tongue.

JASON

And I likewise of thine. But parting is easy.

MEDEA

Say how; what am I to do? for I am fain as thou to go.

JASON

Give up to me those dead, to bury and lament.

MEDEA

No, never! I will bury them myself, bearing them to Hera's sacred field, who watches o'er the Cape, that none of their foes may insult them by pulling down their tombs; and in this land of Sisyphus I will ordain hereafter a solemn feast and mystic rites to atone for this impious murder. Myself will now to the land of Erechtheus, to dwell with Aegeus, Pandion's son. But thou, as well thou mayst, shall die a caitiff's death, thy head crushed 'neath a shattered relic of Argo, when thou hast seen the bitter ending of my marriage.

JASON

The curse of our sons' avenging spirit and of Justice, that calls for blood, be on thee!

MEDEA

What god or power divine hears thee, breaker of oaths and every law of hospitality?

JASON

Fie upon thee! cursed witch! child-murderess!

MEDEA

To thy house! go, bury thy wife.

JASON

I go, bereft of both my sons.

MEDEA

Thy grief is yet to come; wait till old age is with thee too.

JASON

O my dear, dear children!

MEDEA

Dear to their mother, not to thee.

JASON

And yet thou didst slay them?

MEDEA

Yea, to vex thy heart.

JASON

One last fond kiss, ah me! I fain would on their lips imprint.

MEDEA

Embraces now, and fond farewells for them; but then a cold repulse!

JASON

By heaven I do adjure thee, let me touch their tender skin.

MEDEA

No, no! in vain this word has sped its flight.

JASON

O Zeus, dost hear how I am driven hence; dost mark the treatment I receive from this she-lion, fell murderess of her young? Yet so far as I may and can, I raise for them a dirge, and do adjure the gods to witness how thou hast slain my sons, and wilt not suffer me to embrace or bury their dead bodies. Would I had never begotten them to see thee slay them after all!

(*The chariot carries* MEDEA *away.*)

CHORUS (*chanting*)

Many a fate doth Zeus dispense, high on his Olympian throne; oft do the gods bring things to pass beyond man's expectation; that, which we thought would be, is not fulfilled, while for the unlooked-for, god finds out a way; and such hath been the issue of this matter.

THE FROGS

by

ARISTOPHANES

CHARACTERS IN THE PLAY

THE GOD DIONYSUS
XANTHIAS, *his slave*
AESCHYLUS
EURIPIDES
HERACLES
PLUTO
CHARON
AEACUS
A SERVANT OF PLUTO
A CORPSE
A MAIDSERVANT OF PERSEPHONE
A LANDLADY *in Hades*
PLATHANÉ, *her servant*
CHORUS OF FROGS
CHORUS OF INITIATED PERSONS

INTRODUCTION

At the Lenaean festival of 405, Aristophanes produced *The Frogs*, which was awarded the highest prize. The subject of the play is almost wholly literary and its treatment contains astonishingly few passages that can arouse the antipathy of the puritan.

Dionysus, the patron god of tragedy, has deeply mourned the recent death of Euripides, and his nostalgic yearning for the "clever rogue" has finally grown so intense that he has resolved to go down to Hades and bring him back to earth again; the play opens at the commencement of this arduous journey. Since no one but Heracles has ever accomplished such a feat before, Dionysus has acquired a club and slipped a lion's skin over his saffron robe, and in this ludicrous costume he knocks at the house of the very hero he plans to emulate, and obtains advice and directions. With his slave Xanthias accompanying him he soon reaches the Acherusian lake and is ferried across by Charon while the Chorus of Frogs sings lyrics of the rain and the marshes. Xanthias has had to walk around the lake, but he meets his master on the other side, and shortly the real Chorus of the play, composed of initiates into the Mysteries, appears. From them Dionysus learns that he has already reached the house of Pluto, and he knocks at the door. A series of foolish incidents ensues, in which the costume of Heracles alternately arouses the wrath and elicits the blandishments of the enemies and the friends acquired by that hero on his previous visit to the underworld. The former sort of reception induces Dionysus to place the lion's skin on the shoulders of Xanthias, while the latter causes him quickly to abrogate this arrangement. Eventually they enter the house and the stage is left to the Chorus.

They praise the Athenians and gibe at the demagogue Cleophon. Then follows the sound and bold advice that the spectators should restore the oligarchical revolutionaries of 411 to the rights of citizenship.

Then Aeacus, the slave of Pluto, and Xanthias emerge from the house and are engaging in friendly conversation, when a great commotion is heard offstage. In this way the poet introduces the famous and lengthy contest between Aeschylus and Euripides, which occupies the whole of the latter portion of the comedy. The connection of this with what precedes is so loose that some scholars have been led to assume that it was originally composed for an entirely different play and was hurriedly tacked on to the unfinished *Frogs* at the news of the death of Euripides. Dionysus now abandons or forgets the original purpose for which he has come to Hades and announces that the winner of the contest will be the poet whom he will take back to Athens. With their patron god sitting as judge, the two tragedians compare their talents in every department of dramatic art. The contest is extremely close, and Dionysus has great difficulty arriving at a decision; "My choice shall fall on him my soul desires," he finally says, and we remember that it was his ardent and insatiable craving for Euripides that brought him to the underworld. We are greatly surprised when it turns out to be Aeschylus that he wishes to restore to the light of day.

The person and the poetry of Euripides bulk large in the plays of Aristophanes, but it is wholly wide of the mark to speak of him as having *attacked* Euripides; the experiments and the innovations of the restless tragedian provided material for harmless satire; his excessive pathos and ingenious intellectualism were obvious targets for gibes; but he is never accused of pederasty or of cowardice, of venality or of sycophancy, nor is it ever suggested that any of the other tragic poets of the time is even remotely to be compared with him. If we will assume Aristophanes to be speaking through the mask of Dionysus in the final scene of *The Frogs,* we must also remember that the god has no easy time choosing Aeschylus, and that it is his deepest nostalgic emotions that are ultimately decisive.

THE FROGS

(SCENE:—*In the background are two houses, that of* HERACLES *and that of* PLUTO. *Enter* DIONYSUS, *disguised as* HERACLES, *with lion-skin and club, but with the high boots of tragedy and a tunic of saffron silk. He is followed by* XANTHIAS, *seated on a donkey and carrying an immense bale of luggage on a porter's pole. They advance for a while in silence.*)

XANTHIAS (*looking round at his burden with a groan*)
SIR, shall I say one of the regular things
That people in a theatre always laugh at?

DIONYSUS.
Say what you like, except "I'm overloaded."
But mind, not that. That's simply wormwood to me.

XANTHIAS (*disappointed*)
Not anything funny?

DIONYSUS
Not "Oh, my poor blisters!"

XANTHIAS
Suppose I made the great joke?

DIONYSUS.
Why, by all means.
Don't be afraid. Only, for mercy's sake,
Don't . . .

XANTHIAS

Don't do what?

DIONYSUS

Don't shift your luggage pole
Across, and say, "I want to blow my nose."

XANTHIAS (*greatly disappointed*)

Nor that I've got such a weight upon my back
That unless some one helps me quickly I shall sneeze?

DIONYSUS

Oh, please, no. Keep it till I need emetics.

XANTHIAS

Then what's the good of carrying all this lumber
If I mayn't make one single good old wheeze
Like Phrynichus, Amipsias, and Lycis?

DIONYSUS

Ah no; don't make them.—When I sit down there
(*Pointing to the auditorium*)
And hear some of those choice products, I go home
A twelvemonth older.

XANTHIAS (*to himself*)

Oh, my poor old neck:
Blistered all round, and mustn't say it's blistered,
Because that's funny!

DIONYSUS

Airs and insolence!
When I, Dionysus, child of the Great Jug,
Must work and walk myself, and have him riding
Lest he should tire himself or carry things!

XANTHIAS

Am I not carrying things?

DIONYSUS

They're carrying you.

XANTHIAS (*showing the baggage*)

I'm carrying this.

DIONYSUS

How?

XANTHIAS

With my back half broken.

DIONYSUS

That bag is clearly carried by a donkey.

XANTHIAS

No donkey carries bags that *I* am carrying.

DIONYSUS

I suppose you know the donkey's carrying *you*.

XANTHIAS (*turning cross*)

I don't. I only know my shoulder's sore!

DIONYSUS

Well, if it does no good to ride the donkey,
Go turns, and let the poor beast ride on you.

XANTHIAS (*aside*)

Just like my luck—Why wasn't I on board
At Arginusae? Then I'd let you have it.

DIONYSUS

Dismount, you rascal.—Here's the door close by
Where I must turn in first—and I on foot! (*Knocking.*)
Porter! Hi, porter! Hi!

HERACLES (*entering from the house*)

Who's knocking there?
More like a mad bull butting at the door,
Whoever he is . . . (*seeing* DIONYSUS). God bless us, what's all this?

(*He examines* DIONYSUS *minutely, then chokes with silent emotion.*)

DIONYSUS (*aside to* XANTHIAS)

Boy!

XANTHIAS

What, sir?

DIONYSUS

Did you notice?

XANTHIAS

Notice what?

DIONYSUS

The man's afraid.

XANTHIAS

Yes, sir; (*aside*) afraid you're cracked!

HERACLES (*struggling with laughter*)

I wouldn't if I possibly could help it:
I'm trying to bite my lips, but all the same . . . (*Roars with laughter.*)

DIONYSUS

Don't be absurd! Come here. I want something.

HERACLES

I would, but I can't yet shake this laughter off:
The lion-skin on a robe of saffron silk!
How comes my club to sort with high-heeled boots?
What's the idea? Where have you come from now?

DIONYSUS

I've been at sea, serving with Clisthenes.

HERACLES

You fought a battle?

DIONYSUS

Yes: sank several ships,
Some twelve or thirteen.

HERACLES

Just you two?

DIONYSUS

Of course.

XANTHIAS (*aside*)

And then I woke, and it was all a dream!

DIONYSUS

Well, one day I was sitting there on deck
Reading the *Andromeda,* when all at once
A great desire came knocking at my heart,
You'd hardly think . . .

HERACLES

A great desire? How big?

DIONYSUS

Oh, not so big. Perhaps as large as Molon.

HERACLES

Who was the lady?

DIONYSUS

Lady?

HERACLES

Well, the girl?

DIONYSUS

Great Heaven, there wasn't one!

HERACLES

Well, I have always
Considered Clisthenes a perfect lady!

DIONYSUS

Don't mock me, brother! It's a serious thing,
A passion that has worn me to a shadow.

HERACLES

Well, tell us all about it.

DIONYSUS (*with the despair of an artist explaining himself to a common athlete*)

No; I can't.
You never . . . But I'll think of an analogy.
You never felt a sudden inward craving
For . . . pease-broth?

HERACLES

Pease-broth? Bless me, crowds of times.

DIONYSUS

See'st then the sudden truth? Or shall I put it
Another way?

HERACLES

Oh, not about pease-broth.
I see it quite.

DIONYSUS

Well, I am now consumed
By just that sort of restless craving for
Euripides.

HERACLES

Lord save us, the man's dead!

DIONYSUS

He is; and no one in this world shall stop me
From going to see him!

HERACLES

Down to the place of shades?

DIONYSUS

The place of shades or any shadier still.

HERACLES

What do you want to get?

DIONYSUS

I want a poet,
For most be dead; only the false live on.

HERACLES

Iophon's still alive.

DIONYSUS

Well, there you have it,
The one good thing still left us, if it is one.
For even as to that I have my doubts.

HERACLES

But say, why don't you bring up Sophocles
By preference, if you must have some one back?

DIONYSUS

No, not till I've had Iophon quite alone
And seen what note he gives without his father.
Besides, Euripides, being full of tricks,
Would give the slip to his master, if need were,
And try to escape with me; while Sophocles,
Content with us, will be content in Hell.

HERACLES

And Agathon, where is he?

DIONYSUS

Gone far away,
A poet true, whom many friends regret.

HERACLES

Beshrew him! Where?

DIONYSUS

To feast with peaceful kings!

HERACLES

And Xenocles?

DIONYSUS

Oh, plague take Xenocles!

HERACLES

Pythangelus, then?
(DIONYSUS *shrugs his shoulders in expressive silence.*)

XANTHIAS (*to himself*)

And no one thinks of me,
When all my shoulder's skinning, simply skinning.

HERACLES

But aren't there other pretty fellows there
All writing tragedies by tens of thousands,
And miles verboser than Euripides?

DIONYSUS

Leaves without fruit; trills in the empty air,
And starling chatter, mutilating art!
Give them one chance and that's the end of them,
One weak assault on an unprotected Muse.
Search as you will, you'll find no poet now
With grit in him, to wake a word of power.

HERACLES

How "grit"?

DIONYSUS

The grit that gives them heart to risk
Bold things—vast Ether, residence of God,
Or Time's long foot, or souls that won't take oaths
While tongues go swearing falsely by themselves.

HERACLES

You like that stuff?

DIONYSUS

Like it? I rave about it.

HERACLES (*reflecting*)
Why, yes; it's devilish tricky, as you say.

DIONYSUS
"Ride not upon my soul!" Use your own donkey.

HERACLES (*apologising*)
I only meant it was obviously humbug!

DIONYSUS
If ever I need advice about a *dinner*,
I'll come to you!

XANTHIAS (*to himself*)
And no one thinks of me.

DIONYSUS
But why I came in these especial trappings—
Disguised as you, in fact—was this. I want you
To tell me all the hosts with whom you stayed
That time you went to fetch up Cerberus:
Tell me your hosts, your harbours, bakers' shops,
Inns, taverns—reputable and otherwise—
Springs, roads, towns, posts, and landladies that keep
The fewest fleas.

XANTHIAS (*as before*)
And no one thinks of me!

HERACLES (*impressively*)
Bold man, and will you dare . . .

DIONYSUS
Now, don't begin
That sort of thing; but tell the two of us
What road will take us quickest down to Hades,—
And, please, no great extremes of heat or cold.

HERACLES
Well, which one had I better tell you first?—
Which now?—Ah, yes; suppose you got a boatman
To tug you, with a hawser—round your neck . . .

DIONYSUS

A chokey sort of journey, that.

HERACLES

Well, then,

There *is* a short road, quick and smooth, the surface
Well pounded—in a mortar.

DIONYSUS

The hemlock way?

HERACLES

Exactly.

DIONYSUS

Cold and bitter! Why, it freezes
All your shins numb.

HERACLES

Do you mind one short and steep?

DIONYSUS

Not in the least . . . You know I'm no great walker.

HERACLES

Then just stroll down to Ceramicus . . .

DIONYSUS

Well?

HERACLES

Climb up the big tower . . .

DIONYSUS

Good; and then?

HERACLES

. Then watch
And see them start the torch-race down below;
Lean over till you hear the men say "Go,"
And then, go.

DIONYSUS

Where?

HERACLES

Why, over.

DIONYSUS

Not for me.
It'd cost me two whole sausage bags of brains.
I won't go that way.

HERACLES

Well, how *will* you go?

DIONYSUS

The way *you* went that time.

HERACLES (*impressively*)

The voyage is long.
You first come to a great mere, fathomless
And very wide.

DIONYSUS (*unimpressed*)

How do I get across?

HERACLES (*with a gesture*)

In a little boat, like that; an aged man
Will row you across the ferry . . . for two obols.

DIONYSUS

Those two old obols, everywhere at work!
I wonder how they found their way down there?

HERACLES

Oh, Theseus took them!—After that you'll see
Snakes and queer monsters, crowds and crowds.

DIONYSUS

Now don't:
Don't play at bogies! You can never move me!

HERACLES

Then deep, deep mire and everlasting filth,
And, wallowing there, such as have wronged a guest,
Or picked a wench's pocket while they kissed her,
Beaten their mothers, smacked their father's jaws,
Or sworn perjurious oaths before high heaven.

DIONYSUS

And with them, I should hope, such as have learned
Cinesias's latest Battle Dance,
Or copied out a speech of Morsimus!

HERACLES

Then you will find a breath about your ears
Of music, and a light before your eyes
Most beautiful—like this—and myrtle groves,
And joyous throngs of women and of men,
And clapping of glad hands.

DIONYSUS

And who will *they* be?

HERACLES

The Initiated.

XANTHIAS (*aside*)

Yes; and I'm the donkey
Holiday-making at the Mysteries!
But I won't stand this weight one moment longer.
(*He begins to put down his bundle.*)

HERACLES

And they will forthwith tell you all you seek.
They have their dwelling just beside the road,
At Pluto's very door.—So now good-bye;
And a pleasant journey, brother.

DIONYSUS

Thanks; good-bye.
Take care of yourself. (*To* XANTHIAS, *while* HERACLES *returns into the house*) Take up the bags again.

XANTHIAS

Before I've put them down?

DIONYSUS

Yes, and be quick.

XANTHIAS

No, really, sir; we ought to hire a porter.

DIONYSUS

And what if I can't find one?

XANTHIAS

Then I'll go.

DIONYSUS

All right.—Why, here's a funeral, just in time.

(*Enter a* FUNERAL *on the right.*)

Here, sir—it's you I'm addressing—the defunct;
Do you care to carry a few traps to Hades?

THE CORPSE (*sitting up*)

How heavy?

DIONYSUS

What you see.

CORPSE

You'll pay two drachmas?

DIONYSUS

Oh, come, that's rather much.

CORPSE

Bearers, move on!

DIONYSUS

My good man, wait! See if we can't arrange.

CORPSE

Two drachmas down, or else don't talk to me.

DIONYSUS

Nine obols?

CORPSE (*lying down again*)

Strike me living if I will!

(*Exit the* FUNERAL.)

XANTHIAS

That dog's too proud! He'll come to a bad end. —
Well, I'll be porter.

DIONYSUS

That's a good brave fellow.

(*They walk across the stage.* DIONYSUS *peers into the distance.*)

DIONYSUS

What *is* that?

XANTHIAS

That? A lake.

DIONYSUS

By Zeus, it is!
The mere he spoke of.

XANTHIAS

Yes; I see a boat.

DIONYSUS

Yes; by the powers!

XANTHIAS

And yonder must be Charon.

DIONYSUS

Charon, ahoy!

BOTH

Ahoy! Charon, ahoy!

(CHARON *enters. He is an old, grim, and squalid Ferryman, wearing a slave's felt cap and a sleeveless tunic.*)

CHARON

Who is for rest from sufferings and cares?
Who's for the Carrion Crows, and the Dead Donkeys;
Lethé and Sparta and the rest of Hell?

DIONYSUS

I!

CHARON

Get in.

DIONYSUS

Where do you touch? The Carrion Crows,
You said?

CHARON (*gruffly*)

The Dogs will be the place for you.
Get in.

DIONYSUS

Come, Xanthias.

CHARON

I don't take slaves:
Unless he has won his freedom? Did he fight
The battle of the Cold Meat Unpreserved?

XANTHIAS

Well, no; my eyes were very sore just then . . .

CHARON

Then trot round on your legs!

XANTHIAS

Where shall I meet you?

CHARON

At the Cold Seat beside the Blasting Stone.

DIONYSUS (*to* XANTHIAS, *who hesitates*)

You understand?

XANTHIAS

Oh, quite. (*Aside*) Just like my luck.
What can have crossed me when I started out?

(*Exit* XANTHIAS.)

CHARON

Sit to your oar. (DIONYSUS *does his best to obey*) Any more passengers?
If so, make haste. (*To* DIONYSUS) What are you doing there?

DIONYSUS

Why, what you told me; sitting on my oar.

CHARON

Oh, are you? Well, get up again and sit

(*Pushing him down*)

Down there—fatty!

DIONYSUS (*doing everything wrong*)

Like that?

CHARON

Put out your arms
And stretch . . .

DIONYSUS

Like that?

CHARON

None of your nonsense here!
Put both your feet against the stretcher.—Now,
In good time, row!

DIONYSUS (*fluently, putting down his oars*)

And how do you expect
A man like me, with no experience,
No seamanship, no Salamis,—to row?

CHARON

You'll row all right; as soon as you fall to,
You'll hear a first-rate tune that *makes* you row.

DIONYSUS

Who sings it?

CHARON

Certain cycnoranidae.
That's music!

DIONYSUS

Give the word then, and we'll see.

(CHARON *gives the word for rowing and marks the time. A* CHORUS OF FROGS *is heard off stage.*)

FROGS

O brood of the mere and the spring,
Gather together and sing
  From the depths of your throat
  By the side of the boat,
Co-äx, as we move in a ring;

As in Limnae we sang the divine
Nyseïan Giver of Wine,
  When the people in lots
  With their sanctified Pots
Came reeling around my shrine.

Co-äx, co-äx, co-äx,
Brekekekex co-äx.

DIONYSUS

Don't sing any more;
I begin to be sore!

FROGS

Brekekekex co-äx.

Co-äx, co-äx, co-äx,
Brekekekex co-äx!

DIONYSUS

Is it nothing to you
If I'm black and I'm blue?

FROGS

Brekekekex co-äx!

DIONYSUS

A plague on all of your swarming packs.
There's nothing in you except co-äx!

FROGS

Well, and what more do you need?
Though it's none of your business indeed,
When the Muse thereanent
Is entirely content,
And horny-hoof Pan with his reed:

When Apollo is fain to admire
My voice, on account of his lyre
Which he frames with the rushes
And watery bushes—
Co-äx!—which I grow in the mire.

Co-äx, co-äx, co-äx,
Brekekekex co-äx!

DIONYSUS

Peace, musical sisters!
I'm covered with blisters.

FROGS

Brekekekex co-äx.

Co-äx, co-äx, co-äx,
Brekekekex co-äx.
Our song we can double
Without the least trouble:
Brekekekex co-äx.

Sing we now, if ever hopping
Through the sedge and flowering rushes;
In and out the sunshine flopping,
We have sported, rising, dropping,
With our song that nothing hushes

Sing, if e'er in days of storm
Safe our native oozes bore us,
Staved the rain off, kept us warm,
Till we set our dance in form,
Raised our hubble-bubbling chorus:

Brekekekex co-äx, co-äx!

DIONYSUS

Brekekekex co-äx, co-äx!
I can sing it as loud as you.

FROGS

Sisters, that he never must do!

DIONYSUS

Would you have me row till my shoulder cracks?

FROGS

Brekekekex co-äx, co-äx!

DIONYSUS

Brekekekex co-äx, co-äx!
Groan away till you burst your backs.
It's nothing to me.

FROGS

Just wait till you see.

DIONYSUS

I don't care how you scold.

FROGS

Then all day long
We will croak you a song
As loud as our throat can hold.

Brekekekex co-äx, co-äx!!

DIONYSUS

Brekekekex co-äx, co-äx!!
I'll see you don't outdo me in that

FROGS

Well, *you* shall never beat *us*—that's flat!

DIONYSUS

I'll make you cease your song
If I shout for it all day long;
My lungs I'll tax
With co-äx, co-äx
—I assure you they're thoroughly strong—
Until your efforts at last relax:
Brekekekex co-äx, co-äx!!
(*No answer from the* FROGS.)
Brekekekex co-äx, co-äx!!
I knew in the end I should stop your quacks!

CHARON

Easy there! Stop her! Lay her alongside.—
Now pay your fare and go.

DIONYSUS (*peering about him*)

There are the obols.
Ho, Xanthias! . . . Where's Xanthias?—Is that you?

XANTHIAS (*from off stage*)

Hullo!

DIONYSUS

Come this way.

XANTHIAS (*entering*)

Oh, I'm glad to see you!

DIONYSUS (*looking round*)

Well, and what have we here?

XANTHIAS

Darkness—and mud.

DIONYSUS

Did you see any of the perjurers here,
And father-beaters, as he said we should?

XANTHIAS

Why, didn't you?

DIONYSUS

I? Lots.
(*Looking full at the audience.*)
I see them now.
Well, what are we to do?

XANTHIAS

Move further on.
This is the place he said was all aswarm
With horrid beasts.

DIONYSUS

A plague on what he said!
Exaggerating just to frighten me,
Because he knew my courage and was jealous.
Naught lives so flown with pride as Heracles!
Why, my best wish would be to meet with something,
Some real adventure, worthy of our travels!

XANTHIAS (*listening*)

Stay!—Yes, upon my word. I hear a noise.

DIONYSUS (*nervously*)

God bless me, where?

XANTHIAS

Behind.

DIONYSUS

Go to the rear.

XANTHIAS

No; it's in front somewhere.

DIONYSUS

Then get in front.

XANTHIAS

Why, there I see it.—Save us!—A great beast. . . .

DIONYSUS (*cowering behind* XANTHIAS)

What like?

XANTHIAS

Horrid! . . . At least it keeps on changing!
It was a bull; now it's a mule; and now
A fair young girl.

DIONYSUS

Where is it? Let me at it!

XANTHIAS

Stay, sir; it's not a girl now, it's a dog.

DIONYSUS

It must be Empusa!

XANTHIAS

Yes. At least its head
Is all on fire.

DIONYSUS

Has it a leg of brass?

XANTHIAS

Yes, that it has. And the other leg of cow-dung.
It's she!

DIONYSUS

Where shall I go?

XANTHIAS

Well, where shall I?

DIONYSUS (*running forward and addressing the Priest of* DIONYSUS *in his seat of state in the centre of the front row of the audience*)

My Priest, protect me and we'll sup together!

XANTHIAS

We're done for, O Lord Heracles.

DIONYSUS (*cowering again*)

Oh, don't!
Don't shout like that, man, and don't breathe that name

XANTHIAS

Dionysus, then!

DIONYSUS

No, no. That's worse than the other. . . .
Keep on the way you're going.

XANTHIAS (*after searching about*)

Come along, sir.

DIONYSUS

What is it?

XANTHIAS

Don't be afraid, sir. All goes well
And we can say as said Hegelochus,
"Beyond these storms I catch a *piece* of *tail!*"
Empusa's gone.

DIONYSUS

Swear it.

XANTHIAS

By Zeus, she's gone!

DIONYSUS

Again.

XANTHIAS

By Zeus, she's gone!

DIONYSUS

Your solemn oath.

XANTHIAS

By Zeus!!

DIONYSUS (*raising himself*)
Dear me, that made me feel quite pale.

XANTHIAS (*pointing to the Priest*)
And this kind gentleman turned red for sympathy.

DIONYSUS
How can I have sinned to bring all this upon me?
What power is bent on my destruction?

XANTHIAS
The residence of God, or Time's long foot?

DIONYSUS (*listening as flute-playing is heard outside*)
I say!

XANTHIAS
What is it?

DIONYSUS
Don't you hear it?

XANTHIAS
What?

DIONYSUS
Flutes blowing.

XANTHIAS
Yes. And such a smell of torches
Floating towards us, all most Mystery-like!

DIONYSUS
Crouch quietly down and let us hear the music.

(*They crouch down at the left. Music is heard far off.* XANTHIAS *puts down the bundle.*)

CHORUS (*unseen*)
Iacchus, O Iacchus!
Iacchus, O Iacchus!

XANTHIAS

That's it, sir. These are the Initiated
Rejoicing somewhere here, just as he told us.
Why, it's the old Iacchus hymn that used
To warm the cockles of Diagoras!

DIONYSUS

Yes, it must be. However, we'd best sit
Quite still and listen, till we're sure of it.

(*There enters gradually the* CHORUS, *consisting of Men Initiated in the Eleusinian Mysteries. They are led by a hierophant or Initiating Priest, and accompanied by a throng of Worshipping Women. They have white robes, wreaths upon their brows, and torches in their hands.*)

CHORUS (*singing, off stage*)

Thou that dwellest in the shadow
Of great glory here beside us,
Spirit, Spirit, we have hied us
To thy dancing in the meadow!
Come, Iacchus; let thy brow
Toss its fruited myrtle bough;
We are thine, O happy dancer; O our comrade, come and guide us!
Let the mystic measure beat:
Come in riot fiery fleet;
Free and holy all before thee,
While the Charites adore thee,
And thy Mystae wait the music of thy feet!

XANTHIAS

O Virgin of Demeter, highly blest,
What an entrancing smell of roasted pig!

DIONYSUS

Hush! hold your tongue! Perhaps they'll give you some

CHORUS (*singing as they enter*)

Spirit, Spirit, lift the shaken
Splendour of thy tossing torches!
All the meadow flashes, scorches:
Up, Iacchus, and awaken!
Come, thou star that bringest light
To the darkness of our rite,
Till thine old men leap as young men, leap with every thought forsaken
Of the dulness and the fear
Left by many a circling year:
Let thy red light guide the dances
Where thy banded youth advances
To be merry by the blossoms of the mere!

LEADER OF THE CHORUS

Hush, oh hush! for our song begins. Let every one stand aside
Who owns an intellect muddled with sins, or in arts like these untried:
If the mystic rites of the Muses true he has never seen nor sung:
If he never the magical music knew of Cratinus the Bull-eater's tongue:
If he likes in a comedy nothing but riot and meaningless harlequinade:
Or in matters of politics cannot keep quiet and see that cabals be allayed,
But blows up spite and keeps it alight to serve his personal ends:
Or being in power at a critical hour, accepts little gifts from his friends:
Or goes selling a ship, or betraying a fort, or takes to the trade of a smuggler,
Attempting again, in Thorycion's sort,—that pestilent revenue-juggler,—

From Aegina before us to stock Epidaurus with tar and canvas and hide,
Or tries to persuade some friend in the trade for the enemy's ships to provide:
Or a teacher of choirs who forgets his position and damages Hecaté's shrines:
Or the robber of poets, the mere politician, who spites us with pitiful fines
Because we have suitably made him absurd in the God's traditional rhyme:
Behold, I give word: and again give word: and give word for the third, last time:
Make room, all such, for our dance and song.—Up, you, and give us a lay
That is meet for our mirth-making all night long and for this great festival day.

CHORUS (*singing*)

Forth fare all;
This mead's bowers
Bear fresh flowers;
Forth, I call.
Leap, mock, dance, play;
Enough and to spare we have feasted to-day!

March: raise high
Her whose hands
Save these lands;
Raise due cry:
Maid, Maid, save these,
Tho' it may not exactly Thorycion please!

LEADER OF THE CHORUS

One hymn to the Maiden; now raise ye another
To the Queen of the Fruits of the Earth.
To Demeter the Corn-giver, Goddess and Mother
Make worship in musical mirth.

CHORUS (*singing*)

Approach, O Queen of orgies pure,
And us, thy faithful band, ensure
From morn to eve to ply secure
  Our mocking and our clowning:
To grace thy feast with many a hit
Of merry jest or serious wit,
And laugh, and earn the prize, and flit
  Triumphant to the crowning.

LEADER OF THE CHORUS (*speaking*)

Now call the God of blooming mien;
  Raise the mystic chorus:
Our comrade he and guide unseen,
  With us and before us.

CHORUS (*singing*)

Iacchus high in glory, thou whose day
Of all is merriest, hither, help our play;
  Show, as we throne thee at thy Maiden's side,
How light to thee are our long leagues of way.
  Iacchus, happy dancer, be our guide.
Thyself, that poorest men thy joy should share,
Didst rend thy robe, thy royal sandal tear,
  That feet unshod might dance, and robes rent wide
Wave in thy revel with no after care.
  Iacchus, happy dancer, be our guide.

Lo there! but now across the dance apace
A maiden tripped, a maiden fair of face,
  Whose tattered smock and kerchief scarce could hide
The merry bosom peering from its place.
  Iacchus, happy dancer, be our guide.

XANTHIAS (*singing*)

I always liked to follow some one else:
Suppose we join and dance?

DIONYSUS (*singing*)

Why, so say I.

(*They join the dance.*)

LEADER OF THE CHORUS (*singing*)

Perhaps 'twill best beseem us
To deal with Archedemus,
Who is toothless still and rootless, at seven years from birth:

Yet he leads the public preachers
Of those poor dead upper creatures,
And is prince of all the shadiness on earth!

And Clisthenes, says rumour,
In a wild despairing humour
Sits huddled up and tearing out his hair among the graves.

To believe he would incline us
That a person named Sebinus
Is tossing yet unburied on the waves!

While Callias, says tattle,
Has attended a sea-battle,
And lionesses' scalps were the uniform he wore!

DIONYSUS (*singing*)

You'd oblige us much by telling
Me the way to Pluto's dwelling.
We are strangers newly lighted on your shore.

LEADER OF THE CHORUS (*singing*)

No need of distant travel
That problem to unravel;
For know that while you ask me, you are standing at the door.

DIONYSUS (*singing*)

Then up, my lad, be packing!

XANTHIAS (*singing*)

There's the Devil in the sacking:
It can't stay still a second on the floor!

LEADER OF THE CHORUS (*speaking*)

Now onward through Demeter's ring
Through the leaves and flowers,
All who love her junketing,
All who know her powers!
Fare forward you, while I go here
With matron and with maiden,
To make their night-long roaming clear
With tossing torches laden.

CHORUS (*singing*)

Then on 'mid the meadows deep,
Where thickest the rosebuds creep
And the dewdrops are pearliest:
A jubilant step advance
In our own, our eternal dance,
Till its joy the Glad Fates entrance
Who threaded it earliest.

For ours is the sunshine bright,
Yea, ours is the joy of light
All pure, without danger:
For we thine Elect have been,
Thy secrets our eyes have seen,
And our hearts we have guarded clean
Toward kinsman and stranger!

(*The* CHORUS *lines up on one side of the Orchestra.*)

DIONYSUS (*approaching the door of Pluto's house*)

I ought by rights to knock; but how, I wonder.
I don't know how they do knock in this country.

XANTHIAS

Oh, don't waste time. Go in and do your best,
Like Heracles in heart as well as garb.

DIONYSUS (*knocking*)

Ho there!

(*The door opens and a Porter appears, whose dress shows him to be* AEACUS, *the Judge of the Dead.*)

AEACUS

Who summons?

DIONYSUS

Heracles the Brave.

AEACUS

Thou rash, impure, and most abandoned man,
Foul, inly foul, yea, ye foulest upon earth,
Who harried our dog, Cerberus, choked him dumb,
Fled, vanished, and left me to bear the blame,
Who kept him!—Now I have thee on the hip!
So close the black encaverned rocks of Styx
And Acheronian crags a-drip with blood
Surround thee, and Cocytus' circling hounds,
And the hundred-headed serpent, that shall rend
Thy bowels asunder; to thy lungs shall cleave
The lamprey of Tartessus, and thy reins
And inmost entrails in one paste of gore
Tithrasian Gorgons' gorge for evermore!
—To whom, even now, I speed my indignant course!
(*The Porter retires.*)

DIONYSUS (*who has fallen prostrate*)

Please!

XANTHIAS

What's the matter? Quick, get up again
Before they come and see you.

DIONYSUS

But I feel
Faint.—Put a cold wet sponge against my heart.

XANTHIAS (*producing a sponge*)

There; you apply it.

DIONYSUS

Thanks. Where is it?

XANTHIAS

There.

(DIONYSUS *takes and applies it.*)

Ye golden gods, is it there you keep your heart?

DIONYSUS

The nervous shock made it go down and down!

XANTHIAS

You *are* the greatest coward I ever saw,
Of gods or humans!

DIONYSUS

I a coward?—I had
The presence of mind to ask you for a sponge.
Few had done more!

XANTHIAS

Could any one do less?

DIONYSUS

A coward would still be flat there, sniffing salts;
I rose, called for a sponge, and used the sponge.

XANTHIAS

That *was* brave, by Posidon!

DIONYSUS

I should think so.—
And weren't *you* frightened at his awful threats
And language?

XANTHIAS

I? I never cared a rap.

DIONYSUS

Oh, you're a hero, aren't you?—and want glory.
Well, you be *me!* Put on this lion's hide
And take the club—if you're so dauntless-hearted.
I'll take my turn, and be your luggage-boy.

XANTHIAS

Over with both of them! Of course I will.
(*He proceeds to put on the lion-skin.*)
Now watch if Xanthias-Heracles turns faint,
Or shows the same "presence of mind," as you.

DIONYSUS

The true Melitean jail-bird, on my life! . . .
Well, I suppose I'd better take the luggage.

(*The exchange is just effected when the door again opens and there enters a* MAID OF PERSEPHONÉ.)

MAID

Dear Heracles, and is it you once more?
Come in! No sooner did my mistress learn
Your coming, than she set her bread to bake,
Set pots of split-pea porridge, two or three,
A-boiling, a whole ox upon the coals,
Cakes in the oven, and big buns.—Oh, come in.

XANTHIAS (*as* HERACLES)

She is very kind; perhaps some other time.

MAID

Oh, really; but I mustn't let you go!
She's doing everything herself! Braised game,
Spices and fruits and stoups of the sweetest wine—.
Come in with me.

XANTHIAS

Most kind, but . . .

MAID

No excuses.
I won't let go.—A flute-player, very pretty,
Is waiting for you, and two or three such sweet
Young dancing girls.

XANTHIAS (*wavering*)

Did you say dancing girls?

MAID

Yes. Do come in.—They just were going to serve
The fish, and have the table lifted in.

XANTHIAS

I will! I'll chance it!—Go straight in and tell
Those dancing girls that Heracles is coming!
(*The* MAID *retires again.*)
Here, boy, take up the bags and follow me.

DIONYSUS

Stop, please!—You didn't take it seriously
When I just dressed you as Heracles for fun?
You can't be so ridiculous, Xanthias.
Take up the bags at once and bring them in.

XANTHIAS

What? Surely you don't mean to take away
Your own gift?

DIONYSUS

Mean it? No; I'm doing it!
Off with that lion-skin, quick.
(*Begins to strip off the lion-skin by force.*)

XANTHIAS

Help! I'm assaulted . . .
(*Giving way.*)
I leave it with the Gods!

DIONYSUS (*proceeding to dress himself again*)

The Gods, indeed!
What senseless vanity to expect to be
Alcmena's son, a mortal and a slave!

XANTHIAS

Well, take it. I don't care.—The time may be,
God willing, when you'll feel the need of me!

CHORUS (*singing*)

That's the way such points to settle,
Like a chief of tested mettle,
Weather-worn on many seas,
Not in one fixed pattern stopping,
Like a painted thing, but dropping
Always towards the side of ease.
'Tis this instinct for soft places,
To keep warm while others freeze,
Marks a man of gifts and graces,
Like our own Theramenes!

DIONYSUS (*singing*)

Surely 'twould the matter worsen,
If I saw this low-bred person
On his cushions sprawling so,
Served him drinking, watched him winking:—
If he knew what I was thinking—
And he would, for certain, know,
Being a mighty shrewd deviser
Of such fancies—with a blow
P'raps he'd loosen an incisor
From the forefront of my row!

(*During this song there has entered along the street a* LANDLADY, *who is soon followed by her servant,* PLATHANÉ.)

LANDLADY

Ho, Plathané, here, I want you, Plathané! . . .
Here is that scamp who came to the inn before,
Ate sixteen loaves of bread. . .

PLATHANÉ

Why, so it is:
The very man!

XANTHIAS (*aside*)

Here's fun for somebody.

LANDLADY

And twenty plates of boiled meat, half an obol
At every gulp!

XANTHIAS (*aside*)

Some one'll catch it now!

LANDLADY

And all that garlic.

DIONYSUS

Nonsense, my good woman,
You don't know what you're saying.

PLATHANÉ

Did you think
I wouldn't know you in those high-heeled boots?

LANDLADY

And all the salt-fish I've not mentioned yet. . . .

PLATHANÉ (*to* LANDLADY)

No, you poor thing; and all the good fresh cheese
The man kept swallowing, and the baskets with it!

LANDLADY (*to* XANTHIAS)

And when he saw me coming for the money
Glared like a wild bull! Yes, and roared at me!

XANTHIAS

Just what he does! His manners everywhere.

LANDLADY

Tugged at his sword! Pretended to be mad!

PLATHANE

Yes, you poor thing; I don't know how you bore it!

LANDLADY

And we got all of a tremble, both of us,
And ran up the ladder to the loft! And he,
He tore the matting up—and off he went!

XANTHIAS

Like him, again.

PLATHANE

But something must be done!

LANDLADY (*to* PLATHANÉ)

Run, you, and fetch me my protector, Cleon.

PLATHANÉ (*to the* LANDLADY, *as they run excitedly to go off in different directions*)

And you fetch me Hyperbolus, if you meet him. . . .
Then we shall crush him!

LANDLADY (*returning*)

Oh, that ugly jaw!
If I could throw a stone, I'd like to break
Those wicked teeth that ground my larder dry!

PLATHANE (*returning on the other side*)

And I should like to fling you in the pit!

LANDLADY (*turning again as she goes off*)

And I should like to get a scythe, and cut
That throat that swallowed all my sausages.

PLATHANE (*the same*)

Well, I'll go straight to Cleon, and this same day
We'll worm them out in a law-court, come what may!

(*The* LANDLADY *and* PLATHANÉ *go off in different directions.*)

DIONYSUS

Plague take me! No friend left me in the world. . . .
Except old Xanthias!

XANTHIAS

I know, I know!
We all see what you want. But that's enough!
I won't be Heracles.

DIONYSUS

Now don't say that,
Xanthias—old boy!

XANTHIAS

And how am I to be
Alcmena's son—a mortal and a slave?

DIONYSUS

I know you're angry, and quite justly so.
Hit me if you like; I won't say one word back.
But, mark, if ever again in this wide world
I rob you of these clothes, destruction fall
On me myself, my wife, my little ones,—
And, if you like, on the old bat Archedemus!

XANTHIAS

That oath will do. I take it on those terms.

CHORUS (*singing*)

Now 'tis yours to make repayment
For the honour of this raiment;
Wear it well, as erst you wore;
If it needs some renovating,
Think of whom you're personating,
Glare like Heracles and roar.
Else, if any fear you show, sir,
Any weakness at the core,
Any jesting, back you go, sir,
To the baggage as before!

XANTHIAS (*singing*)

Thank you for your kind intention,
But I had some comprehension
  Of the task I undertook.
Should the lion-skin make for profit,
He'll attempt to make me doff it—
  That I know—by hook or crook.
Still I'll make my acting real,
  Peppery gait and fiery look.
Ha! Here comes the great ordeal:
  See the door. I'm sure it shook!

(*The central door opens and the Porter,* AEACUS, *comes out with two other slaves.*)

AEACUS

Here, seize this dog-stealer and lead him forth
To justice, quick.

DIONYSUS (*imitating* XANTHIAS)

Here's fun for somebody.

XANTHIAS (*in a Heraclean attitude*)

Stop, zounds! Not one step more!

AEACUS

You want to fight?
Ho, Ditylas, Sceblyas, and Pardocas,
Forward! Oblige this person with some fighting!

DIONYSUS (*while the Scythians gradually overpower* XANTHIAS)

How shocking to assault the constables—
And stealing other people's things!

AEACUS

Unnatural,
That's what I call it.

DIONYSUS

Quite a pain to see.

XANTHIAS (*now overpowered and disarmed*)
Now, by Lord Zeus, if ever I've been here
Or stol'n from you the value of one hair,
You may take and hang me on the nearest tree! . . .
Now, listen: and I'll act quite fairly by you;
(*Suddenly indicating* DIONYSUS)
Take this poor boy, and put him to the question!
And if you find me guilty, hang me straight.

AEACUS
What tortures do you allow?

XANTHIAS
Use all you like.
Tie him in the ladder, hang him by the feet,
Whip off his skin with bristle-whips and rack him;
You might well try some vinegar up his nose,
And bricks upon his chest, and so on. Only
No scourges made of . . . leek or young shallot.

AEACUS
A most frank offer, most frank.—If my treatment
Disables him, the value shall be paid.

XANTHIAS
Don't mention it. Remove him and begin.

AEACUS
Thank you, we'll do it here, that you may witness
Exactly what he says. (*To* DIONYSUS) Put down your bundle,
And mind you tell the truth.

DIONYSUS (*who has hitherto been speechless with horror, now bursting out*)
I warn all present,
To torture me is an illegal act,
Being immortal! And whoever does so
Must take the consequences.

AEACUS

Why, who *are* you?

DIONYSUS

The immortal Dionysus, son of Zeus;
And this my slave.

AEACUS (*to* XANTHIAS)

You hear his protest?

XANTHIAS

Yes;
All the more reason, that, for whipping him;
If he's a real immortal he won't feel it.

DIONYSUS

Well, but you claim to be immortal too;
They ought to give you just the same as me.

XANTHIAS

That's fair enough. All right; whichever of us
You first find crying, or the least bit minding
Your whip, you're free to say he's no true god.

AEACUS

Sir, you behave like a true gentleman;
You come to justice of yourself!—Now then,
Strip, both.

XANTHIAS

How will you test us?

AEACUS

Easily:
You'll each take whack and whack about.

XANTHIAS

All right.

AEACUS (*striking* XANTHIAS)

There.

XANTHIAS (*controlling himself with an effort*)
Watch now, if you see me even wince.

AEACUS

But I've already hit you!

XANTHIAS

I think not.

AEACUS

Upon my word, it looks as if I hadn't.
Well, now I'll go and whack the other.
(*Strikes* DIONYSUS.)

DIONYSUS (*also controlling himself*)
When?

AEACUS

I've done it.

DIONYSUS (*with an air of indifference*)
Odd, it didn't make me sneeze!

AEACUS

It *is* odd!—Well, I'll try the first again.
(*He crosses to* XANTHIAS.)

XANTHIAS

All right. Be quick. (*The blow falls*) Whe-ew!

AEACUS

Ah, why "whe-ew"?
It didn't hurt you?

XANTHIAS (*recovering himself*)
No; I just was thinking
When my Diomean Feast would next be due.

AEACUS

A holy thought!—I'll step across again.
(*Strikes* DIONYSUS, *who howls.*)

DIONYSUS

Ow-ow!

AEACUS

What's that?

DIONYSUS (*recovering himself*)

I saw some cavalry.

AEACUS

What makes your eyes run?

DIONYSUS

There's a smell of onions!

AEACUS

You're sure it didn't hurt you?

DIONYSUS

Hurt? Not it.

AEACUS

I'll step across again then to the first one.

(*Strikes* XANTHIAS, *who also howls.*)

XANTHIAS

Hi-i!

AEACUS

What is it now?

XANTHIAS

Take out that thorn

(*Pointing to his foot.*)

AEACUS

What does it mean?—Over we go again.

(*Strikes* DIONYSUS.)

DIONYSUS

O Lord! (***hurriedly turning his wail into a line of poetry***)
"of Delos or of Pytho's rock."

XANTHIAS (*triumphantly*)

It hurts. You heard?

DIONYSUS

It doesn't! I was saying
A verse of old Hipponax to myself.

XANTHIAS

You're making nothing of it. Hit him hard
Across the soft parts underneath the ribs.

AEACUS (*to* XANTHIAS)

A good idea! Turn over on your back!

(*Strikes him.*)

XANTHIAS (*as before*)

O Lord!

DIONYSUS

It hurts!

XANTHIAS (*as though continuing*)

"Posidon ruler free
Of cliffs Aegean and the grey salt sea."

AEACUS

Now, by Demeter, it's beyond my powers
To tell which one of you's a god!—Come in;
We'll ask my master. He and Persephassa
Will easily know you, being gods themselves.

DIONYSUS

Most wisely said. Indeed I could have wished
You'd thought of that before you had me swished.

(*They all go into the house. The* CHORUS, *left alone on the stage, turns towards the audience.*)

CHORUS (*singing*)

Draw near, O Muse, to the spell of my song,
Set foot in the sanctified place,
And see thy faithful Athenians throng,

To whom the myriad arts belong,
  The myriad marks of grace,

Greater than Cleophon's own,
On whose lips, with bilingual moan,
    A swallow from Thrace
    Has taken his place
And chirps in blood-curdling tone
On the gibberish-tree's thick branches high
  As he utters a nightingale note,
      A tumultuous cry
      That he's certain to die
  Even with an equal vote!

LEADER OF THE CHORUS

It behoves this sacred Chorus, in its wisdom and its bliss,
To assist the state with counsel. Now our first advice is this:
Let Athenians all stand equal; penal laws be swept away.
Some of us have been misguided, following Phrynichus astray;
Now for all of these, we urge you, let full freedom be decreed
To confess the cause that tripped them and blot out that old misdeed.
Next, no man should live in Athens outcast, robbed of every right.
Shame it is that low-born aliens, just for sharing one sea-fight,
Should forthwith become 'Plataeans' and instead of slaves be masters—
(Not that in the least I blame you for thus meeting our disasters;
No; I pay respectful homage to the one wise thing you've done):
But remember these men also, your own kinsmen, sire and son,
Who have ofttimes fought beside you, spilt their blood on many seas:

Grant for that one fault the pardon which they crave you on their knees.
You whom Nature made for wisdom, let your vengeance fall to sleep;
Greet as kinsmen and Athenians, burghers true to win and keep,
Whosoe'er will brave the storms and fight for Athens at your side!
But be sure, if still we spurn them, if we wrap us in our pride,
Stand alone, with Athens tossing in the long arm of the waves,
Men in days to come shall wonder, and not praise you in your graves.

CHORUS (*singing*)

An' I the make of a man may trow,
And the ways that lead to a fall,
Not long will the ape that troubles us now,
Not long little Cligenes—champion, I vow,
Of rascally washermen all,

Who hold over soap their sway
And lye and Cimolian clay
(Which they thriftily mix
With the scrapings of bricks)—
Not long will our little one stay!
Oh, 'tis well he is warlike and ready to kick
For if once home from supper he trotted,
Talking genially thick
And without his big stick,
We should probably find him garotted.

LEADER OF THE CHORUS

It has often struck our notice that the course our city runs
Is the same towards men and money.—She has true and worthy sons:
She has good and ancient silver, she has good and recent gold.

These are coins untouched with alloys; everywhere their fame is told;
Not all Hellas holds their equal, not all Barbary far and near,
Gold or silver, each well minted, tested each and ringing clear.
Yet, we never use them! Others always pass from hand to hand,
Sorry brass just struck last week and branded with a wretched brand.
So with men we know for upright, blameless lives and noble names,
Trained in music and palaestra, freemen's choirs and freemen's games,
These we spurn for men of brass, for red-haired things of unknown breed,
Rascal cubs of mongrel fathers—them we use at every need!
Creatures just arrived in Athens, whom our city, years ago,
Scarcely would have used as scapegoats to be slaughtered for a show!
Even now, O race demented, there is time to change your ways;
Use once more what's worth the using. If we 'scape, the more the praise
That we fought our fight with wisdom; or, if all is lost for good,
Let the tree on which they hang us be, at least, of decent wood!

(*The door opens, and the two slaves,* AEACUS *and* XANTHIAS, *return.*)

AEACUS

By Zeus, that's what I call a gentleman!
That master of yours!

XANTHIAS

Gentleman? That he is!
There's nothing in his head but wine and wenches!

AEACUS

But not to whip you when you were clean convicted,
A slave caught masquerading as his master!

XANTHIAS (*significantly*)

I'd like to see him try it!

AEACUS

There you go!
The old slave trick, that I'm so fond of too.

XANTHIAS

You like it, eh?

AEACUS

Like it? Why, when I get
Behind my master's back and quietly curse him,
I feel just like the Blessed in the Mysteries!

XANTHIAS

What about muttering as you go outside
After a whacking?

AEACUS

Yes; I like that too.

XANTHIAS (*with increasing excitement*)

And prying into people's secrets, eh?

AEACUS (*the same*)

By Zeus, there's nothing like it in the world!

XANTHIAS

Oh! Zeus makes brethren meet!—And what of list'ning
To what the masters say?

AEACUS

It makes me mad!

XANTHIAS

And telling every word of it to strangers?

AEACUS

Madder than mad, stark staring crimson madder!

XANTHIAS

O Lord Apollo, clap your right hand there,
Give me your cheek to kiss, and you kiss me!
(*They embrace; a loud noise is heard inside the house.*)
But Zeus!—our own Zeus of the Friendly Jailbirds—
What is that noise . . . those shouts and quarrelling . . .
Inside?

AEACUS

That? Aeschylus and Euripides!

XANTHIAS

Eh?

AEACUS

Yes; there's a big business just astir,
And hot dissension among all the dead.

XANTHIAS

About what?

AEACUS

There's a law established here
Concerning all the large and liberal arts,
Which grants the foremost master in each art
Free entertainment at the Central Hearth,
And also a special throne in Pluto's row . . .

XANTHIAS

Oh, now I understand!

AEACUS

To hold until
There comes one greater; then he must make way.

XANTHIAS

But how has this affected Aeschylus?

AEACUS

Aeschylus held the throne of tragedy,
As greatest . . .

XANTHIAS

Held it? Why, who holds it now?

AEACUS

Well, when Euripides came down, he gave
Free exhibitions to our choicest thieves,
Footpads, cut-purses, burglars, father-beaters,
—Of whom we have numbers here; and when they heard
The neat retorts, the fencing, and the twists,
They all went mad and thought him something splendid.
And he, growing proud, laid hands upon the throne
Where Aeschylus sat.

XANTHIAS

And wasn't pelted off?

AEACUS

Not he. The whole folk clamoured for a trial
To see which most was master of his craft.

XANTHIAS

The whole jail-folk?

AEACUS

Exactly;—loud as trumpets.

XANTHIAS

And were there none to fight for Aeschylus?

AEACUS

Goodness is scarce, you know. (*Indicating the audience*)
The same as here!

XANTHIAS

And what does Pluto mean to do about it?

AEACUS

Why, hold a trial and contest on the spot
To test their skill for certain

XANTHIAS (*reflecting*)
But, I say,
Sophocles surely must have claimed the throne?

AEACUS
Not he; as soon as ever he came down,
He kissed old Aeschylus, and wrung his hand,
And Aeschylus made room on half his seat.
And now he means to wait—or so, at least,
Clidemides informs us—in reserve.
If Aeschylus wins the day, he'll rest content:
If not, why then, he says, for poor Art's sake,
He must show fight against Euripides!

XANTHIAS
It is to be, then?

AEACUS
Certainly, quite soon.
Just where you stand we'll have the shock of war.
They'll weigh the poetry line by line . . .

XANTHIAS
Poor thing,
A lamb set in the meat-scale and found wanting!

AEACUS
They'll bring straight-edges out, and cubit-rules,
And folded cube-frames . . .

XANTHIAS
Is it bricks they want?

AEACUS
And mitre-squares and wedges! Line by line
Euripides will test all tragedies!

XANTHIAS
That must make Aeschylus angry, I should think?

AEACUS

Well, he did stoop and glower like a mad bull.

XANTHIAS

Who'll be the judge?

AEACUS

That was a difficulty.
Both found an utter dearth of proper critics;
For Aeschylus objected to the Athenians. . . .

XANTHIAS

Perhaps he thought the jail-folk rather many?

AEACUS

And all the world beside, he thought mere dirt
At seeing what kind of thing a poet was.
So, in the end, they fixed upon your master
As having much experience in the business.
But come in; when the master's face looks grave
There's mostly trouble coming for the slave.

CHORUS (*singing*)

Eftsoons shall dire anger interne be the Thunderer's portion
When his foe's glib tusk fresh whetted for blood he descries;
Then fell shall his heart be, and mad; and a pallid distortion
Descend as a cloud on his eyes.

Yea, words with plumes wild on the wind and with helmets a-glancing,
With axles a-splinter and marble a-shiver, eftsoons
Shall bleed, as a man meets the shock of a Thought-builder's prancing
Stanzas of dusky dragoons.

The deep crest of his mane shall uprise as he slowly unlimbers

The long-drawn wrath of his brow, and lets loose with a roar
Epithets welded and screwed, like new torrent-swept timbers
Blown loose by a giant at war.

Then rises the man of the Mouth; then battleward flashes
A tester of verses, a smooth and serpentine tongue,
To dissect each phrase into mincemeat, and argue to ashes
That high-towered labour of lung!

(*The door opens again. Enter* EURIPIDES, DIONYSUS, *and* AESCHYLUS.)

EURIPIDES

Pray, no advice to me! I won't give way;
I claim that I'm more master of my art.

DIONYSUS

You hear him, Aeschylus. Why don't you speak?

EURIPIDES

He wants to open with an awful silence—
The blood-curdling reserve of his first scenes.

DIONYSUS

My dear sir, I must beg! Control your language!

EURIPIDES

I know him; I've seen through him years ago;
Bard of the "noble savage," wooden-mouthed,
No door, no bolt, no bridle to his tongue,
A torrent of pure bombast—tied in bundles!

AESCHYLUS (*breaking out*)

How say'st thou, Son o' the Goddess of the Greens?—
You dare speak thus of me, you phrase-collector,
Blind-beggar-bard and scum of rifled rag-bags!
Oh, you shall rue it!

DIONYSUS

Stop! Stop, Aeschylus;
Strike not thine heart to fire on rancour old.

AESCHYLUS

No; I'll expose this crutch-and-cripple playwright,
And what he's worth for all his insolence.

DIONYSUS (*to attendants*)

A lamb, a black lamb, quick, boys! Bring it out
To sacrifice; a hurricane's let loose!

AESCHYLUS (*to* EURIPIDES)

You and your Cretan dancing-solos! You
And the ugly amours that you set to verse!

DIONYSUS (*interposing*)

One moment, please, most noble Aeschylus!
And you, poor wretch, if you have any prudence,
Get out of the hailstones quick, or else, by Zeus,
Some word as big as your head will catch you crash
Behind the ear, and knock out all the . . . Telephus!
Nay, Aeschylus, pray, pray control your anger;
Examine and submit to be examined
With a cool head. Two poets should not meet
In fishwife style; but here are you, straight off,
Ablaze and roaring like an oak on fire.

EURIPIDES

For my part I'm quite ready, with no shrinking,
To bite first or be bitten, as he pleases.
Here are my dialogue, music, and construction;
Here's Peleus at your service, Meleager,
And Aeolus, and . . . yes, Telephus, by all means!

DIONYSUS

Do you consent to the trial, Aeschylus? Speak.

AESCHYLUS

I well might take objection to the place;
It's no fair field for him and me.

DIONYSUS

Why not?

AESCHYLUS

Because my writings haven't died with me,
As his have; so he'll have them all to hand. . . .
However, I waive the point, if you think fit.

DIONYSUS

Go, some one, bring me frankincense and fire
That I may pray for guidance, to decide
This contest in the Muses' strictest ways;
To whom, meantime, uplift your hymn of praise!

CHORUS (*singing*)

All hail, ye nine heaven-born virginal Muses,
Whiche'er of ye watch o'er the manners and uses
Of the founts of quotation, when, meeting in fray—
All hearts drawn tense for who wins and who loses—
With wrestling lithe each the other confuses,
Look on the pair that do battle to-day!
These be the men to take poems apart
By chopping, riving, sawing;
Here is the ultimate trial of Art
To due completion drawing!

DIONYSUS

Won't you two pray before you show your lines?

AESCHYLUS (*going up to the altar*)

Demeter, thou who feedest all my thought,
Grant me but worthiness to worship thee!

DIONYSUS (*to* EURIPIDES)

Won't you put on some frankincense?

EURIPIDES (*staying where he is*)

Oh, thank you;
The gods I pray to are of other metal!

DIONYSUS

Your own stamp, eh? New struck?

EURIPIDES

Exactly so.

DIONYSUS

Well, pray away then to your own peculiar.

EURIPIDES (*esoterically*)

Ether, whereon I batten! Vocal cords!
Reason, and nostrils swift to scent and sneer,
Grant that I duly probe each word I hear.

CHORUS (*singing*)

All of us to hear are yearning
Further from these twins of learning,
What dread road they walk, what burning
Heights they climb of speech and song.
Tongues alert for battle savage,
Tempers keen for war and ravage,
Angered hearts to both belong.
He will fight with passes witty
Smooth and smacking of the city,
Gleaming blades unflecked with rust;
He will seize—to end the matter—
Tree-trunks torn and clubbed, to batter
Brains to bits, and plunge and scatter
Whole arena-fulls of dust!

LEADER OF THE CHORUS

Now, quick to work. Be sure you both do justice to your cases,
Clear sense, no loose analogies, and no long commonplaces.

EURIPIDES

A little later I will treat my own artistic mettle,
This person's claims I should prefer immediately to settle.
I'll show you how he posed and prosed; with what audacious fooling

He tricked an audience fresh and green from Phrynichus's schooling.
Those sole veiled figures on the stage were first among his graces,
Achilles, say, or Niobé, who never showed their faces,
But stood like so much scene-painting, and never a grunt they uttered!

DIONYSUS

Why, no, by Zeus, no more they did!

EURIPIDES

And on the Chorus spluttered
Through long song-systems, four on end, the actors mute as fishes!

DIONYSUS

I somehow loved that silence, though; and felt it met my wishes
As no one's talk does nowadays!

EURIPIDES

You hadn't yet seen through it!
That's all.

DIONYSUS

I really think you're right! But still, what made him do it?

EURIPIDES

The instinct of a charlatan, to keep the audience guessing
If Niobé ever meant to speak—the play meantime progressing!

DIONYSUS

Of course it was! The sly old dog, to think of how he tricked us!—
Don't (*to* AESCHYLUS) ramp and fume!

EURIPIDES

We're apt to do so when the facts convict us!
—Then after this tomfoolery, the heroine, feeling calmer,
Would utter some twelve wild-bull words, on mid-way in the drama,
Long ones, with crests and beetling brows, and gorgons round the border,
That no man ever heard on earth.

AESCHYLUS

The red plague . . . !

DIONYSUS

Order, order!

EURIPIDES

Intelligible—not one line!

DIONYSUS (*to* AESCHYLUS)

Please! Won't your teeth stop gnashing?

EURIPIDES

All fosses and Scamander-beds, and bloody targes flashing,
With gryphon-eagles bronze-embossed, and crags, and riders reeling,
Which somehow never quite joined on.

DIONYSUS

By Zeus, sir, quite my feeling!
A question comes in Night's long hours, that haunts me like a spectre,
What kind of fish or fowl you'd call a "russet hippalector."

AESCHYLUS (*breaking in*)

It was a ship's sign, idiot, such as every joiner fixes!

DIONYSUS

Indeed! I thought perhaps it meant that music-man Eryxis!

[EURIPIDES

You like then, in a tragic play, a cock? You think it mixes?]

AESCHYLUS (*to* EURIPIDES)

And what did you yourself produce, O fool with pride deluded?

EURIPIDES

Not "hippalectors," thank the Lord, nor "tragelaphs," as you did—
The sort of ornament they use to fill a Persian curtain!
—I had the Drama straight from you, all bloated and uncertain,
Weighed down with rich and heavy words, puffed out past comprehension.
I took the case in hand; applied treatment for such distension—
Beetroot, light phrases, little walks, hot book-juice, and cold reasoning;
Then fed her up on solos. . . .

DIONYSUS (*aside*)

With Cephisophon for seasoning!

EURIPIDES

I didn't rave at random, or plunge in and make confusions.
My first appearing character explained, with due allusions,
The whole play's pedigree.

DIONYSUS (*aside*)

Your own you left in wise obscurity!

EURIPIDES

Then no one from the start with me could idle with security.
They had to work. The men, the slaves, the women, all made speeches,
The kings, the little girls, the hags . . .

AESCHYLUS

Just see the things he teaches!
And shouldn't you be hanged for that?

EURIPIDES

No, by the lord Apollo!
It's democratic!

DIONYSUS (*to* EURIPIDES)

That's no road for you, my friend, to follow;
You'll find the "little walk" too steep; I recommend you quit it.

EURIPIDES

Next, I taught all the town to talk with freedom.

AESCHYLUS

I admit it.
'Twere better, ere you taught them, you had died amid their curses!

EURIPIDES

I gave them canons to apply and squares for marking verses;
Taught them to see, think, understand, to scheme for what they wanted,
To fall in love, think evil, question all things. . . .

AESCHYLUS

Granted, granted!

EURIPIDES

I put things on the stage that came from daily life and business.
Where men could catch me if I tripped; could listen without dizziness
To things they knew, and judge my art. I never crashed and lightened
And bullied people's senses out; nor tried to keep them frightened
With Magic Swans and Aethiop knights, loud barb and clanging vizor!
Then look at my disciples, too, and mark what creatures his are!

Phormisius is his product and the looby lump Megaenetus,
All trumpet, lance, moustache, and glare, who twist their clubs of pine at us;
While Clitophon is mine, sirs, and Theramenes the Matchless!

DIONYSUS

Theramenes! Ah, that's the man! All danger leaves him scratchless.
His friends may come to grief, and he be found in awkward fixes,
But always tumbles right end up, not aces—no: all sixes!

EURIPIDES (*more rapidly*)

This was the kind of lore I brought
To school my town in ways of thought;
I mingled reasoning with my art
And shrewdness, till I fired their heart
To brood, to think things through and through;
And rule their houses better, too.

DIONYSUS (*still more rapidly*)

Yes, by the powers, that's very true!
No burgher now, who comes indoors,
But straight looks round the house and roars:
"Where is the saucepan gone? And who
Has bitten that sprat's head away?
And, out, alas! The earthen pot
I bought last year is not, is not!
Where are the leeks of yesterday?
And who has gnawed this olive, pray?"
Whereas, before they took his school,
Each sat at home, a simple, cool,
Religious, unsuspecting fool,
And happy in his sheep-like way!

CHORUS (*singing*)

Great Achilles, gaze around thee!
'Twill astound thee and confound thee

Answer now: but keep in bound the
  Words that off the course would tear,
Bit in teeth, in turmoil flocking.
Yes: it's monstrous—shameful—shocking--
  Brave old warrior. But beware!

Don't retort with haste or passion;
Meet the squalls in sailor fashion,
  Mainsail reefed and mast nigh bare;
Then, when safe beyond disaster
You may press him fiercer, faster,
Close and show yourself his master,
  Once the wind is smooth and fair!

LEADER OF THE CHORUS

O thou who first of the Greeks did build great words to heaven-high towers,
And the essence of tragedy-padding distilled, give vent to thy pent-up showers

AESCHYLUS

I freely admit that I take it amiss, and I think my anger is just,
At having to answer a man like this. Still, lest I should seem nonplussed,
Pray, tell me on what particular ground a poet should claim admiration?

EURIPIDES

If his art is true, and his counsel sound; and if he brings help to the nation,
By making men better in some respect.

AESCHYLUS

And suppose you have done the reverse.
And have had upon good strong men the effect of making them weaker and worse,
What, do you say, should your recompense be?

DIONYSUS

The gallows! You needn't ask him.

AESCHYLUS

Well, think what they were when he had them from me!
Good six-footers, solid of limb,
Well-born, well-bred, not ready to fly from obeying their country's call,
Nor in latter-day fashion to loiter and lie, and keep their consciences small;
Their life was in shafts of ash and of elm, in bright plumes fluttering wide,
In lance and greaves and corslet and helm, and hearts of sevenfold hide!

EURIPIDES (*aside*)

Oh, now he's begun and will probably run a whole armourer's shop on my head!
(*To* AESCHYLUS) Stop! How was it due in especial to you, if they were so very—well-bred?

DIONYSUS

Come, answer him, Aeschylus! Don't be so hot, or smoulde in silent disdain.

AESCHYLUS (*crushingly*)

By a tragedy 'brimming with Ares!'

DIONYSUS

A what?

AESCHYLUS

The "Seven against Thebes."

DIONYSUS

Pray explain

AESCHYLUS

There wasn't a man could see that play but he hungered for havoc and gore

DIONYSUS

I'm afraid that tells in the opposite way. For the Thebans profited more,
It urged them to fight without flinching or fear, and they did so; and long may you rue it!

AESCHYLUS

The same thing was open to all of you here, but it didn't amuse you to do it!
Then next I taught you for glory to long, and against all odds stand fast;
That was "The Persians," which bodied in song the noblest deed of the past.

DIONYSUS

Yes, yes! When Darius arose from the grave it gave me genuine joy,
And the Chorus stood with its arms a-wave, and observed, "Yow-oy, Yow-oy!"

AESCHYLUS

Yes, that's the effect for a play to produce! For observe, from the world's first start
Those poets have all been of practical use who have been supreme in their art.
First, Orpheus withheld us from bloodshed impure, and vouchsafed us the great revelation;
Musaeus was next, with wisdom to cure diseases and teach divination.
Then Hesiod showed us the season to plough, to sow, and to reap. And the laurels
That shine upon Homer's celestial brow are equally due to his morals!
He taught men to stand, to march, and to arm. . . .

DIONYSUS

So that was old Homer's profession?
Then I wish he could keep his successors from harm, like

Pantacles in the procession,
Who first got his helmet well strapped on his head, and then tried to put in the plume!

AESCHYLUS

There be many brave men that he fashioned and bred, like Lamachus, now in his tomb.
And in his great spirit my plays had a part, with their heroes many and brave—
Teucers, Patrocluses, lions at heart; who made my citizens crave
To dash like them at the face of the foe, and leap at the call of a trumpet!—
But no Stheneboea I've given you, no; no Phaedra, no heroine-strumpet!
If I've once put a woman in love in one act of one play, may my teaching be scouted!

EURIPIDES

No, you hadn't exactly the style to attract Aphroditê!

AESCHYLUS

I'm better without it.
A deal too much of that style she found in some of your friends and you,
And once, at least, left you flat on the ground!

DIONYSUS

By Zeus, that's perfectly true.
If he dealt his neighbours such rattling blows, we must think how he suffered in person.

EURIPIDES

And what are the public defects you suppose my poor Stheneboea to worsen?

AESCHYLUS (*evading the question with a jest*)

She makes good women, and good men's wives, when their hearts are weary and want ease,

Drink jorums of hemlock and finish their lives, to gratify Bellerophontes!

EURIPIDES

But did I invent the story I told of—Phaedra, say? Wasn't it history?

AESCHYLUS

It was true, right enough; but the poet should hold such a truth enveloped in mystery,
And not represent it or make it a play. It's his duty to teach, and you know it.
As a child learns from all who may come in his way, so the grown world learns from the poet.
Oh, words of good counsel should flow from his voice—

EURIPIDES

And words like Mount Lycabettus
Or Parnes, such as you give us for choice, must needs be good counsel?—Oh, let us,
Oh, let us at least use the language of men!

AESCHYLUS

Flat cavil, sir! cavil absurd!
When the subject is great and the sentiment, then, of necessity, great grows the word;
When heroes give range to their hearts, is it strange if the speech of them over us towers?
Nay, the garb of them too must be gorgeous to view, and majestical, nothing like ours.
All this I saw, and established as law, till you came and spoilt it.

EURIPIDES

How so?

AESCHYLUS

You wrapped them in rags from old beggarmen's bags, to express their heroical woe,
And reduce the spectator to tears of compassion!

EURIPIDES

Well, what was the harm if I did?

AESCHYLUS (*evading the question as before*)

Bah, your modern rich man has adopted the fashion, for remission of taxes to bid;
"He couldn't provide a trireme if he tried"; he implores us his state to behold.

DIONYSUS

Though rags outside may very well hide good woollens beneath, if it's cold!
And when once he's exempted, he gaily departs and pops up at the fishmongers' stalls.

AESCHYLUS (*continuing*)

Then, next, you have trained in the speechmaking arts nigh every infant that crawls.
Oh, this is the thing that such havoc has wrought in the wrestling-school, narrowed the hips
Of the poor pale chattering children, and taught the crews of the pick of the ships
To answer back pat to their officer's nose! How unlike my old sailor of yore,
With no thought in his head but to guzzle his brose and sing as he bent at the oar!

DIONYSUS

And spit on the heads of the rowers below, and garotte stray lubbers on shore!
But our new man just sails where it happens to blow, and argues, and rows no more!

AESCHYLUS (*more rapidly*)

What hasn't he done that is under the sun,
And the love-dealing dames that with him have begun?
One's her own brother's wife;
One says Life is not Life;

And one goes into shrines to give birth to a son!
Our city through him is filled to the brim
With monkeys who chatter to every one's whim;
Little scriveners' clerks
With their winks and their larks,
But for wrestle or race not a muscle in trim!

DIONYSUS (*still more rapidly*)

Not a doubt of it! Why, I laughed fit to cry
At the Panathenaea, a man to espy,
Pale, flabby, and fat,
And bent double at that,
Puffing feebly behind, with a tear in his eye;

Till there in their place, with cord and with brace,
Were the Potters assembled to quicken his pace;
And down they came, whack!
On sides, belly, and back,
Till he blew out his torch and just fled from the race.

CHORUS (*singing*)

Never were such warriors, never
Prize so rich and feud so keen:
Dangerous, too, such knots to sever:
He drives on with stern endeavour,
He falls back, but rallies ever,
Marks his spot and stabs it clean!

Change your step, though! Do not tarry;
Other ways there be to harry
Old antagonists in art.
Show whatever sparks you carry,
Question, answer, thrust and parry—
Be they new or ancient, marry,
Let them fly, well-winged and smart!

If you fear, from former cases,
That the audience p'raps may fail

To appreciate your paces,
Your allusions and your graces,
Look a moment in their faces!
  They will tell another tale.

Oft from long campaigns returning
Thro' the devious roads of learning
  These have wandered, books in hand:
Nature gave them keen discerning
Eyes; and you have set them burning!
Sharpest thought or deepest yearning—
  Speak, and these will understand.

EURIPIDES

Quite so; I'll turn then to his prologues straight,
And make in that first part of tragedy
My first review in detail of this Genius!
His exposition always was obscure.

DIONYSUS

Which one will you examine!

EURIPIDES

Which? Oh, lots!
First quote me that from the Oresteia, please.

DIONYSUS

Ho, silence in the court! Speak, Aeschylus.

AESCHYLUS (*quoting the first lines of The Choephori*)

"Guide of the Dead, warding a father's way,
Be thou my light and saviour, where I pray,
In this my fatherland, returned, restored."

DIONYSUS (*to* EURIPIDES)

You find some false lines there?

EURIPIDES

About a dozen!

DIONYSUS

Why, altogether there are only three!

EURIPIDES

But every one has twenty faults in drawing!

(AESCHYLUS *begins to interrupt.*)

DIONYSUS

No, stop, stop, Aeschylus; or perhaps you'll find
Your debts run up to more than three iambics.

AESCHYLUS (*raging*)

Stop to let *him* speak?

DIONYSUS

Well, that's my advice.

EURIPIDES

He's gone straight off some thousand miles astray.

AESCHYLUS

Of course it's foolery—but what do *I* care?
Point out the faults.

EURIPIDES

Repeat the lines again.

AESCHYLUS

"Guide of the Dead, warding a father's way, . . .

EURIPIDES

Orestes speaks those words, I take it, standing
On his dead father's tomb?

AESCHYLUS

I don't deny it.

EURIPIDES

Then what's the father's way that Hermes wards?
Is it the way Orestes' father went,
To darkness by a woman's dark intent?

AESCHYLUS

No, no! He calls on Eriunian Hermes,
Guide of the Dead, and adds a word to say
That office is derived from Hermes' father.

EURIPIDES

That's worse than I supposed! For if your Hermes
Derives his care of dead men from his father, . . .

DIONYSUS (*interrupting*)

Why, resurrectioning's the family trade!

AESCHYLUS

Dionysus, dull of fragrance is thy wine!

DIONYSUS

Well, say the next; and (*to* EURIPIDES) you look out for slips.

AESCHYLUS

"Be thou my light and saviour where I pray
In this my fatherland returned, restored."

EURIPIDES

Our noble Aeschylus repeats himself.

DIONYSUS

How so?

EURIPIDES

Observe his phrasing, and you'll see.
First to this land "returned" and then "restored";
'Returned' is just the same thing as 'restored.'

DIONYSUS

Why, yes! It's just as if you asked your neighbour,
'Lend me a pail, or, if not that, a bucket.'

AESCHYLUS

Oh, too much talking has bemuzzed your brain!
The words are not the same; the line is perfect.

DIONYSUS

Now, is it really? Tell me how you mean.

AESCHYLUS

Returning home is the act of any person
Who has a home; he comes back, nothing more;
An exile both returns and is restored!

DIONYSUS

True, by Apollo! (*To* EURIPIDES) What do you say to that?

EURIPIDES

I don't admit Orestes was restored.
He came in secret with no legal permit.

DIONYSUS

By Hermes, yes! (*aside*) I wonder what they mean!

EURIPIDES

Go on then to the next.

(AESCHYLUS *is silent*.)

DIONYSUS

Come, Aeschylus,
Do as he says; (*to* EURIPIDES) and you look out for faults.

AESCHYLUS

"Yea, on this bank of death, I call my lord
To hear and list. . . ."

EURIPIDES

Another repetition!
"To hear and list"—the same thing palpably!

DIONYSUS

The man was talking to the dead, you dog,
Who are always called three times—and then don't hear.

AESCHYLUS

Come, how did *you* write prologues?

EURIPIDES

Oh, I'll show you.
And if you find there any repetitions
Or any irrelevant padding,—spit upon me!

DIONYSUS

Oh, do begin. I mustn't miss those prologues
In all their exquisite exactitude!

EURIPIDES

"At first was Oedipus in happy state."

AESCHYLUS

He wasn't! He was born and bred in misery.
Did not Apollo doom him still unborn
To slay his father? . . .

DIONYSUS (*aside*)

His poor unborn father?

AESCHYLUS

"A happy state at first," you call it, do you?

EURIPIDES (*contemptuously resuming*)

"At first was Oedipus in happy state,
Then changed he, and became most desolate."

AESCHYLUS

He didn't. He was never anything else!
Why, he was scarcely born when they exposed him
In winter, in a pot, that he might never
Grow up and be his father's murderer.
Then off he crawled to Polybus with sore feet,
Then married an old woman, twice his age,
Who further chanced to be his mother, then
Tore out his eyes: the lucky dog he was!

DIONYSUS

At least he fought no sea-fight with a colleague
Called Erasinides!

EURIPIDES

That's no criticism,
I write my prologues singularly well!

AESCHYLUS

By Zeus, I won't go pecking word by word
At every phrase; I'll take one little oil-can,
God helping me, and send your prologues pop!

EURIPIDES

My prologues pop . . . with oil-cans?

AESCHYLUS

Just one oil-can!
You write them so that nothing comes amiss,
The bed-quilt, or the oil-can, or the clothes-bag,
All suit your tragic verse! Wait and I'll prove it.

EURIPIDES

You'll prove it? Really?

AESCHYLUS

Yes.

DIONYSUS

Begin to quote.

EURIPIDES

"Aegyptus, so the tale is spread afar,
With fifty youths fled in a sea-borne car,
But, reaching Argos . . ."

AESCHYLUS

Found his oil-can gone!

DIONYSUS

What's that about the oil-can! Drat the thing!
Quote him another prologue, and let's see

EURIPIDES

"Dionysus, who with wand and fawn-skin dight
On great Parnassus races in the light
Of lamps far-flashing, . . ."

AESCHYLUS

Found his oil-can gone!

DIONYSUS

Alas! again the oil-can finds our heart!

EURIPIDES (*beginning to reflect anxiously*)

Oh, it won't come to much, though! Here's another,
With not a crack to stick the oil-can in!
"No man hath bliss in full and flawless health;
Lo, this one hath high race, but little wealth;
That, base in blood, hath . . ."

AESCHYLUS

Found his oil-can gone!

DIONYSUS

Euripides!

EURIPIDES

Well?

DIONYSUS

Better furl your sails;
This oil-can seems inclined to raise the wind!

EURIPIDES

Bah, I disdain to give a thought to it!
I'll dash it from his hands in half a minute.
(*He racks his memory.*)

DIONYSUS

Well, quote another;—and beware of oil-cans.

EURIPIDES

"Great Cadmus long ago, Agenor's son,
From Sidon racing, . . ."

AESCHYLUS

Found his oil-can gone!

DIONYSUS

Oh, this is awful! Buy the thing outright,
Before it messes every blessed prologue!

EURIPIDES

I buy him off?

DIONYSUS

I strongly recommend it.

EURIPIDES

No; I have many prologues yet to cite
Where he can't find a chink to pour his oil.
"As rapid wheels to Pisa bore him on,
Tantalian Pelops . . ."

AESCHYLUS

Found his oil-can gone.

DIONYSUS

What did I tell you? There it sticks again!
You might let Pelops have a new one, though—
You get quite good ones very cheap just now.

EURIPIDES

By Zeus, not yet! I still have plenty left.
"From earth King Oeneus, . . ."

AESCHYLUS

Found his oil-can gone!

EURIPIDES

You *must* first let me quote one line entire!
"From earth King Oeneus goodly harvest won,
But, while he worshipped, . . ."

AESCHYLUS

Found his oil-can gone!

DIONYSUS

During the prayers! Who can have been the thief!

EURIPIDES (*desperately*)

Oh, let him be! I defy him answer this—
"Great Zeus in heaven, the word of truth has flown, . . ."

DIONYSUS

O mercy! *His* is certain to be gone!
They bristle with long oil-cans, hedgehog-wise,
Your prologues; they're as bunged up as your eyes!
For God's sake change the subject.—Take his songs!

EURIPIDES

Songs? Yes, I have materials to show
How bad his are, and always all alike.

CHORUS (*singing*)

What in the world shall we look for next?
Aeschylus' music! I feel perplexed
    How he can want it mended.
I have always held that never a man
Had written or sung since the world began
    Melodies half so splendid!
(Can he really find a mistake
    In the master of inspiration?
    I feel some consternation
For our Bacchic prince's sake!)

EURIPIDES

Wonderful songs they are! You'll see directly;
I'll run them all together into one.

DIONYSUS

I'll take some pebbles, then, and count for you.

EURIPIDES (*singing*)

"O Phthian Achilles, canst hark to the battle's man-slaying
  shock,
        Yea, shock, and not to succour come?
Lo, we of the mere give worship to Hermes, the fount of our
  stock,
        Yea, shock, and not to succour come!"

DIONYSUS

Two shocks to you, Aeschylus, there!

EURIPIDES (*singing*)

"Thou choice of Achaea, wide-ruling Atrides, give heed to my schooling!
Yea, shock, and not to succour come."

DIONYSUS

A third shock that, I declare!

EURIPIDES (*singing*)

"Ah, peace, and give ear! For the Bee-Maids be near to ope wide Artemis' portals.
Yea, shock-a-nock a-succour come!
Behold it is mine to sing of the sign of the way fate-laden to mortals;
Yah, shocker-knocker succucum!"

DIONYSUS

O Zeus Almighty, what a chain of shocks!
I think I'll go away and take a bath;
The shocks are too much for my nerves and kidneys'

EURIPIDES

Not till you've heard another little set
Compounded from his various cithara-songs.

DIONYSUS

Well then, proceed; but don't put any shocks in!

EURIPIDES (*singing*)

"How the might twin-throned of Achaea for Hellene chivalry bringeth
Flattothrat toflattothrat!
The prince of the powers of storm, the Sphinx thereover he wingeth
Flattothrat toflattothrat!
With deedful hand and lance the furious fowl of the air
Flattothrat toflattothrat!

That the wild wind-walking hounds unhindered tear
Flattothrat toflattothrat!
And War toward Ajax leaned his weight,
Flattothrat toflattothrat!"

DIONYSUS

What's Flattothrat? Was it from Marathon
You gathered this wool-gatherer's stuff, or where?

AESCHYLUS

Clean was the place I found them, clean the place
I brought them, loath to glean with Phrynichus
The same enchanted meadow of the Muse.
But any place will do for *him* to poach,
Drink-ditties of Meletus, Carian pipings,
And wakes, and dancing songs.—Here, let me show you!
Ho, some one bring my lyre! But no; what need
Of lyres for this stuff? Where's the wench that plays
The bones?—Approach, Euripidean Muse,
These songs are meet for your accompaniment!

DIONYSUS

This Muse was once . . . no Lesbian; not at all!

AESCHYLUS (*to* EURIPIDES)

"Ye halcyons by the dancing sea
Who babble everlastingly,
While on your bathing pinions fall
The dewy foam-sprays, fresh and free;
And, oh, ye spiders deft to crawl
In many a chink of roof and wall,
While left and right, before, behind,
Your fingers wi-i-i-ind
The treasures of the labouring loom,
Fruit of the shuttle's minstrel mind,
Where many a songful dolphin trips
To lead the dark-blue-beakèd ships
And tosses with aerial touch

Temples and race-courses and such.
O bright grape tendril's essence pure,
Wine to sweep care from human lips;
Grant me, O child, one arm-pressúre!"
(*Breaking off.*)
That foot, you see?

DIONYSUS

I do.

AESCHYLUS

And he?

EURIPIDES

Of course I see the foot!

AESCHYLUS

And this is the stuff to trial you bring
And face my songs with the kind of thing
That a man might sing when he dances a fling
To mad Cyrené's flute!

There, that's your choral stuff! But I've not finished,
I want to show the spirit of his solos!
(*Sings again; mysteriously.*)
"What vision of dreaming,
Thou fire-hearted Night,
Death's minion dark-gleaming,
Hast thou sent in thy might?
And his soul was no soul, and the Murk was his mother, a horror to sight!
Black dead was his robe, and his eyes
All blood, and the claws of him great;
Ye maidens, strike fire and arise;
Take pails to the well by the gate,
Yea, bring me a cruse of hot water, to wash off this vision of fate.
Thou Sprite of the Sea,
It is e'en as I feared!

Fellow-lodgers of me,
What dread thing hath appeared?
Lo, Glycé hath stolen my cock, and away from the neighbourhood cleared!

(*Wildly.*)

(Ye Nymphs of the Mountain give aid!
And what's come to the scullery-maid?)

(*Tearfully.*)

And I—ah, would I were dead!—
To my work had given my mind;
A spindle heavy with thread
My hands did wi-i-i-ind,
And I meant to go early to market, a suitable buyer to find!

(*Almost weeping.*)

—But he rose, rose, in the air
On quivering blades of flight;
He left me care, care;
And tears, tears of despair,
Fell, fell, and dimmed my sight!
(*Recovering himself; in florid, tragic style.*)

Children of Ida's snows,
Cretans, take up your bows,
And ring the house with many a leaping limb!
And thou, fair maid of bliss,
Dictynna, Artemis,
Range with thy bandogs through each corner dim;
Yea, Thou of twofold Fires,
Grant me my deep desires,
Thou Zeus-born Hecaté; in all men's eyes
Let the detective sheen
Flashed from thy torches keen,
Light me to Glycé's house, and that lost fowl surprise!"

DIONYSUS

Come, stop the singing.

AESCHYLUS

I've had quite enough!
What I want is to bring him to the balance;
The one sure test of what art is worth!

DIONYSUS

So that's my business next? Come forward, please;
I'll weigh out poetry like so much cheese!
(A large pair of scales is brought forward.)

CHORUS *(singing)*

Oh, the workings of genius are keen and laborious!
Here's a new wonder, incredible, glorious!
Who but this twain have the boldness of brain
To so quaint an invention to run?
Such a marvellous thing, if another had said it had
Happened to him, I should never have credited;
I should have just thought that he must
Simply be talking for fun!

DIONYSUS

Come, take your places by the balance.

AESCHYLUS *and* EURIPIDES

There!

DIONYSUS

Now, each take hold of it, and speak your verse,
And don't let go until I say "Cuckoo."

AESCHYLUS *and* EURIPIDES
(taking their stand at either side of the balance)

We have it.

DIONYSUS

Now, each a verse into the scale!

EURIPIDES

"Would God no Argo e'er had winged the brine."

AESCHYLUS

"Sperchius, and ye haunts of grazing kine!"

DIONYSUS

Cuckoo! Let go.—Ah, down comes Aeschylus
Far lower.

EURIPIDES

Why, what can be the explanation?

DIONYSUS

That river he put in, to wet his wares
The way wool-dealers do, and make them heavier!
Besides, you know, the verse you gave had wings!

AESCHYLUS

Well, let him speak another and we'll see.

DIONYSUS

Take hold again then.

AESCHYLUS *and* EURIPIDES

There you are.

DIONYSUS

Now speak.

EURIPIDES

"Persuasion, save in speech, no temple hath."

AESCHYLUS

"Lo, one god craves no offering, even Death."

DIONYSUS

Let go, let go!

EURIPIDES

Why, his goes down again!

DIONYSUS

He put in Death, a monstrous heavy thing!

EURIPIDES

But my Persuasion made a lovely line!

DIONYSUS

Persuasion has no bulk and not much weight.
Do look about you for some ponderous line
To force the scale down, something large and strong.

EURIPIDES

Where have I such a thing, now? Where?

DIONYSUS (*mischievously*)

I'll tell you:
"Achilles has two aces and a four!"—
Come, speak your lines; this is the final bout.

EURIPIDES

"A mace of weighted iron his right hand sped."

AESCHYLUS

"Chariot on chariot lay, dead piled on dead."

DIONYSUS

He beats you this time too!

EURIPIDES

How does he do it?

DIONYSUS

Two chariots and two corpses in the scale—
Why, ten Egyptians couldn't lift so much!

AESCHYLUS

Come, no more line-for-lines! Let him jump in
And sit in the scale himself, with all his books,
His wife, his children, his Cephisophon!
I'll back two lines of mine against the lot!

(*The central door opens and* PLUTO *comes forth.*)

PLUTO (*to* DIONYSUS)

Well, is the strife decided?

DIONYSUS

I won't decide! The men are both my friends;
Why should I make an enemy of either?
The one's so good, and I so love the other!

PLUTO

In that case you must give up all you came for!

DIONYSUS

And if I do decide?

PLUTO

Why, not to make
Your trouble fruitless, you may take away
Whichever you decide for.

DIONYSUS

Hearty thanks!
Now, both, approach, and I'll explain.—I came
Down here to fetch a poet: "Why a poet?"
That his advice may guide the city true
And so keep up my worship! Consequently,
I'll take whichever seems the best adviser.
Advise me first of Alcibiades,
Whose birth gives travail still to mother Athens.

PLUTO

What is her disposition towards him?

DIONYSUS

Well,
She loves and hates, and longs still to possess.
I want the views of both upon that question!

EURIPIDES

Out on the burgher, who to serve his state
Is slow, but swift to do her deadly hate,
With much wit for himself, and none for her.

DIONYSUS

Good, by Posidon, that!—And what say you?
(*To* AESCHYLUS.)

AESCHYLUS

No lion's whelp within thy precincts raise;
But, if it *be* there, bend thee to its ways!

DIONYSUS

By Zeus the Saviour, still I can't decide!
The one so fine, and the other so convincing!
Well, I must ask you both for one more judgment;
What steps do you advise to save our country?

EURIPIDES

I know and am prepared to say!

DIONYSUS

Say on.

EURIPIDES

Where Mistrust now has sway, put Trust to dwell
And where Trust is, Mistrust; and all is well.

DIONYSUS

I don't quite follow. Please say that again,
Not quite so cleverly and rather plainer.

EURIPIDES

If we count all the men whom now we trust,
Suspect; and call on those whom now we spurn
To serve us, we may find deliverance yet.

DIONYSUS

And what say you?

AESCHYLUS

First tell me about the city;
What servants does she choose? The good?

DIONYSUS

Great Heavens

She loathes them!

AESCHYLUS

And takes pleasure in the vile?

DIONYSUS

Not she, but has perforce to let them serve her!

AESCHYLUS

What hope of comfort is there for a city
That quarrels with her silk and hates her hodden?

DIONYSUS

That's just what *you* must answer, if you want
To rise again!

AESCHYLUS

I'll answer there, not here.

DIONYSUS

No; better send up blessing from below.

AESCHYLUS

Her safety is to count her enemy's land
Her own, yea, and her own her enemy's;
Her ships her treasures, and her treasure dross!

DIONYSUS

Good;—though it all goes down the juror's throat!

PLUTO

Come, give your judgment!

DIONYSUS

Well, I'll judge like this;
My choice shall fall on him my soul desires!

EURIPIDES

Remember all the gods by whom you swore
To take me home with you, and choose your friend!

DIONYSUS

My tongue hath sworn;—but I'll choose Aeschylus!

EURIPIDES

What have you done, you traitor?

DIONYSUS

I? I've judged
That Aeschylus gets the prize. Why shouldn't I?

EURIPIDES

Canst meet mine eyes, fresh from thy deed of shame?

DIONYSUS

What is shame, that the . . . Theatre deems no shame!

EURIPIDES

Hard heart! You mean to leave your old friend dead?

DIONYSUS

Who knoweth if to live is but to die? . . .
If breath is bread and sleep a woolly lie?

PLUTO

Come in, then, both.

DIONYSUS

Again?

PLUTO

To feast with me
Before you sail.

DIONYSUS

With pleasure! That's the way
Duly to crown a well-contented day!

CHORUS (*singing*)

O blessed are they who possess
An extra share of brains!
'Tis a fact that more or less
All fortunes of men express;
As now, by showing
An intellect glowing,
This man his home regains,
Brings benefit far and near
To all who may hold him dear,
And staunches his country's tear,—
All because of his brains!

Then never with Socrates
Make one of the row of fools
Who gabble away at ease,
Letting art and music freeze,
And freely neglect
In every respect
The drama's principal rules!
Oh, to sit in a gloomy herd
A-scraping of word on word,
All idle and all absurd,—
That is the fate of fools!

PLUTO

Then farewell, Aeschylus! Go your ways,
And save your town for happier days
By counsel wise; and a school prepare
For all the fools—there are plenty there!
And take me some parcels, I pray; this sword
Is for Cleophon; these pretty ropes for the board
Of providers. But ask them one halter to spare
For Nicomachus; one, too, is Myrmex's share.
And, along with this venomous
Draught for Archenomus,
Take them my confident prayer,

That they all will come here for a visit, and stay.
And bid them be quick; for, should they delay,
Or meet my request with ingratitude, say
 I will fetch them myself, by Apollo!
And hurry the gang of them down with a run
All branded and chained—with Leucolophus' son
 The sublime Adimantus to follow!

AESCHYLUS

I will do as you wish.—And as for my throne,
I beg you let Sophocles sit there alone,
On guard, till perchance I return some day;
For he—all present may mark what I say—
 Is my second in art and in wit.
And see, above all, that this devil-may-care
Child of deceit with his mountebank air
Shall never on that imperial chair
 By the wildest of accidents sit!

PLUTO (*to the* CHORUS)

With holy torches in high display
 Light ye the Marchers' triumphal advance;
Let Aeschylus' music on Aeschylus' way
 Echo in song and in dance!

LEADER OF THE CHORUS

Peace go with him and joy in his journeying! Guide ye our poet
Forth to the light, ye powers that reign in the Earth and below it;
Send good thoughts with him, too, for the aid of a travailing nation,
So shall we rest at the last, and forget our long desolation,
War and the clashing of wrong.—And for Cleophon, why, if he'd rather,
Let him fight all alone with his friends, in the far-off fields of his father.

GLOSSARY

The following classes of proper names have been omitted from this Glossary: 1. Geographical names of purely ornamental or entirely obvious significance; 2. Personal names introduced for merely genealogical reasons; 3. The names of a large number of Persian generals; 4. Names of persons in Comedy, about whom nothing is known beyond what can be deduced from the contexts in which they are mentioned. Not all the omissions are covered by these categories, but it is hoped that nothing really important has failed of treatment.

ABAE. An old town in Phocis, noted for its temple and oracle of Apollo.

ACASTUS. Brother of Alcestis and son of Pelias, King of Iolcus. He drove Jason and Medea into exile after the latter had contrived the death of Pelias. He likewise exiled Peleus who had fallen in love with his wife Hippolyte.

ACHAEA. In Homer this is practically the equivalent of Hellas, and Achaeans, Argives, and Danaans indifferently denote what a later age called Hellenes. The tragic dramatists are wont to imitate the epic poet in this usage.

ACHERON. A river in the Underworld.

ACHILLES. Son of Peleus and Thetis, father of Neoptolemus, the greatest of the Greek warriors before Troy, finally slain by Paris.

ACRISIUS. See DANAE.

ADIMANTUS. An Athenian general suspected of treachery at the battle of Aegospotami; he was also a friend of Alcibiades.

ADMETUS. King of Pherae in Thessaly, husband of Alcestis, son of Pheres.

AEACUS. Father of Peleus, Telamon, and Psamathe; so famous for his justice that he became one of the judges in the Underworld.

AEGEUS. An early king of Athens, the father of Theseus.

AEGINA. An island in the Saronic Gulf.

AEGIPLANCTUS. A mountain in Megaris.

AEGISTHUS. Son of Thyestes, and cousin of Agamemnon.

AENEAS. Trojan hero in the *Iliad*. After the fall of Troy, according to the legend, he led a band of Trojan survivors to Italy, where his descendants founded Rome.

AEOLUS. Ruler of Thessaly, ancestor of the Aeolians.

AETNA. A volcanic mountain in the northeast of Sicily. One of the Titans was believed to have been buried under it by the victorious Zeus.

AETOLIA. A wild and mountainous region in western Greece. In mythology it is the scene of many hunting legends.

AGAMEMNON. Son of Atreus, brother of Menelaus, king of Mycenae, leader of the Greek forces against Troy.

AGATHON. A fifth-century Athenian tragic dramatist whose personal delicacy and precious style are frequently satirized by Aristophanes.

AGENOR. Son of Poseidon, king of Phoenicia, father of Cadmus.

AJAX. Name of two Greek heroes in the Trojan War. One was the son of Telamon and was a perfect soldier, tall, strong, tireless, reliable. The other was the son of Oileus, small but swift; he often acted in conjunction with his bulkier namesake.

ALCESTIS. Daughter of Pelias, and wife of Admetus, King of Thessaly.

ALCIBIADES. An Athenian, son of Clinias, born around 450. Of a noble and wealthy family, gifted with beauty of person and an irresistible charm of manner, he might have become one of the greatest statesmen in Athens' history if he had possessed more self-control and stability. But the wildness of his life and the insecurity of his policy prevented the populace from ever quite placing complete confidence in him, and his magnificent ambitions experienced a series of frustrations.

ALCMENA. Wife of Amphitryon and mother, by Zeus, of Heracles.

ALTHAEA. Wife of Oeneus, a king of Calydon. Dionysus had been her lover.

AMAZONS. A race of belligerent women who lived without contact with men, according to mythology, in the Caucasian regions, from which they were reputed to have made a number of invasions of Asia Minor and other countries. In the reign of Theseus they attacked Attica, and in the Trojan War they played a late and ineffective part. An attack on them was one of the exploits of Heracles.

AMIPSIAS. A successful fifth-century Athenian comic poet.

AMPHION. Son of Zeus by Antiope, whom Lycus of Thebes had ill-treated. Amphion and his brother Zethus accordingly attacked and captured the city, eventually putting to death Lycus and his wife Dirce. The city was then fortified with a wall. Later Amphion married Niobe and became by her the father of numerous progeny, but Apollo killed them all and Amphion ended his own life because of his grief.

AMPHITRITE. A daughter of Nereus, wife of Poseidon. Goddess of the sea, and mother of Triton.

AMPHITRYON. See ALCMENE.

ANTIGONE. The daughter of Oedipus and Jocasta.

APHRODITE. The Greek goddess of love. Her cult was practised chiefly in Cyprus; hence she is called Cypris. Other seats of her worship were Cythera and Paphos.

APIAN. An older equivalent of Argive.

APOLLO. Often called Phoebus. In tragedy he is usually the god of healing, of prophecy, and of music. Notable points in connection with him are: his building of the Trojan walls with Poseidon; his consistent support of Troy in the Trojan War; his unusual gift of prophecy to Cassandra.

ARACHNE. A mountain in Argolis.

ARCADIA. Anglicized into Arcady. The mountainous central region of the Peloponnesus, suited only to stock-raising. The god Pan was extensively worshipped there. A later and romantic age idealized the pastoral life of Arcadia into what has ever since been connoted by the name.

ARCHEDEMUS. A demagogue, who initiated the prosecution of the Generals, after Arginusae.

ARCTURUS. A star, whose morning rising in September indicated the vintage season, and the time when the cattle came down from their upland pastures.

ARES. The Greek god of war. The Areopagus at Athens was often called, by a doubtful etymology, the Hill of Ares.

ARGINUSAE. Three islands off the Asia Minor coast, opposite Mitylene. The greatest naval battle of the Peloponnesian War took place here in 406 and the Athenian fleet won a brilliant victory, but the commanding officers, either because of a storm or in a moment of negligence, failed to pick up the men who were left on the disabled ships or were in the sea, and when they returned to Athens they were condemned to death. The incident is full of strange and unexplained factors, and we can never hope to understand it fully.

ARGIVES. Inhabitants of Argos, or Greeks generally.

ARGO. The name of the ship in which Jason and his heroic crew set out to fetch the Golden Fleece.

ARGOLIS. Often Anglicized into The Argolid. The later and more restricted name for the region of the Peloponnesus in which the town of Argos was situated, roughly the northeast corner.

ARGOS. A city in the northeast corner of the Peloponnesus; also the region in which this city was situated, The Argolid. This region was one of the centers of the Achaean or Mycenaean civilization and plays a large rôle in Greek mythological history. In later historical times Argos was often at war with Sparta, and in the Peloponnesian War she played a clever and generally neutral game, profiting immensely from the conflict between the chief states of Greece. On occasion she sided definitely with Athens, but was never of any great or permanent use to her.

ARGUS. A son of Earth, endowed with a hundred eyes and thus proverbial for vigilance. It was he whom Hera set to watch over Io, and he was finally slain by Hermes at the command of Zeus; his eyes were than transferred to the tail of the peacock.

ARIADNÉ. Daughter of Minos and Pasiphae. She fell in love with Theseus, was deserted by him on the island of Naxos, where Dionysus found her.

ARIMASPI. A people who supposedly dwelt in the north of Scythia.

ARTEMIS. Daughter of Zeus and Leto, twin sister of Apollo, born at Delos, the virgin goddess of the hunt, also identified with the Moon; protectress of animals and especially of their young, she was also thought to preside over human childbirth. At Tauris human sacrifices were made to a goddess whom the Greeks called Artemis.

ASCLEPIUS. A son of Apollo who learned to heal the sick and revive the dead; slain by Zeus; he was later deified and became the god of medicine.

ASOPUS. A river in Boeotia.

ATE. Daughter of Eris and Zeus, an ancient goddess, who led men into rash actions.

ATHAMAS. In a tragedy by Sophocles called *Athamas* this king of Orchomenus was brought in with a chaplet on his head, about to be sacrificed.

ATHENE. Also called Pallas, a virgin goddess, daughter of Zeus, special protectress of Athens. Although regularly thought of as a warrior goddess, she was also the patroness of peaceful arts and of wisdom. Her epithet Polias means "guardian of cities."

ATHOS. A mountain on a peninsula which projects from Chalcidice in Macedonia.

ATLAS. A Titan who was condemned to hold the heavens on his shoulders. The name is also given to the mountain range of northwestern Africa.

ATREIDAE. A patronymic referring to Agamemnon and Menelaus, the sons of Atreus.

ATREUS. The son of Pelops and the father of Agamemnon and Menelaus.

AULIS. A harbour in Boeotia from which the Greek expedition sailed against Troy.

BACCHUS. Dionysus.

BELLEROPHON. The rider of the winged steed Pegasus, by whose aid he slew the Chimaera.

BISTONES. A people of Thrace.

BOEBIAN. Referring to a lake in Thessaly.

BOEOTIA. A fertile region in Greece, northwest of Attica, allied with Sparta in the Peloponnesian War.

BOREAS. The North Wind.

BOSPHORUS. The channel between the Black Sea and the Sea of Marmora.

BYBLINE. Mythical mountains in Africa.

CADMUS. The legendary founder of Thebes. Hence the Thebans are often called Cadmeans.

CALCHAS. Agamemnon's seer.

CALLIAS. Wealthy scion of an illustrious family, who squandered all his riches in extravagant living.

CANOBUS or CANOPUS. A city on the coast of lower Egypt, in the Nile delta.

CARCINUS. A tragic poet, who had three sons of very diminutive stature. One was named Xenocles; the names of the others are uncertain. All three wrote tragedies and introduced an inordinate amount of new-fangled dancing into their productions. The Greek *karkinos* also means "crab."

CARIA. A country in the southwest of Asia Minor; the inhabitants seem to have been exceptionally stupid and coarse.

CASSANDRA. Daughter of Priam and Hecuba. She possessed the gift of prophecy from Apollo who ordained subsequently that no one should believe her.

CASTALIA. A fountain on Mt. Parnassus.

CASTOR. See DIOSCURI.

CENCHREAE. A town in the Argolid.

CEPHISOPHON. A domestic slave of Euripides, whom Aristophanes accuses of composing parts of the dramatist's works.

CEPHISUS or CEPHISSUS. A stream in Attica. The god of the stream called Cephisus was an ancestor of Creusa.

CERAMICUS. The name of two sections of Athens. The one referred to in *The Frogs* was an attractive suburb in which those who had given their lives for the state were buried.

CERBERUS. A dog stationed at the entrance to Hades, to keep the living from getting in and the dead from getting out. He was proverbially fierce and difficult to handle.

CHALCIS. A Euboean city, on the Euripus. So many colonies were sent out from Chalcis to the three-fingered Macedonian peninsula in the northern Aegean that that region was called Chalcidice. The colonies there were mostly subject to Athens in the fifth century, but they frequently revolted.

CHALYBES. A people who dwelt on the south shore of the Black Sea.

CHARITES. The Graces.

CHARON. The ferryman of the Styx.

CHARYBDIS. A monster who swallowed down the waters of the sea thrice daily and thrice daily spewed them forth again. Opposite SCYLLA.

CHRYSEIS. Agamemnon's favorite concubine at Troy.

CILICIA. A district in the southeast of Asia Minor.

CIMMERII. A people who lived near the Caspian Sea.

CIMOLIAN CLAY. A sort of fuller's-earth, from Cimolus, a tiny island north of Melos.

CIMON. A great Athenian statesman and general in the period immediately following the Persian Wars. He was the leader of the conservative group, which had as one of its chief objectives the maintenance of friendship with Sparta.

CINESIAS. A popular dithyrambic poet, famous for his thinness and misbehaviour. He was reported to have smeared excrement on the statues of Hecate. The point of the jest in *The Frogs* (1437) is somewhat obscure.

CITHAERON. A range of mountains separating Boeotia from Megaris and Attica.

CLEON. The most renowned of the Athenian demagogues. A tanner by trade, he soon turned to politics, and from the death of Pericles in 429 to his own in 422 he was the most powerful man in Athens. Aristophanes constantly attacks his rapacity, sham patriotism, vulgarity and jingoism; his status as a citizen is also questioned. For a defense of the man, see Grote's *History of Greece*.

CLEOPHON. A demagogue who violently opposed peace in the last years of the Peloponnesian War.

CLINIAS. The father of Alcibiades.

CLISTHENES. Athens' most noted homosexual, at whom Aristophanes never tires of poking fun.

CLITOPHON. A dilettante in philosophy.

COCYTUS. A river in the Underworld.

COLCHIS. A country at the extreme east of the Black Sea.

CORINTH. A city on the Isthmus, famous for its prostitutes.

CORYCIA. A nymph, from whom a cave on Mt. Parnassus was named. It was near the fountain of Castalia.

CRATINUS. An older comic poet; in 423 he won the first prize and neatly turned the tables on Aristophanes, who had cast slurs on his senility the year before.

CREON. 1. Brother of Jocasta. 2. A legendary king of Corinth.

CRETE. A large island south of the Aegean, in the fifth century famous for looseness of morals, but in the Heroic Age more highly respected.

CRONUS. Father of Hera, Poseidon, and Zeus. He was deprived of his throne by Zeus.

CYBELE. An Asiatic goddess identified with Rhea. Her worship was wild and orgiastic in character, and hence it became closely connected with that of Dionysus.

CYCLOPES. One-eyed giants, assistants of Hephaestus, who were supposed to dwell likewise as shepherds in Sicily.

CYCNUS. A famous robber slain by Heracles.

CYLLENE. A mountain in the Peloponnesus, sacred to Hermes.

CYPRIS. Aphrodite.

CYPRUS. A large island in the Mediterranean, south of Cilicia.

CYRENE. The name of a famous courtesan, perhaps of Corinthian origin, nicknamed *dodekamechanos* to indicate her mastery of no less than a dozen methods of making love.

CYTHERA. An island off the southern tip of the Peloponnesus, famous for its worship of Aphrodite.

DANAAN. Equivalent of Greek.

DANAE. Daughter of Acrisius, king of Argos, who confined her in a brazen tower, since an oracle had told him that she would bear a child who would kill him. Zeus visited her in a shower of gold, and she gave birth to Perseus. Acrisius shut mother and child in a chest, cast it into the sea, but both were rescued.

DARIUS. King of Persia, father of Xerxes.

DAULIS or DAULIA. An ancient town in Phocis.

DELOS. A small island in the Aegean, birthplace of Apollo and Artemis.

DELPHI. A town in Phocis, site of a famous oracular shrine of Apollo and of the Pythian Games.

DEMETER. Goddess of agriculture, mother of Persephone.

DEO. Another name for Demeter.

DICTYNNA. Another name for Artemis.

DIOMEAN FEAST. A festival held in honour of Heracles in the Attic deme of Diomea.

DIOMEDES. Son of Tydeus. A Greek hero in the Trojan War.

DIONYSUS. Son of Zeus and Semele, god of wine and of the productive power of nature, patron of drama at Athens. His worship was orgiastic and when first introduced into Greece was strongly opposed by the staid. He had an oracular shrine in Thrace.

DIOSCURI. Castor and Pollux, sons of Leda and Tyndareus, or, according to another tradition, of Leda and Zeus. They were hence brothers of Helen. Castor was famed for his skill in dealing with horses, and Pollux for his skill in boxing. Both were regarded as protectors of sailors.

DIRCE. Wife of Lycus, an ancient king of Thebes. A famous fountain there took its name from her.

DITYLAS. A Scythian name, like the Sceblyas and Pardocas which immediately follow it.

DODONA. An ancient oracle of Zeus in Epirus. The sounds made by the wind in the sacred oaks were interpreted by the priests.

DRYAS. Father of the Thracian king Lycurgus.

ELECTRA. Daughter of Agamemnon and Clytemnestra.

ELECTRYON. Father of Alcmena. Amphitryon was exiled from Mycenae for killing him.

ELEUSIS. A town near Athens, where the mysteries in honour of Demeter and Persephone were celebrated.

EMPUSA. A terrible spectre haunting lonely places at night and associated with Hecate. The Empusa had the power of taking on any shape or likeness.

EPAPHUS. The son of Io and Zeus.

EPIDAURUS. A town in Argolis on the Saronic gulf.

ERASINIDES. One of the Arginusae generals who were put to death.

ERECHTHEUS. A legendary king of Athens. The Athenians were often called Erechtheidae after him.

ETEOCLES. Son of Oedipus and Jocasta.

ETRURIA. A country in central Italy.

EUBOEA. A long and narrow island northeast of the Attic and Boeotian coasts, subject to Athens.

EUMELUS. Son of Admetus and Alcestis.

EURIPUS. The channel between Euboea and Boeotia.

EURYDICE. The wife of Creon, king of Thebes.

EURYSTHEUS. King of Argos, enemy and master of Heracles to whom he assigned the twelve labours.

EUXINE. The Black Sea.

FLATTOTHRAT. An onomatopoeic word designed to imitate the twanging of strings on a lyre.

GERYON. A triple-bodied monster whose cattle Heracles carried off.

GLYCE. "Sweet."

GORGONS. Three horrible sisters, of whom Medusa was the most renowned in mythology. They had serpents on their heads instead of hair, and were endowed with wings, claws, and enormous teeth. Anyone who looked at Medusa's head was turned to stone.

GORGOPIS. A bay near Corinth.

GRAEAE. Three old women, who possessed but one eye and one tooth, which they could loan to one another.

HADES. The god of the Underworld. It is also used as a name for the Underworld.

HAEMON. A Theban, the son of Creon.

HARMONIA. Daughter of Ares and Aphrodite, who became the wife of Cadmus.

HARPIES. Monstrous birds with heads of maidens.

HECATE. A confusing divinity, identified with the Moon, Artemis, and Persephone, and invoked by sorcerers. She is the great sender of visions, of madness, and of sudden terror. Sometimes she is called one of the Titans, sometimes, as Artemis, the daughter of Leto.

HECTOR. Son of Priam and Hecuba, the leading hero of the Trojans.

HECUBA. Queen of Troy, the wife of Priam.

HEGELOCHUS. An Athenian actor who, in a performance of Euripides' *Orestes* had made a slight and fatal slip in diction; he had pronounced *galen' horo* (*galena* with the final *a* elided) so that it sounded like *galen horo* (*galen* without any *a* to elide). This created a ridiculous line, for instead of saying, "After the storm I perceive the calm," he tragically declaimed, "After the storm I perceive the cat."

HELEN. Daughter of Zeus and Leda, sister of the Dioscuri. Paris stole her from her husband Menelaus and thus precipitated the Trojan War.

HELICON. A celebrated range of mountains in Boeotia, sacred to Apollo and the Muses.

HELIOS. The god of the Sun.

HEPHAESTUS. God of fire and metallurgy, associated with all volcanic places, particularly Lemnos and Aetna.

HERA. Sister and wife of Zeus. A goddess associated with Argos, who is portrayed as jealous and hostile to all the women loved by Zeus, and to his irregular offspring.

HERACLES. A Greek hero, later deified, son of Zeus and Alcmena. Through the trickery of the jealous Hera, Eurystheus was given power over

Heracles and the hero was forced to exert his great strength in the performance of labours for his master.

HERMES. Son of Zeus and Maia, a god of various attributes. Messenger of the Olympians, he was also the guide of the souls of the dead. Trickery and thievery were his innate talents. As bringer of good luck he was called Eriunian.

HERMIONE. Daughter of Menelaus and Helen.

HESIOD. A famous early Greek poet, born at Ascra in Boeotia, probably toward the end of the ninth century; he is the author of *Works and Days,* a didactic poem which gives a great deal of sound and practical advice on agriculture.

HESIONE. Daughter of Oceanus and wife of Prometheus.

HIPPODAMIA. Daughter of Oenomaus and wife of Pelops.

HYDRA. A monster slain by Heracles whose blood he used to poison his arrows.

HYMEN. The god of marriage. The *Hymen Hymenaeus* was the song sung at weddings.

HYPERBOLUS. An Athenian demagogue, whom Aristophanes constantly attacks. He had been a seller of lamps. It was he that proposed an expedition against Carthage. In general he seems to have been, in the eyes of the comic poet, a sort of poor imitation of Cleon and there is little that is cast up at him which is not also found in the attacks on Cleon.

IACCHUS. A son of Zeus and Demeter, partly identified with Dionysus.

IDA. A mountain in the Troad, the scene of the judgment of Paris.

ILION. An alternate name for Troy.

INACHUS. Son of Oceanus and Tethys, the father of Io. He was the first king of Argos, and gave his name to the river Inachus there.

INO. Daughter of Cadmus, with whom Athamas had illicit relations. Hera drove him mad and he slew one of his and Ino's children. Ino took the other and threw herself into the sea; both were changed into marine deities, Ino becoming Leucothea, or Leucothoe, and the son, Melicertes, Palaemon.

IO. Daughter of Inachus.

IOLCUS. A town in Thessaly where Pelias and Jason lived.

IONIA. The fringe of Greek settlements on the coast of Asia Minor, from Miletus to Phocaea. The Ionic dialect was also spoken in the northern islands and in Euboea. The Ionians were regarded as cowardly and lascivious by the other Greeks.

IOPHON. Son of Sophocles; it was suspected that the father was partly responsible for the virtues of the son's compositions.

IPHIGENIA. Daughter of Agamemnon and Clytemnestra, sacrificed by her father at Aulis, that the Greek expedition might sail for Troy.

ISMENE. Daughter of Oedipus and Jocasta.

ISMENUS. A river near Thebes, by whose side was a temple of Apollo.

ISTER. The Danube.

ITHACA. An island in the Ionian Sea, the home of Odysseus.

ITYS. Son of Tereus and Procne, slain by his mother. In a parallel myth his name is Itylus.

JASON. A Greek hero, the leader of the Argonauts, and husband of Medea.

JOCASTA. Wife of Laius, and mother of Oedipus.

LABDACUS. A king of Thebes, the father of Laius. The name Labdacidae is often given to his descendants.

LACONIA. A region in the southeastern Peloponnesus, chief town Sparta.

LAERTES. Father of Odysseus.

LAIUS. A king of Thebes, the husband of Jocasta, and father of Oedipus by whom he was killed.

LAMACHUS. An Athenian general, one of the most dependable soldiers that the city possessed.

LARISSA. A town in eastern Thessaly.

LEDA. Wife of Tyndareus, King of Sparta, by whom or by Zeus she became the mother of the Dioscuri, Clytemnestra, and Helen. The legends record that Zeus visited her in the form of a swan.

LEMNOS. A large volcanic island in the Aegean. A myth told that the Lemnian women had murdered all their husbands.

LERNA. A district in Argolis where Heracles slew the Hydra.

LESBOS. A large island off the Asia Minor coast. The word Lesbian had in ancient times sometimes the same connotations that it does today.

LETHE. A river in Hades, from which the souls of the departed drank and were rendered quite oblivious of their past experiences.

LETO. Mother of Apollo and Artemis, hence, occasionally, also of the Moon and of Hecate.

LEUCOLOPHUS. The father of Adimantus.

LIMNA. A sea-coast town in Troezen.

LOXIAS. Alternate name for Apollo.

LYCABETTUS. A mountain in Attica.

LYCAON. Son of Ares with whom Heracles fought.

LYCEAN. "Light-bringing," an epithet of Apollo. The Lyceum in Athens was a gymnasium in the vicinity of the temple of Lycean Apollo.

LYCIA. A small district in southern Asia Minor.

LYCURGUS. A mythical king in Thrace who persecuted Dionysus. For this act he was driven mad by the gods.

LYCUS. A mythical tyrant of Thebes, who sought to kill the children of Heracles. Also the patron hero of the Athenian law-courts.

LYDIA. A country in southwestern Asia Minor. Many Athenian slaves were Lydians.

MACISTUS. An unknown mountain in Euboea.

MAENADS. A name given to the frenzied worshippers of Dionysus.

MAEOTIS. The Sea of Azov. The Amazons lived in this area.

MAIA. The mother of Hermes.

MARATHON. A village in a plain on the east shore of Attica, site of the Athenian defeat of the Persians in 490.

MEDEA. A Colchian princess, who, after aiding the Argonauts, returned with Jason to Greece as his wife.

MEDUSA. One of the Gorgons.

MEGAREUS. A son of Creon who was defender of Thebes.

MELANTHIUS. A tragic poet, brother of Morsimus. His dramas seem to have been almost as unpleasant as his personality; a glutton and a leper, he was noted for his flattery and his pederasty, and his voice is reputed to have been exceptionally harsh.

MELETUS. A writer of drinking-songs and bad tragedies, but much better known as one of the accusers of Socrates.

MELOS. An island in the Aegean, birthplace of Diagoras the atheist.

MENELAUS. King of Sparta, son of Atreus, brother of Agamemnon, husband of Helen, father of Hermione and Megapenthes.

MENOECEUS. Father of Jocasta and Creon

MEROPE. Wife of the Corinthian king, Polybus. The foster-mother of Oedipus.

MESSAPIUS. A mountain in Boeotia, near Euboea.

MINOS. King of Crete, husband of Pasiphae, and father of Phaedra and Ariadne.

MINOTAUR. A Cretan monster, half man and half bull, born of a union between Pasiphae and a bull. The Minotaur, to whom the Athenians had to make annual human sacrifice, was finally slain by Theseus.

MITYLENE. (Also spelled Mytilene.) The chief city on the island of Lesbos. In 428 Mitylene, followed by all the other towns on the island except Methymna, had revolted. After the revolt had been suppressed and Lesbos recovered in the following year, a debate was held at Athens as to suitable punishment. Led on by Cleon's oratory the Assembly voted a wholesale massacre, but rescinded the decree the next day. A ship was sent out to overtake the previous one bearing the fateful command, and an exciting race across the Aegean was narrowly won by the pursuers. The bribe which Cleon is accused of having taken from the Mitylenaeans must have been connected with some later incident.

MOLON. An otherwise unknown man, reported to have been of gigantic stature.

MOLOSSI. A people who inhabited Epirus.

MORSIMUS. A writer of very bad tragedies, brother of Melanthius.

MUSAEUS. A very ancient poet of Thrace.

MYCENAE. An ancient city in Argolis, Agamemnon's kingdom.

MYSIA A district in northwestern Asia Minor.

MYSTAE. Initiates into the Mysteries.

NAXOS. An island in the Aegean.

NEOPTOLEMUS. The son of Achilles.

NEREUS. A sea god, father of th Nereids.

NICOMACHUS. A corrupt under-secretar in the public service.

NIOBE. Daughter of Tantalus, wife o Amphion of Thebes, mother of fourteen children, because of which sh thought herself superior to Leto. Al her offspring were slain by Apoll and Artemis and Niobe herself wa turned by Zeus into a stone on Mt Sipylus in Lydia, which shed tears i the summer.

NYSA. The legendary scene of the nurture of Dionysus. There are severa places which are given this name.

OCEANUS. The god of the water whic was believed to surround the whol earth. He was the husband o Tethys.

ODYSSEUS. King of Ithaca, son o Laertes, husband of Penelope, fathe of Telemachus. Famous for his crafti ness and adroitness, he is usually th villain of the tragic plots in whic he appears.

OEDIPUS. King of Thebes, son of Laiu and Jocasta, father of Eteocles, Polyneices, Antigone, and Ismene. It wa his sad fate unwittingly to kill hi father and to marry his mother.

OENEUS. King of Pleuron and Calydo in Aetolia, father of Tydeus, Melea ger, Althaea, and Deianeira.

OENOMAUS. King of Pisa in Elis. Pelop contested with him in a famou chariot race.

OLYMPIA. A place in Elis, in the Peloponnesus, where the Olympic game were celebrated every four years citizens of every state in Greece too part. A famous temple of Zeus wa located there.

OLYMPUS. A mountain between Macedonia and Thessaly. In Greek mythology it is regarded as the home of the gods

ORESTES. Son of Agamemnon and Clytemnestra, brother of Electra.

ORPHEUS. A mythical character, regarded as a great poet. A mystery religion developed out of the stories of his life and death.

PALLAS. Athene.

PAN. An originally Arcadian god of flocks and shepherds. Sudden terror (panic) was caused by him.

PANATHENAEA. A festival of Athene, celebrated in Athens every five years. It was accompanied by feasting and a number of ceremonial performances, choral poetry, dancing, etc.

PANDION. King of Athens and father of Aegeus.

PAPHOS. A town on the west coast of Cyprus, celebrated as the chief centre of Aphrodite's worship.

PARIS. Son of Hecuba and Priam, who carried off Helen, the wife of Menelaus. Aphrodite promised Helen to him, if he gave her the award for beauty in her contest with Hera and Athene.

PARNASSUS. A mountain near Delphi, the haunt of Apollo and the Muses.

PARNES. A well-wooded mountain in Attica.

PASIPHAE. See MINOS and MINOTAUR.

PATROCLUS. A Greek hero in the Trojan War. He was Achilles' closest friend and was slain by Hector.

PEGASUS. See BELLEROPHON.

PELASGUS. A mythical king of Argos. Sometimes the Greeks as a whole are called Pelasgians because of a tradition which said that a Pelasgus, not the Argive king, was the ancestor of the earliest inhabitants of Greece.

PELEUS. Son of Aeacus and King of Phthia. Husband of Thetis and father of Achilles.

PELIAS. King of Iolcus, father of Alcestis and Acastus. He sent Jason on the quest for the Golden Fleece. On Jason's return, Medea deceitfully persuaded Pelias' daughters that they could restore their father's youth by cutting him to pieces and boiling him.

PELION. A mountain in Thessaly.

PELOPS. He came to Greece as an exile from Phrygia. He married Hippodamia, daughter of Oenomaus, and was the ancestor of the house of Atreus, whose members are called Pelopidae. The Peloponnesus takes its name from him.

PERSEPHASSA. Persephone.

PERSEPHONE. The daughter of Zeus and Demeter, who became the wife of Hades and the queen of the Underworld.

PERSEUS. A mythical hero, son of Zeus and Danae. He was the slayer of Medusa.

PHAEDRA. Daughter of Minos and wife of Theseus.

PHASIS. A river in Colchis, flowing into the east end of the Euxine.

PHERAE. An ancient town in Thessaly.

PHERES. Father of Admetus.

PHILOMEL. Daughter of Pandion and sister of Procne.

PHINEUS. King of Salmydessus in Thrace. He blinded his sons because of a false accusation by their stepmother against them. The gods then blinded him and sent the Harpies to torment him. He was delivered from these monsters by two of the Argonauts.

PHOCIS. A country in northern Greece in which the Delphic oracle was situated.

PHOEBUS. See APOLLO.

PHOENICIA. A country on the extreme eastern shore of the Mediterranean.

PHORCYS. A sea deity, father of the Graeae and the Gorgons.

PHORMISIUS. A very hairy man who was rather important politically in the years following the Sicilian expedition.

PHRYGIAN. Trojan; Phrygia was a country in northwestern Asia Minor.

PHRYNICHUS. A comic poet, a contemporary and rival of Aristophanes.

PHTHIA. A district in southeastern Thessaly, the realm of Achilles.

PIERIA. A district on the southeast coast of Macedonia, an early haunt of the Muses.

PIRENE. A famous fountain at Corinth, where Bellerophon caught Pegasus.

PISA. A district in Elis in the Peloponnesus.

PLATAEA. A Boeotian town near the Attic border. The sympathies of the inhabitants had always been with Athens, and they aided the Athenians at Marathon. In 479 the final defeat of the Persians on land took place near Plataea, and her territory was proclaimed inviolable thereafter.

PLATHANE. "Bread-pan."

PLEIADES. A constellation.

PLEISTHENES. One tradition makes him the father of Agamemnon and Menelaus.

PLEURON. An ancient city in Aetolia.

PLUTO. The supreme god of the Underworld.

POLIAS or POLIEUS. "Guardian of Cities."

POLLUX. See DIOSCURI.

POLYBUS. King of Corinth, the foster-father of Oedipus

POLYDORUS. 1. Father of Labdacus. 2. Son of Hecuba and Priam.

POLYNEICES. Son of Oedipus and Jocasta. His name means literally "much-wrangling."

POSEIDON. God of the sea; also the causer of earthquakes. He was a brother of Zeus and the father of Cyclopes. Horse-racing was under his patronage.

PRIAM. King of Troy during the Trojan War.

PROCNE. A daughter of Pandion, who slew her son Itys in order to avenge herself on Tereus, her husband, who had sought to put her out of the way and to marry Philomela, her sister. Procne was changed into a nightingale, Tereus into a hoopoe.

PROMETHEUS. One of the Titans, a great benefactor of mankind. He stole fire from heaven and brought it to earth, thereafter teaching men all the useful arts. Zeus punished him by chaining him to a rock in the Caucasus and sending an eagle to eat his liver. He was finally freed by Heracles.

PYTHIAN. Pertaining to the Delphian Apollo.

RHEA. Wife of Cronus and mother of Demeter, Hera, Hades, Poseidon, and Zeus. Later she was identified with Cybele.

SALAMIS. An island off the coasts of Attica and Megara, scene of the decisive defeat of the Persian navy in 480. From the sixth century Salamis had been subject to Athens.

SALMYDESSUS. A town in Thrace on the shores of the Black Sea.

SARDIS. The capital of Lydia, fabulously wealthy.

SARONIC GULF. A bay of the Aegean Sea between Attica and Argolis.

SCAMANDER. A famous river in the Troad.

SCYLLA. A sea monster, living in a cave on the Italian side of the straits between Italy and Sicily.

SCYTHIANS. A rude nomadic people dwelling northeast of Thrace; the Athenians employed Scythian archers as policemen.

SEBINUS. An Athenian, whose name suggests *binein*, "to make love to."

SEMELE. Daughter of Cadmus and mother of Dionysus.

SIDON. A city in Phoenicia.

SIPYLIAN. Referring to a mountain in Phrygia.

SISYPHUS. Son of Aeolus, King of Corinth, and founder of the royal house there. For his wickedness in life he was severely punished in the Underworld. One tradition makes him the father of Odysseus.

SPARTA. The chief town in Laconia, head of the Peloponnesian Confederacy.

SPERCHEIUS. A river in southern Thessaly.

SPHINX. A monster who proposed a riddle to the Thebans and killed all who could not solve it. Oedipus gave her the correct answer, whereupon she slew herself.

STHENELUS. 1. The father of Eurystheus. 2. The son of Capaneus and squire of Diomedes. 3. A tragic actor.

STHENOBOEA. The Potiphar's wife of Greek mythology. She fell in love with Bellerophon, and when that chaste hero would have nothing to do with her, she compassed his death by slandering him to her husband.

STRYMON. An important river in Macedonia.

TANTALUS. The father of Pelops. He was a king either of Lydia or Argos or Corinth. For divulging secrets entrusted to him he was punished horribly in the Underworld.

TARTARUS. The Underworld.

TARTESSUS. A town in Spain; the lampreys caught there were a great delicacy in the ancient world. The name, however, suggests Tartarus and thus has a terrifying sound.

TEIRESIAS. A blind Theban seer.

TELAMON. Son of Aeacus, brother of Peleus, and father of Ajax. He was one of the Argonauts.

TELEMACHUS. Son of Odysseus and Penelope.

TELEPHUS. A son of Heracles, who became king of Mysia. He attempted to keep the Greek expedition against Troy from landing on the coast of Asia Minor, but Dionysus made him trip over a vine and he was wounded by Achilles. An oracle informed him that the wound could be healed only by the man who had inflicted it and the Greeks were simultaneously informed that Telephus was indispensable to them. Achilles healed the wound and Telephus gave valuable directions for reaching Troy. Euripides had made Telephus the hero of a tragedy by that name, and had brought him on the stage in the beggarly disguise in which he effected entrance into the Greek camp.

TEREUS. See PROCNE.

TETHYS. The wife of Oceanus.

THEBES. The chief city in Boeotia, allied with Sparta. Also the name of a city in Egypt and of one in Cilicia.

THEMIS. A goddess, the personification of law, custom, and equity.

THEMISCYRA. A region near the Sea of Azov, where the Amazons lived.

THERAMENES. Leader of the moderately anti-democratic group in Athens after the Sicilian expedition. He strove always to avoid extremes and was thus forced to transfer his allegiance repeatedly. This earned him the nickname *kothornos*, "buskin."

THERMODON. A river on whose banks the Amazons were supposed to have dwelt.

THESEUS. King of Attica, son of Aegeus and Aethra, father of Hippolytus, Demophoön, Acamas, and Melanippus. He was the most famous and most active of the legendary heroes of Athens.

THESPROTIA. A district in Epirus.

THESSALY. A large region in northern Greece, noted for its horses and its witchcraft.

THETIS. A sea goddess, the wife of Peleus and mother of Achilles.

THRACE. An extensive country northeast of Greece, in mythology famous for its prophetic minstrels, in historical times for its warlike inhabitants and rigorous climate.

THYESTES. Brother of Atreus.

THYIAD. A Bacchant.

TIRYNS. An ancient town in Argolis.

TITANS. Giants, born of Earth and Heaven, who warred against the gods.

TITHRASIAN. From the Attic deme Tithras.

TRITON. A sea divinity, son of Poseidon and Amphitrite. When he blew his trumpet he calmed the sea.

TROEZEN. A town in southeastern Argolis.

TYDEUS. One of the seven champions who attacked Thebes. The father of Diomedes.

TYNDAREUS. King of Sparta, husband of Leda, and the putative or actual father of Castor, Polydeuces, Helen, and Clytemnestra.

TYPHO. A many-headed monster.

TYRRHENIA. An alternate name for Etruria.

XANTHIAS. A frequent slave-name, from Xanthus, a river in Lydia.

XENOCLES. See CARCINUS.

ZETHUS. A Theban, the brother of Amphion.

ZEUS. The chief god of the ancient Greeks, the ruler of the heavens.

MODERN LIBRARY COLLEGE EDITIONS

AQUINAS, ST. THOMAS: *Introduction to Saint Thomas Aquinas* (30974)
ARISTOTLE: *Introduction to Aristotle* (30973)
AUSTEN, JANE: *Pride and Prejudice* (30987)
BALZAC, HONORE DE: *Pere Goriot and Eugenie Grandet* (30902)
BELLAMY, EDWARD: *Looking Backward 2000–1887* (32980)
BLAKE, WILLIAM: *Selected Poetry and Prose* (30986)
BOSWELL, JAMES: *The Life of Samuel Johnson* (30962)
BRADFORD, WILLIAM: *Of Plymouth Plantation* (32602)
BRONTE, EMILY: *Wuthering Heights* (30904)
BROWNING, ROBERT: *Poetry of Browning* (30943)
CAMUS, ALBERT: *The Plague* (30969)
CHEKHOV, ANTON: *Best Plays by Chekhov* (30984)
CHOPIN, KATE: *The Awakening and Selected Stories* (32667)
CICERO, MARCUS TULLIUS: *The Basic Works* (30955)
COLERIDGE, SAMUEL TAYLOR: *Selected Poetry and Prose* (30952)
CRANE, STEPHEN: *The Red Badge of Courage* (30945)
DANTE: *The Divine Comedy,* (30907)
DEFOE, DANIEL: *Moll Flanders* (30908)
DONNE, JOHN: *Poetry and Prose* (30989)
DOSTOYEVSKY, FYODOR: *The Best Short Stories* (30966)
DOSTOYEVSKY, FYODOR: *The Brothers Karamazov* (30912)
DOSTOYEVSKY, FYODOR: *Crime and Punishment* (30911)
EMERSON, RALPH WALDO: *The Selected Writings* (32662)
FAULKNER, WILLIAM: *Absalom, Absalom!* (30978)
FAULKNER, WILLIAM: *Intruder in the Dust* (30988)
FAULKNER, WILLIAM: *Light in August* (30968)
FAULKNER, WILLIAM: *The Sound and the Fury* (30994)
FIELDING, HENRY: *Joseph Andrews* (30916)
FIELDING, HENRY: *Tom Jones* (30915)
FLAUBERT, GUSTAVE: *Madame Bovary* (32986)
FRANKLIN, BENJAMIN: *The Autobiography of Benjamin Franklin* (32669)
HALLINE, ALLAN G., (Ed.): *Six Modern American Plays* (30985)
HAMILTON, ALEXANDER; JAY, JOHN; AND MADISON, JAMES: *The Federalist: A Commentary on the Constitution of the United States* (30961)
HARDY, THOMAS: *Tess of the D'Urbervilles* (30946)
HARRIS, BRICE, (Ed.): *Restoration Plays* (30979)
HAWTHORNE, NATHANIEL: *The Scarlet Letter* (30921)

HEGEL, GEORG WILHELM FREIDRICH: *The Philosophy of Hegel* (30976)
HERODOTUS: *The Persian Wars* (30954)
IBSEN, HENRIK: *Eight Plays* (32865)
JAMES, HENRY: *The Bostonians* (30959)
JAMES, HENRY: *The Portrait of a Lady* (30947)
JOHNSON, JAMES WELDON, (Ed.): *Utopian Literature* (30996)
LOOMIS, ROGER SHERMAN AND LOOMIS, LAURA HIBBARD, (Ed.): *Medieval Romances* (30970)
MACHIAVELLI, NICCOLO: *The Prince and the Discourses* (30925)
MALRAUX, ANDRE: *Man's Fate* (30975)
MANN, THOMAS: *Death in Venice* (30999)
MANN, THOMAS: *The Magic Mountain* (30993)
MELVILLE, HERMAN: *Moby Dick* (30926)
MILTON, JOHN: *Paradise Lost* (30994)
MOLIERE: *Eight Plays* (30929)
OATES, WHITNEY J. AND O'NEILL, EUGENE, JR., (Ed.): *Seven Famous Greek Plays* (30930)
O'NEILL, EUGENE: *The Later Plays* (30991)
PLATO: *The Work of Plato* (30971)
POE, EDGAR ALLAN: *The Selected Poetry and Prose* (30958)
PROUST, MARCEL: *Swann's Way* (30967)
QUINTANA, RICARDO, (Ed.): *Eighteenth-Century Plays* (30980)
SHELLEY, PERCY BYSSHE: *Selected Poetry and Prose* (30950)
SOLOMON, ROBERT C., (Ed.): *Existentialism* (31704)
SWIFT, JONATHAN: *Gulliver's Travels and Other Writings* (30932)
TACITUS: *The Complete Works* (30953)
TENNYSON, ALFRED LORD: *Selected Poetry* (30960)
THACKERAY, WILLIAM MAKEPEACE: *Vanity Fair* (30933)
THOREAU, HENRY DAVID: *Walden and Other Writings* (32666)
THUCYDIDES: *The Peloponnesian War* (32978)
TOCQUEVILLE, ALEXIS DE: *Democracy in America* (32675)
TOLSTOY, LEO: *Anna Karenina* (30936)
TROLLOPE, ANTHONY: *Berchester Towers and The Warden* (30937)
TURGENEV, IVAN S.: *Fathers and Sons* (30938)
VOLTAIRE: *Candide and Other Writings* (30964)
WHITMAN, WALT: *Leaves of Grass and Selected Prose* (32661)
WINE, M. L., (Ed.): *Drama of The English Renaissance* (30866)
WORDSWORTH, WILLIAM: *Selected Poetry* (30941)